CHANGE for PUBLIC EDUCATION

CHANGE
for PUBLIC
EDUCATION

Practical
Approaches
for the
21st Century

Vito Germinario, Ed.D.
Henry G. Cram, Ed.D.

TECHNOMIC
PUBLISHING CO., INC.
LANCASTER · BASEL

Change for Public Education
a TECHNOMIC®publication

Published in the Western Hemisphere by
Technomic Publishing Company, Inc.
851 New Holland Avenue, Box 3535
Lancaster, Pennsylvania 17604 U.S.A.

Distributed in the Rest of the World by
Technomic Publishing AG
Missionsstrasse 44
CH-4055 Basel, Switzerland

Printed in the United States of America
10 9 8 7 6 5 4 3 2 1

Main entry under title:
   Change for Public Education: Practical Approaches for the 21st Century

A Technomic Publishing Company book
Bibliography: p. 203
Includes index p. 213

Library of Congress Catalog Card No. 97-62360
ISBN No. 1-56676-611-7

To my "amigos", Marie Gdula, Paul Lempa and Jim Wasser for their unconditional friendship, support and love. – Vito Germinario

To my wife Maria and my children Christopher and Paige who have patiently encouraged and supported me throughout the preparation of this book. – Henry Cram

CONTENTS

ACKNOWLEDGEMENTS

The Moorestown Township and Rancocas Valley Regional High School Public School systems whose programs, practices and dedicated staff provided the framework for this publication

The authors are also indebted to Cheryl Haines for her assistance in research and editing, Jeff Stern for his technological assistance in preparing the manuscript for publication and Karen Phillips for typing the manuscript.

To Dr. Vito Germinario for providing the opportunity to collaborate with him in committing to writing the many ideas we have shared and to all the talented professionals with whom I have worked who provided me guidance in finding solutions and the motivation to rethink the way we get things done.

The demands on public education to prepare students for the twenty-first century are a dramatic departure from the mission for which the American system of public education was orginally designed over 100 years ago. More students than ever before will need to be equipped with a level of skills and knowledge that were formerly reserved for only the best and the brightest. These changes in expectation come at a time when the fastest growing segments of the student population (immigrant, poor, and minority students) are those with whom our schools have been historically least successful.

America's demographics and the rigors of preparing students for the new millennium will require a dramatic change in what we teach, how we are teaching, and how we measure both student and teacher performance. Those changes will have to be made at the classroom level by enlightened teachers capable of rethinking every aspect of the educational process in terms of what they are doing and how they will get things done.

If schools for the twenty-first century are going to be different, the role of the teacher will need to be transformed from the relatively independent and isolated position it currently is to one that will involve teachers in working relationships with other professionals, parents, and the full range of community members. While educators and, in particular, administrators, acknowledge this, little in the way of systematic collaboration can be seen in most reform efforts. By the very nature of what teachers do in their classrooms, they are leaders. Yet those leadership abilities have not been used outside the classroom.

In developing this new paradigm for school leadership, traditional beliefs and hierarchical relations must be challenged. This is by no means an easy task. For decades the structure of schools has done little to allow and encourage teachers to seek new roles in influencing and reshaping educational practices. Interestingly, teachers are held accountable for a system that they had little opportunity to help design. It is no wonder, then, that teachers are reluctant to change, take risks, or challenge the status quo. The inherent distrust that is perpetuated in the limitation of leadership opportunities based on traditional role expectation will only serve to inhibit the type of pervasive change needed to meet the needs of students in the twenty-first century.

The challenge then exists to develop both the culture and the vehicles to thrust teachers into leadership roles. Clearly, concepts related to culture and leadership opportunity are both interactive and cyclical. That is, while culture influences risk taking and willingness to change, establishing vehicles for teachers to assume meaningful leadership roles likewise influences school culture. These opportunities for teacher leaders are possible on a broad continuum of informal to formal with an impact on both individual and school-wide practices.

This book provides a summary of much of what we need to know and a conceptual framework of practical strategies to assist educators in planning for and bringing forth the requisite changes. Changes in philosophy, behavior, and practice can position a school to meet the challenges of today and the next century.

To facilitate its use the book has been organized into eleven chapters that suggest an interdependent sequence that exists among the areas of school reform that must be considered and addressed. It presents, by chapter, issues which stand alone but are interrelated in their potential to bring about substantive change. Each chapter provides the background and information on the selected topic and concludes with practical strategies to foster effective practices for the twenty-first century. The individual chapters combine to provide the reader with a systemic, interrelated model for a comprehensive school improvement process.

Chapter 1 provides an overview of the topics that schools will need to address and what truly competent teachers will need to master. Chapter 2 describes strategies for the selection, induction, and retention of a high-quality professional staff. Chapters 3 through 8 identify what teachers need to know about curriculum, instruction, assessment, the use of time, technology, and collaboration. Chapters 9 and 10 provide models for the differentiated training, development, and supervision of teachers. Chapter 11 provides a unified model describing the interrelatedness of the concepts that lead to effective schooling in the twenty-first century.

It is hoped that this book will serve as a guide to program planning. Additionally, the practical strategies and processes provided in each chapter can be used to initiate change in the school or improve current practices. We have both the knowledge and skills to make a difference. We require only the will and the way to bring about the required changes. The very nature of American education is at risk if we fail to act. Hopefully, this book about change will provide the basis and impetus for every educator to begin the process.

CHAPTER 1

Schools of the Twenty-First Century
Establishing a Framework for Success

In many respects schools are already in the twenty-first century. The initiatives developed throughout this decade will define the competencies and the character of the next generation. During the past 20 years, much research has been generated about what constitutes effective schools and viable learning experiences for our students. This research and ensuing dialogue have generated much debate concerning the fundamental aspects of the goals of education, school governance structures, and the changing roles of parents, teachers, and administrators in the schools of the future.

General agreement exists that the demands on public education to prepare students for the twenty-first century are dramatically different from the mission of public education designed over 100 years ago. Yet attempts at systematic reform have generally failed.

By most measures, United States students perform poorly in comparison to students in other industrial and technologically advanced nations. While some question exists as to the validity of these comparisons, it is clear that many schools are not meeting the challenges of effectively educating our youth.

Much has been written concerning the underlying causes for failure to effectively sustain school reform. In general, this failure has been fostered by a reliance on untested theory, an ill-defined premise for the need for change, and a failure to recognize the dynamics of schools and school staff as a social system.

All too often, attempts at educational change are implemented in response to crisis or the need to try a promising innovation. These approaches often lead to short-lived "tinkering" whose origins are not founded in research or whose implementation is resisted by various stakeholders within the school community.

1

Cawelti and Roberts (1993), after analyzing the results of over 10,000 surveys sent to high school principals throughout the country, concluded that "there's a lot of activity going on, but there have been very few schools that have been able to put it all together" (p. 4).

Glickman (1993) discovered that activities in and of themselves can become the goal. He found that many schools are equating measures of activities with actual improvement of performance. While such measures have a legitimate function, they should not be used as a substitute for student learning outcomes.

The scope, nature, and magnitude of the kinds of issues that need to be addressed make it unlikely that change will come quickly or easily. The generally conservative nature of education, the resistance of organizations to change, the unique problems presented by the bureaucratic nature of schools, and the tradition of autonomy among teachers make the task so overwhelming that it might easily be abandoned. Yet enough is known about the teaching–learning process to guide the transformation of classroom and school practices. In many instances, resistance to change is inevitable. The primary task of managing this change is not technical but motivational. Thus, a critical part of improving schools for the twenty-first century is dependent upon an organization's ability to build commitment among those who must implement it. Evans (1993) describes five dimensions of this readiness for change: (1) the content of reform, (2) the faculty's willingness and capacity for change, (3) the strength of the school as an organization, (4) support and training, and (5) leadership.

To that end, the goal in planning for successful transformation is to create a professional culture in which instruction and curriculum decisions are based on informed research; support inquiry and cooperative collaboration; and establish a primary concern for the successful achievement of all students (Ogden and Germinario, 1995).

Connor (1993) describes three levels of change occurring, sometimes simultaneously, to facilitate this process:

- Renewal activities help the school do what it is already doing, only better and in a more efficient manner.
- Reform-driven activities alter existing procedures and requirements and enable the school to adapt to new circumstances or requirements.
- Restructuring activities change fundamental practices and relationships within the school and between the school and the greater community.

Using this framework, the school community is empowered to establish a clear vision for their school, which is the centerpiece for school improvement and reform. This vision must focus on several central themes; a brief identification and description of these concepts are provided below.

CURRICULUM

Despite ongoing reform efforts, the nature of classroom practice, the processes, and the content of instruction in public school classrooms today are little different from what they were in 1980 or 1970 (Smith and O'Day, 1990).

The most important issues in curriculum development are deciding what learning content and learning experiences will most benefit students in the future. Decisions as to the nature of what students should know will drive expected learning outcomes and standards. These decisions are eventually translated into a coherent curriculum that is not simply a collection of disparate pieces but provides a sense of unity, connectedness, relevance, and authenticity.

Within this context, curriculum for the twenty-first century should be framed around a set of guiding principles including: success for all learners; appropriate content; integration and authenticity; social and cultural responsibility; critical thinking and reasoning; use of technology; and standards and accountability.

Success for All Learners

While teachers often speak of reaching all students, a disparity exists between the ideal and what actually happens (Lortre, 1975). Curriculum for the twenty-first century must emphasize learning outcomes where each student demonstrates competencies before moving on.

Appropriate Content

Discussions regarding the development of a core set of knowledge that students should learn at a given grade level have become the centerpiece of educational reform in many states. Using a modified Delphi approach, Uchida et al. (1996) obtained consensus from a panel of over fifty leaders in education, business, and government. From their responses a list of major academic content areas students need to master for success in the twenty-first century was developed. This list includes:

(1) Math, logic, and reasoning skills; functional and operational literacy; and an understanding of statistics
(2) Critical interpersonal skills including speaking, listening, and the ability to be part of a team
(3) Effective information accessing and processing skills using technology

(4) Writing skills to enable students to communicate effectively

(5) Knowledge of American history and government to function in a democratic society, and an understanding of issues surrounding patriotism

(6) A scientific knowledge base, including applied science

(7) An understanding of the history of the world and of world affairs

(8) Multicultural understanding including insights into diversity and the need for an international perspective

(9) Knowledge of foreign languages

(10) Knowledge of world geography

Integration and Authenticity

Relevant linkages among learning objectives are critical to the curriculum of the twenty-first century. When such a curriculum is in place, young people are more likely to integrate educational experiences into their schemes of meaning, which in turn broadens and deepens their understanding of themselves and their world (Beane, 1995).

Social and Cultural Responsibilities

Curriculum must prepare students to understand their society and its multiplicity of cultures. A school that is truly committed to teaching about diversity reinforces the curriculum with ongoing interdisciplinary opportunities for students to learn about culture, develop cultural sensitivity, examine their own biases (and the biases of others), and develop skills necessary to communicate effectively with all types of people and to survive in a multicultural world. Specific objectives common to multicultural programs include:

- knowing about and feeling proud of one's own culture and ethnic identity
- knowing about and appreciating cultures different from one's own
- recognizing contributions that all types of people—women and men, young and old, rich and poor, including those from minority and nontypical cultures—have made to the school, community, nation, and world
- developing skills for communicating effectively with people from different backgrounds
- recognizing and refusing to accept any behavior based on stereotypes, prejudice, or discrimination
- recognizing the economic interdependence among nations

Critical Thinking and Reasoning

Schools of the twenty-first century must promote increasing opportunities for students to take greater responsibilities for their learning. Students are confronted with information at an astounding rate. Increasingly, students must be prepared to identify, analyze, manipulate, and draw conclusions about what they see, hear, and read.

Technology

Technology is one way to provide significant tools for teachers and students to develop an information-rich instructional environment to solve problems more efficiently, enhance thinking operations, organize and process information, communicate ideas, learn new information, reinforce prior learning, and apply learning to future life situations.

The research on student learning clearly reflects the importance of technology in today's schools. Specifically, the effective use of technology can be linked to improved problem-solving skills and increased student motivation and higher levels of academic achievement. It is extremely important that today's schools have the capability of delivering instruction in a climate that is conducive to learning and can facilitate technology as a learning tool.

Computers and other technology are fast becoming a frequent sight in America's classrooms. Unfortunately, all too often they are used as electronic workbooks or viewed as a separate type of content. Curriculum for the twenty-first century must infuse technology into the content of every learning unit. The interactive, high-performance uses of technology could allow students to solve real-world problems, retrieve information from electronic libraries, perform scientific simulations and experiments, "travel" to far away places, and analyze large volumes of information.

Standards and Accountability

"What gets measured gets done" (Peters, 1987, p. 480). Systematic data collection of student outcomes must become part of the curriculum for the twenty-first century. The primary principle of this activity, however, must be to improve student learning. This process should be consistent with current knowledge about how learning takes place and provide continuous feedback for the student.

Methods of assessment must be linked to authentic learning objectives and include methods such as observations, interviews, projects, tests, experiments, portfolios, and journals.

INSTRUCTION

Curriculum may be considered the heart of educational reform. Instruction is clearly the muscle. The delivery of content in a relevant, interactive, and systematic fashion will ensure student learning. Most authors make explicit reference to the influence of constructivism on effective instruction. Brooks and Brooks (1993) summarize the major principles associated with this concept:

- The learner is an active maker of meaning.
- Learning at its best is socially constructed.
- Learners interact with each other.
- Learners apply knowledge in solving contextualized and meaningful problems.
- Learning results in conceptual or behavioral change.
- Optimal learning involves metacognition (reflecting about one's learning throughout the process).

To successfully integrate these principles into instructional delivery systems, teachers must look for ways to make learning more meaningful and collaborative. Increasingly, the world will become the classroom using both technological and human resources to promote authentic learning experiences.

PROFESSIONAL DEVELOPMENT

The framework for school improvement primarily comes from the thoughts and actions of professionals in the school. It is well documented that staff development and school improvement are undeniably related. Yet despite widespread interest and school district initiatives in staff development, much remains to be learned about the effectiveness of the process. All too often, schools embark on one set of training after another or provide isolated in-service experiences in an attempt to influence individual or school development (Ogden and Germinario, 1995).

Typically, a staff development system is developed to generate three kinds of efforts (Joyce and Showers, 1989): an *individual* component to enrich an individual's content knowledge or clinical competence as an instructor, principal, etc.; a *collective* component requiring the cooperative enterprise of the entire staff; and a *systematic* component embodying a district wide initiative requiring a coordinated effort among all branches of the school district organization.

In many respects, staff development outcomes must be reconceptualized from seeing each stage of a teacher's professional life as distinct and separate to a more holistic view of the development of a teacher from a novice to an advanced practitioner (Dilworth and Imig, 1995).

To facilitate this change in the way we organize staff development, we must change the way we think about educators as professionals. Essentially, we must shift the emphasis of the process from external and organizationally initiated to a more internal and reflective emphasis. The outcome of such a transformation will increasingly guide staff members from generic in-service and training experiences to self-initiated *professional* development.

Smylie and Conyers (1991) suggest that we must organize professional development opportunities that reflect the following paradigm shifts:

- from a deficit-based to a competency-based approach in which teachers' knowledge, skills, and experiences are considered assets
- from replication to reflection, in which teachers focus less on transfer of knowledge and strategy to more on analytical and reflective learning
- from learning separately to learning together, in which teachers are jointly responsible for their work in classrooms, and their wisdom and experiences are perceived as professional resources
- from centralization to decentralization, in which the role of a school system's central administration shifts from identifying and organizing staff development activities to facilitating those activities that school-based staff have determined important

TECHNOLOGY

Our society is experiencing a scientific and technological revolution of unprecedented proportions. Technology has changed much in the way we work and live. However, that technology has not substantially changed the way teachers teach and students are expected to learn.

Regardless of the reason, the teacher-centered mode for instructional delivery continues to be standard school practice. In spite of a large body of research supporting more dynamic instructional strategies, today's classrooms are still dominated by a "chalk and talk" mentality.

Cuban (1995) provides several reasons why teachers have been slow to use technology in their classrooms:

(1) Most teachers have limited access to equipment; additionally, newly purchased technologies often become obsolete.

(2) The century-old form of age-graded schools with self-contained classrooms, curriculum divided into discrete segments of knowledge, and a schedule that brings students and teachers together for short periods of

time places strong parameters on the integration of any innovation, including technology.

(3) The predominate role of teacher as gatekeeper of knowledge continues to be expected and, in most cases, rewarded.

In reality, the demands of classroom life make it difficult for teachers to integrate new methods into their classrooms. The requirements to cover local- and state-mandated curriculums, the perplexities involved in addressing the diverse social and behavioral needs of students, and the general lack of systemic technology training add to the difficulties of integrating technology into today's classrooms. Thus, most teachers are casual or non-users, but an increased number of computers (and other technologies) have encouraged some teachers to experiment in employing technology. These classrooms are won over one at a time, making general application slow.

Today any teacher, school, or school district that is attempting to maximize its efficiency and ultimately student learning must consider how technology is integrated into the daily lives of students. Microcomputers, CD-ROMs, the Internet, interactive video, local- and wide-area networks, e-mail, voice mail, and other technologies offer powerful tools to increase student learning. Likewise, technology can facilitate connections between and within schools enabling students, teachers, and administrators to work in an information-rich, collaborative environment. Technology can provide a vehicle to enrich the relationship between schools and homes. Likewise, technology can provide access between schools and the larger community.

The United States Office of Technology Assessment (1995) has identified the potential benefits of technology in education. They include:

(1) Changing teaching and learning
- resources for teaching abstract concepts, complex systems, problem solving and basic skills
- resources for group work and collaborative inquiry
- adaptable to various student learning styles and special needs
- teachers report they (1) expect more of students, (2) are more comfortable with students working independently, (3) present more complex materials, (4) tailor instruction more to individual needs, (5) adopt new roles so that there is more "guide on the side" than "sage on the stage," and (6) spend less time lecturing so that classrooms are more student centered.

(2) Assisting with daily tasks
- preparing lesson plans: On-line databases, CD-ROMs, videodisks, and other electronic sources help teachers create, customize, and update lessons.

- tracking student progress: Gradebook programs and databases update student profiles and maintain records.
- communicating: Telephone, voice-mail, and e-mail help teachers to contact parents, other teachers, or administrators to plan meetings and discuss student and administrative concerns.

(3) Enhancing professional development
- "just in time" training and support: Satellite, video, cable, and computers give access to new ideas, master teachers, and other experts for training and follow-up.
- formal courses and advanced degrees: Distance learning technologies are used for courses not available locally.
- informal educational opportunities: On-line contact with teacher colleagues and other experts is available.

(4) Preparing new teachers
- models of effective teaching: Video can take prospective teachers into classrooms to watch effective teachers in action.
- computer and video simulations and case studies: These can give prospective teachers practice solving teaching challenges in a non-threatening environment.
- electronic networks: These minimize isolation during field experiences and provide support and interaction with college faculty or mentors.

Simply placing technology into the classroom won't significantly change teaching and learning. Additionally, technology in and of itself will not produce school improvement. Instead, it must be looked upon as a powerful tool for teaching students more efficiently and promoting the intellectual inquiry needed for students to adapt to a world where the only constant is rapid change.

COLLABORATION

To be truly successful, teachers of the future must transform the relative isolation in which they operate to extensive collaborative time for teachers to undertake and sustain school improvement. This collaboration may be more important than equipment, facilities, or even staff development (Fullan and Miles, 1992).

Within the school and throughout the community teachers, parents, students, and other community members will need to become primary participants in the process of defining the mission and structure of public education. They will need to be involved in identifying more effective and efficient ways of using resources and of ensuring the maintenance of high-quality standards. Essentially, these collaborations should be focused upon three major elements: collaboration within the school, collaboration with parents, and collaboration with the greater community.

Collaboration within the School

Collaborative schools provide a collegial climate and appropriate opportunities for professionals in the school to work together toward a common vision of school improvement. Additionally, it places significant emphasis on cooperative activities to promote professional development.

Because collaborative schools are a composite of beliefs and practices, it is easier to describe than define. This description of collaboration includes the following essential elements:

- the belief, based on effective schools research, that the quality of education is largely determined by what happens at the school site
- the conviction, also supported by research findings, that instruction is most effective in a school environment characterized by norms of collegiality and continuous improvement
- the belief that teachers are professionals who should be given responsibility for the instructional process and held accountable for its outcomes
- the use of a wide range of practices and structures that enable administrators and teachers to work together on school improvement
- the involvement of teachers in decisions about school goals and the means for achieving them

Collaboration with Parents

Research strongly supports parent involvement in schools. When parents are meaningfully involved in their child's education, children achieve at a higher level and have more positive attitudes toward school (Jones, 1991). Yet meaningful parent involvement is only achieved when the school creates an environment that makes parents feel welcome, reaches out in a wide variety of ways, connects parents to needed resources, and provides systematic opportunities for participation. Epstein (1988) suggests that a comprehensive program of parent involvement should include: (1) techniques to help parents create home environments conducive to learning, (2) frequent and clear communications from teachers to parents about pupil progress, (3) the use of parents as resources in school (i.e., volunteers), (4) teacher guidance with educational activities in the home, and (5) involvement in school governance through such vehicles as the PTA and school planning committees.

Although approaches and strategies may vary, in schools focused on excellence the principal and staff realize that parents and the school are linked by the common goal of providing the best for the child. To facilitate this relationship, successful schools have developed partnerships with parents to ensure that:

- Parents have a real voice in shaping the school's educational program.
- Parents are helped to increase their effectiveness in working with their children both in school and at home.
- Parents are given through both formal and informal vehicles specific information regarding their child's performance and progress in school.
- Parents' concerns regarding their parenting role are facilitated through parent training opportunities.
- Parents are provided with the necessary resources and networks to ensure greater control over their own lives and their child's future (Ogden and Germinario, 1995).

Collaboration with the Community

Classroom activities in the twenty-first century cannot be limited by the physical space in the school. In a real sense, opportunities for student learning will be part of a total culture, a culture not confined to discrete places or restrictive times.

Additionally, schools will enrich their resources by coordinated functions and articulation agreements between schools and business entities. These may include loaning personnel for teaching and consulting, establishing satellite school operations within business facilities, furnishing schools with computers, and establishing preschool or day-care programs (Rudiger and Krinsky, 1992). Organizing and working with community resources will become a critical skill for all school personnel.

ORGANIZATION AND TIME

To be truly effective, teachers must organize instructional time to provide learning opportunities that are less fragmented, less hurried, and more intensive.

In a review of the use of time and organizational factors in high schools, Canady and Rettig (1995) detail the inherent problems in the typical student schedule. These problems include:

- adding to the impersonal nature of the school
- exacerbating discipline problems
- limiting instructional possibilities for teachers

- prohibiting flexible time to meet individual students' learning needs
- resulting in "non-user friendly" workplaces for staff

In most schools, the organizational use of time allocated within the school day has not changed in decades. Looking at classroom time as distinct periods for the delivery of distinct content is contrary to what we know about how students learn and often promotes irrelevance between learning activities.

All school professionals must become aware of the constraints and benefits associated with how they organize the school day. Teachers particularly skilled in organizing and using time well find the opportunity to use instructional techniques and strategies that add meaning and depth to students' learning activities.

There is a very strong interconnectiveness associated with the concepts discussed above. While each in and of itself warrants study, and, if appropriate, implementation, the major benefits associated with them are truly derived when they are looked upon as necessary pieces in an integrated system for school improvement.

It would be impractical to believe that each of these concepts is of equal importance to each school. Similarly, it is not prudent to expect all major stakeholders in the school community to embrace the need for and the significance of change. All too often educators have attempted to jump in to solve a problem without first understanding the full scope of the problem. Thus, implementing wide-reaching change in schools has, more often than not, proven ineffective.

A more prudent way of influencing school improvement efforts may be through a process of *systematic tinkering*. Unlike the isolated nonconnective efforts that many schools have embraced to improve schools, systematic tinkering provides a clear vision of where a school wants to go and how it will get there and applies different degrees of emphasis and resources to different elements of the overall improvement model.

The basic premise for such an approach lies in the differences in adult and child learning. Adults bring a much more highly developed set of beliefs about what works and doesn't work in a given situation. Educators, like all adult professionals, have been socialized into a set of norms and values specific to ways of doing what is right for them. To some degree teachers develop a set of survival skills to meet the demands of the profession and the ever increasing complexities of students. Thus, for successful change in our schools, we must direct our emphasis to the classroom and its teachers. Teachers will ultimately determine the extent to which school innovations translate into meaningful results.

While not fashionable in the eyes of some reformers, this more incremental approach embraces the realities of life in today's schools and is built around the following assumptions:

- Use what we already know and what is supported in the research and operationalized in current practice.
- Keep what is good in our classrooms and schools.
- Recognize organizational constraints, limitations, and the inherent instinct to resist change.
- Accept that teachers are the major participants and contributors in the school improvement process.
- Value the role and participation of parents and community members in the improvement of schools.
- Transform an administrator from a manager to a collaborative leader.

The preparation of teachers and administrators for the challenges of the twenty-first century will only be successful if we recognize how schools currently operate and ultimately accept change. Working within this context, schools (and the individuals who work in them), can change standard practices in a way that preserves what is effective and simultaneously transition into needed change. The cumulative impact of small improvements will be dramatic. The litmus test for this change will not be the extent of a school's innovations but rather the solid, purposeful, enduring results it obtains for its students (Glickman, 1993).

SUMMARY

This chapter provided an overview of the major elements associated with effective schooling in the twenty-first century. It acknowledged the interconnectiveness of the elements and provided an organizational context for systematic implementation within the parameters of current school life.

Subsequent chapters will provide a historical foundation, a conceptual framework, and examples of practical applications for each of these elements. Additionally, a model aimed at describing the interrelations of the elements will be developed.

REFERENCES

Beane, James A. (1995). *Toward a Coherent Curriculum. The 1995 ASCD Yearbook,* Alexandria, VA: Association for Supervision and Curriculum Development.

Brooks, J. G. and M. G. Brooks (1993). *In Search of Understanding: The Case for Constructivist Classrooms.* Alexandria, VA: Association for Supervision and Curriculum Development.

Canady, Robert L. and Michael D. Rettig (1995). *Block Scheduling: A Catalyst for Change in High Schools.* Princeton, NJ: Eye on Education.

Cawelti, Gordon and Art Roberts. (1993). *Redesigning General Education in American High Schools.* Alexandria, VA: Association for Supervision and Curriculum Development.

Connor, D. (1993). *Managing at the Speed of Change.* New York: Villard Books.

Cuban, Larry (1995). "Reality bytes." *Electronic Learning,* 14(8): 18–19.

Dilworth, Mary E. and David G. Imig. (1995). "Professional Teacher Development." *The EIRC Review,* 3(3): 5–11.

Epstein, Joyce (1988). "How Do We Improve Programs for Parent Involvement?" *Educational Horizons* (66): 58–59.

Evans, Robert (1993). "The Human Face of Reform." *Educational Leadership,* 51(1): 19–23.

Fullan, M. and M. Miles (1992). "Getting Reform Right: What Works and What Doesn't." *Phi Delta Kappan,* 745–752.

Glickman, Carl D. (1993). *Reviewing America's Schools: A Guide for School-based Action.* San Francisco, CA: Jossey-Boss.

Jones, Linda T. (1991). *Strategies for Involving Parents in Their Children's Education,* Fastback, No. 315, Bloomington, IN. Phi Delta Kappan Educational Foundation.

Joyce, Bruce and Beverly Showers. (1989). *Student Achievement Through Staff Development.* White Plains, NY: Longman, Inc.

Lortre, D. C. (1975). *Schoolteacher: A Sociological Study.* Chicago, IL: University of Chicago Press.

Office of Technology Assessment. (1995). *Teachers & Technology: Making the Connection.* Washington, D.C.: U.S. Government Printing Office.

Ogden, Evelyn H. and Vito Germinario. (1995). *The Nation's Best Schools: Blueprints for Excellence, Volume II—Middle and Secondary Schools.* Lancaster, PA: Technomic Publishing Company, Inc.

Peters, Thomas (1987). *Thriving on Chaos.* New York: Alfred A. Knopf.

Rudiger, Charles W. and Ira W. Krinsky (1992). "Getting to 2001." *International Journal of Educational Reform,* 1(3): 285–290.

Smith, M. and J. O'Day. Position Paper on Education Reform Decade. Stanford University Center for Policy Resources in Education, 1990.

Smylie, Mark A. and John G. Conyers (1991). "Changing Conceptions of Teaching Influence the Future of Staff Development." *Journal of Staff Development,* 12(1): 12–16.

Uchida, Donna, Marion Cetron and Floretta McKenzie (1996). *Preparing Students for the Twenty-first Century.* Reston, VA: American Association of School Administrators.

CHAPTER 2

Selection, Recruitment, Induction, and Relations of Teachers

Schools are only as good as their teachers. While the reform movement has cited the need for cultural and curricular changes in our schools, a common theme for school improvement is the attitude and skill of the classroom teacher. In fact, to a large degree teachers are the main constant within the school organization. The average teacher in the United States spends about 23 years in the same district, most in the same school, and many in the same classroom. During this time they will have four or five principals; five or six superintendents; and over 100 board of education members. Yet despite the influences parents, administrators, and board members may have on school improvement and practice, it is the teacher who will dictate the success of any change in school operation.

While the importance of hiring and keeping talented, qualified teachers is undeniable, little research is available to guide personnel practices. Specifically, the research to date has not sufficiently addressed questions such as (1) what criteria need to be assessed in hiring teachers, (2) which of those criteria are the most important in the process, and (3) what variables influence hiring decisions (Place and Drake, 1994).

One of the most significant reasons why meaningful research is not available is that often the medium for doing such research is the job interview. This line of research produces disappointing validity coefficients, at least in part because of insufficient control over the variable being studied (Young and Ryerson, 1986).

Despite the absence of research to guide personnel practices, enough is known from practices throughout our nation's schools to establish effective parameters for hiring qualified teachers. This chapter will present those processes in three distinct sections: recruitment, selection, and retaining teachers.

15

RECRUITMENT

Like any other school practice, recruitment efforts must be carefully planned and go beyond merely interviewing and hiring candidates. Wise et al. (1987) in a study of teacher recruitment provide three basic requirements for effective recruiting:

- Schools must have something to sell potential candidates—tangibles such as adequate salaries and attractive working conditions.
- Schools must sell themselves to the right candidates, that is, those who meet the district's needs.
- Schools must follow up on the job offers they make and reduce procedural barriers that exist for teachers to accept employment.

The purpose of recruitment is to provide a large enough group of candidates so that school officials can select the qualified candidates it needs. An important part of the recruiting process is developing a written statement of the content of the job. This is commonly referred to as a *job description.* Once the position description has been determined, an accompanying *job specification* is developed identifying the background, educational level, experiences, and personal characteristics an individual must have to effectively perform in the position. While not an uncommon practice, all too often job descriptions and specifications are outdated and given little credence in the recruiting process.

As teaching has become more complex, the need to develop operational standards to guide recruiting (and initial screening) have become more important. No longer can school officials use existing structure to get a "feel" for potential teachers. Instead, characteristics embodied in a contemporary job description might include:

- understanding and implementing effective teaching models
- using computer-assisted instruction
- teaching higher-level thinking skills
- implementing mastery teaching
- applying technologies such as interactive video in the classroom
- using computers for classroom management, grading, reporting, etc.
- teaching to different learning styles
- using hands-on approaches in mathematics and science
- effectively implementing "time-on-task"
- putting research-based instructional skills into practice (Steuteville-Brodinsky et al., 1989)

A similar list of skills necessary for effective teaching has been developed by the National Association of Secondary School Principals (1996). In a partnership with the Carnegie Foundation for the Advancement of Teaching, in the high school of the twenty-first century seven critical instructional skills were identified:

(1) Each high school teacher will have a broad base of academic knowledge with depth in at least one subject area.
(2) Teachers will use a variety of strategies and settings that identify and accommodate individual learning styles to engage students.
(3) Teachers will be coaches and facilitators of learning to promote more active involvement of students in their own learning.
(4) Teachers will teach in ways that help students to develop into competent problem solvers and critical thinkers.
(5) Teachers will convey a sense of caring to their students so that their students feel that their teachers share a stake in their learning.
(6) Teachers will use technology in their instruction in ways that improve student learning.
(7) Teachers will integrate assessment into instruction so that assessment does not merely measure students, but becomes part of the learning process itself.

Upon establishment of the characteristics necessary for successful employment, sources for job candidates must be identified. The most common sources are *internal,* through employee referrals and existing temporary employees, and *advertising,* primarily through newspapers, professional journals, and outside referral sources such as employment services, special events and job fairs, and professional networking. Of course, special effort must be given to the hiring of minority or under-represented candidates within the school/district. The Marietta, Georgia, School District (Fielder, 1993) has developed a series of successful strategies to increase staff diversity. With the commitment of the entire administrative staff to increase minority candidates to teach within the school district, the following activities were initiated:

(1) Increase in visiting and recruiting efforts in traditionally black colleges and universities
(2) Increase in recruiting area to encompass the entire United States, which was accomplished through the assistance of a minority-owned recruiting firm in the Southeast
(3) Cooperative recruiting efforts with other school districts to share cost of advertising in national publications targeted at minorities, such as *Black Collegian*

(4) The initiation of the "Grow Your Own" scholarship program jointly formed by the Marietta School District and Kennesaw State College, which provides scholarships to perspective teachers in return for agreeing to teach in the school district

(5) The development of the Minority Applicant Support Program, which pairs minority applicants with current minority employees in the district

The National Commission on Teaching and America's Future provides a vision and strategies for the development of a twenty-first-century teaching profession that can facilitate the nation's educational goals (Darling-Hammond, 1996). The commission urges a complete overhaul of teacher preparation and professional development to ensure that they reflect current knowledge and practice. This redesign would create a continuum of standards from recruitment and preservice education through licensing, hiring, and induction. One recommendation is the overhaul of teacher recruitment to ensure qualified teachers in every classroom. Specific recommendations included the following actions:

- Increase the ability of financially disadvantaged districts to pay for qualified teachers and insist that school districts hire only qualified teachers.
- Redesign and streamline hiring at the district level—principally by creating a central "electronic hiring hall" for all qualified candidates and establishing cooperative relationships with universities to encourage early hiring of teachers.
- Eliminate barriers to teacher mobility by promoting reciprocal interstate licensing and by working across states to develop portable pensions.
- Provide incentives (including scholarships and premium pay) to recruit teachers for high-need subjects and locations.
- Develop high-quality pathways to teaching for recent graduates, mid-career changers, paraprofessionals already in the classroom, and military and government retirees.

As the demand for more qualified teachers increases over the next decade, recruitment will become of ever increasing significance. The National Center for Education Statistics estimates schools will need to employ between 400,000 and 600,000 additional teachers over the next decade to keep up with rising enrollment. It is predicted this increase will come in the midst of a cycle that should bring massive teacher retirements (Haselkorn, 1996).

SELECTION

The selection of qualified teachers is probably the surest way to improve the quality of education for students in our schools. While this statement seems quite simplistic, little evidence exists that schools have systematically addressed the selection of teachers as the foundation for school improvement efforts.

"If a caring, qualified teacher for every child is the most important ingredient in education reform, then it should no longer be the factor that is most frequently overlooked" (Darling-Hammond, 1996, p. 194).

Schools often lose the best candidates because of the inability of staff to identify those candidates who have the most potential for success. Most frequently this is a function of the screening and interviewing process.

Place and Drake (1994) report that no difference exists between principals at either the elementary or high school level on the priority of the criteria they set for hiring employees. The criteria in the order of priority by all principals included: (1) enthusiasm for teaching, (2) communication skills, (3) interviewer's evaluation, (4) former teaching performance, (5) verbal fluency, (6) specialized knowledge, (7) reference information, (8) grade point average, and (9) self-purposing behaviors. While the list may provide a valuable generalization about the highest and lowest priorities principals place on hiring teachers, little evidence exists that these priorities lead to the selection of the best qualified candidate. In fact, given the lack of research to guide hiring practices, it is likely that, as well meaning as school personnel may be, they may simply perpetuate the hiring of people who demonstrate those traits that help them successfully gain employment.

Given these challenges, it is important that school personnel systematize the screening, interviewing, and selection process. It would seem most appropriate to first examine the most frequently used screening process—the interview.

The Structured Interview

The structured interview uses a standard list of questions that provide focus to hiring decisions. The questions often require applicants to be reflective and offer substantive responses. Pawlas (1995) describes a type of structured interview called "target selection" where the applicant responds to a list of prepared questions and is evaluated based on the STAR (Situation, Task, Action, Result) procedure. Each applicant responds to a question by describing the situation, the action taken, and the result of that action. Over thirty different interview questions are then asked in four separate categories. The categories and a sample question within each category are provided below:

(1) Teacher relationships with students
   • You give an assignment. A student ridicules the assignment, saying it doesn't make sense. What would you do?

- How would you challenge the slow learner and the advanced student within the same class?

(2) Teacher relationships with colleagues
- What kind of teachers do you prefer to work with? Why?
- What qualities do you have that would enhance our teaching staff?

(3) Teacher relationships with parents
- A parent walks into your room before the school day begins, yelling and complaining about something you don't even understand. The parent is obviously very upset. What would you do?
- Describe the reasons why you would contact parents.

(4) Instructional techniques
- How would you integrate technology into the curriculum you would teach?
- What rules do you have for your classroom?

(5) A potpourri of topics and background information
- Why did you choose to become a teacher?
- Tell me about three people who have most influenced your own education and educational career.

Pawlas (1995) further asserts that applicants' responses should indicate they understand the purposes, methods, and materials of instruction, and (among other things) they are enthusiastic about teaching and are eager to improve their competencies.

Haberman (1995) identifies seven aptitudes of teachers that go beyond instructional and relationship skills. They are considered equally powerful in discriminating between "stars and quitters"; a brief explanation follows:

- organizational ability: the predisposition and ability to engage in planning and gathering of materials
- physical/emotional stamina: the ability to persist in situations characterized by violence, death, and other crises
- teaching style: the predisposition to engage in coaching rather than directive teaching
- explanations of success: the predisposition to emphasize a student's effort rather than ability
- basis of rapport: the approach to student involvement. Whose classroom is it? Whose work is to be protected?
- readiness: the approach to prerequisite knowledge. Who should be in this classroom?

It is important to note that whatever set of questions is used within the structured interview, the main purpose of the interview is to eliminate from consideration candidates who, for whatever reason, are clearly unqualified or do not "fit" the job expectations. To some extent, the interview validates (or invalidates) the initial recruitment and screening efforts. That is, through questioning school personnel can determine the utility of a candidate's potential beyond initial impressions and a review of certification, licenses, etc.

Additionally, structured interviews should be held at various levels within the school organization. Teachers, administrators, and, if deemed appropriate, parents or school-based improvement teams, bring different perspectives to the needs of children and provide valuable insight into the selection of quality teachers.

OBSERVING THE CANDIDATE AT WORK IN THE CLASSROOM

Observing candidates teaching is probably the best way to judge whether they possess the human, organizational, and instructional skills needed to promote student learning.

Within the district there are several ready sources of candidates whose work can be directly observed: substitute teachers, student teachers, and teacher assistants. Most school districts have the opportunity to hire fully licensed substitute teachers in a variety of subject/grade areas. In some respects substitutes are subject to the same observations and expectations as regular staff members. When interviewed, substitute teachers who express interest in full-time employment can be taken through the same rigors of selection as candidates for permanent positions. That is, a modified, structured interview and classroom observations should be a routine part of their selection and induction process.

Student teachers are very often available through local colleges and universities. Having worked under the direct supervision of one of the district's skilled, experienced teachers, the student teacher is acquainted with the expectations of the district. Similarly, a careful analysis of the student teacher's potential as it relates to the district's/school's needs can be accomplished.

Many school districts develop partnerships with local colleges and universities to provide a steady source of student teachers. If such a partnership is initiated, it is important that the same expectations for hiring teachers, substitute teachers, etc. be maintained when accepting a student teacher. Simply stated, it would be inappropriate to accept a student teacher whose skills and background show little potential for enriching the lives of students in the classroom.

Occasionally, a school district may hire a licensed teacher to serve as a teaching assistant. This often occurs when an experienced teacher may be reentering the job market or when a recent college graduate is unable to find a teaching job. Again, the opportunities to assess the teaching assistant's work ethic, relationship with students, etc. are easily attainable. While information about direct teaching skills may not be observed, information concerning the teaching assistant's potential can prove valuable.

In spite of its inherent difficulties, direct observation of candidates coming from other districts is very important. While this should not be a routine procedure for all candidates, it is best used as a final assessment for candidates who will most probably be offered employment. These observations can serve two valuable purposes: (1) it provides a final reassurance that the candidate of choice can "deliver" the strategies and outcomes discussed during the various stages of the screening and interview process, and (2) it can provide an initial assessment of where the candidate is best placed in the district's/school's professional development program.

INDUCTION OF BEGINNER TEACHERS

Few things in education are more difficult than one's first year as a teacher. The research on new teacher attrition is disturbing:

- Almost 15% of new teachers leave teaching after 1 year.
- Between 40–50% of new teachers leave after fewer than 7 years.
- As a group, the most academically talented teachers are the least likely to stay in the profession.
- Young teachers, when compared to more experienced teachers, report more emotional exhaustion and a greater degree of depersonalization (Tonnesen and Patterson, 1992).

Although the reasons for these phenomena vary, there is significant support that the difficulties are environmental in nature. Gordon (1991) has identified six such environmental factors: (1) difficult work assignments, (2) unclear expectations, (3) inadequate resources, (4) isolation, (5) role conflict, and (6) reality shock.

What happens during the first few months after a teacher is hired establishes that teacher's future attitude about himself or herself and about the profession. A school's failure to adequately induct, orient, and support these teachers leads to an excessive "dropout rate."

All too often novice teachers (or experienced teachers new to the school) are handed their textbooks and their keys with the assumption that they will be happy and productive. While some, through trial and error, may eventually find a degree of success, formal induction into the school will provide a systematic path to help ensure both teacher satisfaction and, more importantly, student learning.

While the term *induction* is not new, the particular meaning that it has now taken on is somewhat different from meanings it has formerly been given. Whereas induction often referred to the informal, or reactionary, and ritualistic socialization of new teachers, its use now refers to more sophisticated and systematic efforts to initiate, shape, and sustain the initial experiences of prospective career teachers (DeBolt, 1992).

Induction programs have become increasingly more popular throughout the last decade. Realizing the greater challenge facing today's novice teachers, school districts have initiated programs to help new teachers met the current demands of teaching. These challenges, associated with the diverse nature of children in classrooms, the extensive curricular expectations to teach more, the greater variety of instructional tools from which to choose, and increasing accountability from school officials and parents, all lead to the complexities associated in teaching in today's schools.

Once in the classroom, novice teachers experience a sense of panic, feeling that their teacher education programs left them ill-prepared to deal with actual classroom life. Almost invariably, new teachers engage in stressful trial-and-error periods during which they figure out what works, with survival as their primary goal. No longer having the safety nets associated with student teaching, the teachers are awakened to the stark reality that the accountability for planning, organization of instruction, and assessment of students is now solely their responsibility.

Induction programs are aimed at minimizing the stresses associated with beginning teaching by providing programs that seek to add to the experiences of becoming a teacher. Huling-Asten et al. (1989) list five common goals of programs designed to assist beginner teachers:

(1) To improve teaching performance
(2) To increase the retention of promising beginner teachers
(3) To promote the personal and professional well-being of beginner teachers
(4) To satisfy mandated requirements related to induction
(5) To transmit the culture of the school (and the teaching profession) to beginner teachers

Huling-Asten et al. (1989) have condensed a somewhat different set of goals that represent a more comprehensive view of the purpose of induction programs:

(1) Provide continuing assistance to reduce the problems known to be common to beginner teachers.
(2) Support development of the knowledge and the skills needed by beginner teachers to be successful in their initial teaching positions.

(3) Integrate beginner teachers into the social system of the school district and the community.
(4) Provide an opportunity for beginner teachers to analyze and reflect on their teaching with coaching from veteran support teachers.
(5) Initiate and build a foundation with new teachers for the continued study of teaching.
(6) Increase the positive attitudes of beginner teachers about teaching.
(7) Increase the retention of good beginner teachers in the profession.

In pursuit of goals such as these, induction programs have been developed into ongoing vehicles involving new teachers in a wide variety of activities. While programs may vary from providing intensive and continuing support to less structured or more informal "buddy" systems, the most effective programs are carefully planned and provide a variety of activities for the orientation and support of beginner teachers.

Strategies to assist in this process can include the use of support groups. The use of such groups is not for personal "therapy" but rather as an opportunity for relaxed reflection concerning the professional demands that novice teachers experience (Thies-Sprinthall and Gerler, 1990). These groups provide support and challenge (Hall and Loucks, 1978) for personal adaptation to teaching by providing the following stages for personalizing staff development:

- awareness—"I'm not concerned about new ideas or methods."
- informational—"Maybe I need to find out more about the requirements."
- personal—"How will this affect me?"
- management—"How can I organize my methods to control the class?"
- consequence—"How does my teaching affect the pupils?"
- collaboration—"Now I'm ready to share my ideas with other teachers."
- refocusing—"I'm developing new methods that are working even better."

One promising program increasingly used by successful schools is *peer mentoring*. While traditionally an informal relationship between new and veteran teachers, mentoring has emerged as a central theme of many induction programs. Mentoring, as the term suggests, provides for an experienced teacher to assist the new teacher as he or she faces the challenges of teaching. Anderson and Shannon (1988) offered a definition of mentoring that includes the following attributes:

- the process of nurturing
- the act of serving as a role model

- a provision for the five fundamental functions of the mentor—teaching, sponsoring, encouraging, counseling, and befriending
- a focus on professional and personal development
- an ongoing, caring relationship

Typically, mentors, who are usually excellent teachers, good role models, and positive people, are matched with new teachers within their discipline or grade level. Program design includes a mechanism that (1) promotes interaction, including class visitation, between new and veteran teachers, (2) shares research and experiences on effective teaching strategies, and (3) disseminates information on school policies, procedures, and routines. Often, specific times are provided within the workday to facilitate these activities. In a few schools (and mandated in a few states) a stipend is paid to the mentor for this assignment.

Galvey-Hjornevik (1985) found consistent evidence to support the importance of mentorship programs. The contention is made that the assignment of an appropriate support teacher is likely to be the most powerful and cost-effective intervention in an induction program. In fact, most of the beginning teachers in the study reported that having a mentor was the single most helpful aspect of induction activities because it provided a resource to turn to on a daily basis, if and when problems arose.

As one would guess, induction–mentor programs also have benefits for experienced teachers who have an active role in program development and implementation. A review of the specific benefits includes:

- a mechanism to revitalize teachers who experience mid-career doldrums
- a vehicle to provide developmentally appropriate professional growth opportunities for experience teachers
- a way to demonstrate appreciation and recognition of exceptional teachers
- an approach to develop and retain a high-quality teaching staff (Killon, 1990)

Finally, Tonnesen and Paterson (1992) provide a comprehensive summary of examples of concepts and activities that principals in schools with effective induction programs have employed.

- Treat new teachers like guests in your home; courtesy, acceptance, and support are crucial.
- Introduce them to everyone on the school staff. Set up meetings for beginner teachers and others—teachers, librarians, psychologists, nurses, and assistant principals—to exchange ideas.
- Hold individual and group orientation sessions.
- Meet regularly with new teachers. Discuss experiences and techniques that might help them.

- Visit new teachers' classrooms frequently.
- Assign strong, experienced teachers as mentors, and arrange for new teachers to meet their mentors before the school year begins.
- Offer praise and encouragement, but nip small problems in the bud before they become big problems.

RETENTION OF EFFECTIVE TEACHERS

Maintaining an effective school system requires the retention of the outstanding teachers that make up the lifeblood of every school. Approximately 40–50% of all teachers leave the profession within 7 years. Increasing numbers of teachers state that, if they had it to do over again, they probably would not choose to teach in public schools. In a very real sense, teachers' satisfaction with the workplace depends on the environment in which they work and the success of their experiences in the classrooms. To this end, schools have actively engaged and empowered teachers to seek self-fulfillment and satisfaction. Strategies such as improving the management of existing resources, involving teachers in school-based decision making, minimizing bureaucracy, empowering teachers through greater knowledge about teaching and learning, and breaking down teacher isolation through team teaching and planning, are all efforts to professionalize teaching so that our best teachers remain in the profession (Ogden and Germinario, 1995).

Respondents to a survey conducted by the Steuteville-Brodinsky et al. (1989), ranked in order of importance fifteen factors that school districts considered "effective in retaining good teachers." These factors included:

(1) Involvement of teachers in decisions that affect them
(2) Salary schedule with annual increments acceptable to teachers
(3) Consistent policies on discipline, homework, and parent conferences
(4) Giving teachers a voice, role, and vote on professional issues
(5) Principals trained in listening skills and human relations
(6) Mechanisms for teacher recognition, rewards, and praise
(7) Fair, effective teacher evaluation system
(8) Safe, clean schools
(9) Time for professional activities
(10) In-service education activities developed *with* teachers
(11) Establishing a career ladder for teachers
(12) Faculty meetings that are interesting, useful, and effective
(13) Reassignment policies acceptable to teachers

(14) Merit pay

(15) Effective grievance procedures

It is not by chance that the meaningful involvement of teachers is a significant feature associated with teacher retention in a school or district. A common theme that has been promoted throughout this book is that teacher involvement should be tailored to their respective career stage and skill level. Thus, asking beginner teachers to serve on a school-based council for school improvement would not be as beneficial as their participation in discussion groups for teaching strategies. Conversely, the involvement of skilled, experienced staff in action research that ultimately impacts in classroom or school successes would have a much more profound impact on their level of readiness and satisfaction.

Regardless of the vehicles used for teacher involvement, the goal of the activities should be to promote a sense of empowerment and ownership toward individual and school-wide professional development.

Maintaining teacher job satisfaction in an attempt to motivate and keep the most capable teachers is critical to the success of school improvement. Reforms related to school restructuring, site-based management, empowering teachers, and implementing career ladders attempt to enrich the professional lives of teachers. Yet research conducted over the last decade yields no simple solution for increasing job satisfaction among educators (Hartzell and Wenger, 1989). Job satisfaction for teachers tends to be multidimensional rather than unidimensional in nature and, more often than not, is not consistently related to predictable demographic variables. Although job dissatisfaction for teachers is commonly related to (1) negative student attitudes and discipline problems, (2) disappointment and stress, (3) low salaries, (4) poor working conditions, and (5) lack of professional recognition, little support is given to a categorical list of predictions. Instead, job dissatisfaction variables tend to revolve around a teacher's sense of powerlessness to appreciably affect the lives of students and satisfy the need to achieve, advance, and become self-actualized (Ellis, 1988).

Research conducted over the last decade provides no categorical steps to increasing job satisfaction among educators, yet variables such as management style of the principal, demographics, financial support, and class size find some support in the literature. Additionally, a school culture that stresses accomplishment and recognition is likely to elicit job satisfaction and commitment, whereas a culture emphasizing personal relationships and informal influence are of lesser importance. In most cases, clearly defined and reinforced lines of power have a negative influence on job satisfaction. Finally, teacher job satisfaction and commitment are most often associated with the behaviors of the school principal.

The research (Hartzell and Wenger, 1989) suggests that principals who develop and maintain satisfied teachers are those who

- structure work opportunities that can fulfill higher-order needs for recognition and self-actualization in teachers
- create a school climate for participatory management and teacher involvement in decision making
- nurture teacher autonomy, empowerment, and professional involvement
- cultivate, maintain, and use consideration behaviors, demonstrating concern for their employees, as well as for the task to be completed

In addition to involving teachers in meaningful ways within the school, strategies must be developed to recognize their respective individual and collective efforts. Through intrinsic and external reward opportunities and incentives, schools can provide teachers with a sense of accomplishment, power, prestige, and, in some cases, money, so that students can continue to benefit from a teacher's expertise. In a general sense, the purpose of recognition and incentive programs is to establish an environment in which special achievements and contributions of faculty and staff are recognized and applauded on a regular, systematic basis. In so doing, the faculty and staff will be encouraged to develop and sustain the efforts to teach children.

Linda Darling-Hammond (1996) describes schools as having few ways of encouraging and supporting teachers or rewarding increases in their knowledge and skills. She supports a career continuum that places teaching at the top of organizational development. She also supports increased expertise by (1) recognizing teacher accomplishments, (2) anticipating that teachers will continue to teach while taking on other roles that will allow them to share their knowledge, and (3) promoting continued skill development related to clear standards.

The need to recognize teacher accomplishments is a common theme in the literature associated with teacher satisfaction. Some suggestions for recognition that are repeatedly heard include (a) plaques of commendation, (b) recognition in staff notes or district newsletters, (c) written praise with evaluation, (d) written notes of appreciation by the superintendent or principal, (e) verbal compliments, (f) parent–teacher organization awards, and (g) teacher of the month or teacher appreciation days.

While the benefit of involvement and recognition of teachers for their role in professional development and school governance is important, they are not likely to stay unless they are compensated fairly for their level of training and performance on the job. For the most part, highly effective teachers (with similar levels of experience) receive the same rewards as mediocre teachers. Frequently, merit pay is discussed as a means to recognize exemplary teachers.

Merit pay has periodically been implemented (and frequently discarded) as a means of promoting tangible rewards for notable teacher performance. Very few school districts have successfully implemented such systems. In most cases, teacher unions look upon merit systems as an ineffective vehicle for school reform. Yet the success of a merit pay program depends primarily on careful, cooperative planning involving all constituencies who will be affected, so that the resultant plan is affordable, acceptable to teachers, and adapted to the needs of the district. Criteria for awards should reflect the goals of the program and should be applied fairly and consistently by trained evaluators. Failure of merit pay programs normally results from ambiguous or inconsistent standards, remote or authoritarian planning, or arbitrary award determinations (all of which engender teacher opposition), or from unforeseen administrative complexities and budget limitations.

Shaten (1983) describes five mechanisms to reward teachers that can be incorporated into a merit system:

(1) A base salary at three levels:
- a probationary/apprentice category, with a beginning salary competitive with the salary paid to comparable professionals
- a master teacher category with a salary at least $4,000 per year above the top of the probationary/apprentice scale
- a superior teacher category with a salary at least $4,000 per year above the master teacher category

(2) Individual teacher bonuses based upon outstanding student achievement and performance, as agreed upon prior to the presentation of the material to be learned, using valid instruments of measurement for the skill, content, processes, or use of the curriculum

(3) Department, team, school, or district-wide bonuses based on student achievement, recognition, and involvement outside the school but related to school programs

(4) Professional growth and involvement in other facets of the school, district, regional, or national organizations

(5) Extra-duty assignments based on current contractual obligations such as athletic coaching, dramatics, publications, student government, clubs, musical organizations, etc.

Despite its complexity, merit or other forms of differential rewards can have an impact on the retention of effective teachers. An initiative that has gained considerable recognition, the National Certification of Teachers, can be a viable mechanism to reward teachers using independent, external criteria and procedures. The National Board for Professional Teaching Standards was established in 1987 in response to a recommendation that the Carnegie

Task Force on Teaching as a Profession put forth in *A Nation Prepared: Teachers for the 21st Century (1986)*.

The National Board sets high and rigorous standards for what accomplished teachers should know and be able to do and certifies teachers who meet those standards. Teachers who earn National Board Certification have demonstrated through performance-based assessments that they

- are committed to students and their learning
- know the subjects they teach and how to teach those subjects to students
- are responsible for managing and monitoring student learning
- think systematically about their practice and learn from experience
- are members of learning communities (NBPTS, 1994)

Standards based on these five propositions are either completed or in progress for more than thirty different fields or teaching specialties. These fields, organized by subject and student developmental level, are the ones in which National Board Certification will be offered. Because the standards describe the skills, knowledge, and dispositions of accomplished teachers, they provide a model for how effective teaching can improve what and how students learn (Buday and Kelly, 1996).

The maintenance of a quality teaching staff is the most significant element of school improvement. Continued emphasis must be placed on this phenomenon if we are to prepare students for the rigors of life in the twenty-first century.

SUMMARY

This chapter provided a framework for the successful selection, recruitment, induction, and retention of a quality teaching staff. While the limited research in these areas does not point to categorical cause- and- effect relationships, enough is known to help guide planning and practice. Importantly, success for twenty-first-century schools and the teachers who work in them must be guided by systematic efforts to select, train, and keep quality professionals. The critical elements presented in this chapter must be part of an organized process to promote the mission of the school and to foster an environment that promotes success.

REFERENCES

Anderson, E. M. and A. L. Shannon. (1988). "Toward a Conceptualization of Mentoring." *Journal of Teacher Education.* 39(1): 38–42.

Buday, Mary Catherine and James A. Kelly. (1996). "National Board Certification and the Teaching Profession's Commitment to Quality Assurance." *Kappan.* 78(3): 215–219.

Darling-Hammond, Linda. (1996). "What Matters Most: A Competent Teacher for Every Child." *Kappan.* 78(3): 193–200.

DeBolt, Gary P. (1992). *Teacher Induction and Monitoring.* Albany, NY: State University of New York Press.

Ellis, Nancy H. (1988). "Job Redesign: Can It Influence Teacher Motivation?" Paper presented at the *Annual Meeting of New England Educational Research Organization.* Rockport, ME. April, 1988.

Fielder, Donald J. (1993). "Wanted: Minority Teachers—Strategies for Increasing Staff Diversity." *The Executive Educator.* 15(5): 33–34.

Galvey-Hjornevik, C. (1985). *Teacher Mentors: A Review of the Literature.* Austin, TX: The University of Texas at Austin, The Research and Development Center for Teacher Education, ERIC No. ED 263105.

Gordon, Stephen P. (1991). *How to Help Beginning Teachers Succeed.* Alexandria, VA: Association for Supervision and Curriculum Development.

Haberman, Martin. (1995). "Selecting Star Teachers for Children and Youth in Urban Poverty." *Kappan.* 76: 777–781.

Hall, G. and S. Loucks. (1978). "Teacher Concern as a Basis for Facilitating and Personalizing Staff Developing." *Teacher College Record.* 80(1): 36–53.

Hartzell, Gary and Marc Wenger. (1989). "Manage to Keep Teachers Happy." *The School Administrator.* 46(10): 22–24.

Haselkorn, David. (1996). *Breaking the Class Ceiling: Paraeducator Pathways in Teaching.* Belmont, MA: Recruiting New Teachers, Inc.

Huling-Asten, L., S. J. Odell, P. Ishler, L. S. Kay, and R. A. Edelfet. (1989). *Assisting the Beginning Teacher.* Reston, VA: Association of Teacher Educators.

Killon, Joellen P. (1990). "The Benefits of Induction Programs for Experienced Teachers." *Journal of Staff Development.* 11(4): 32–36.

A Nation Prepared: Teachers for the 21st Century. (1986). Washington, D.C.: Carnegie Task Force on Teaching.

The National Association of Secondary School Principals. (1996). *Breaking Ranks: Changing an American Institution.* Alexandria, VA: Author.

National Board for Professional Teaching Standards. (1994). *What Teachers Should Know and Be Able to Do.* Southfield, MI: Author.

Ogden, Evelyn H. and Vito Germinario. (1995). *The Nation's Best Schools: Blueprints for Excellence. Volume II—Middle and Secondary Schools.* Lancaster, PA: Technomic Publishing Co., Inc.

Pawlas, George E. (1995). "The Structured Interview: Three Dozen Questions to Ask Prospective Teachers." *NASSP Bulletin.* 79: 62–65.

Place, A. William and Thelbert L. Drake. (1994). "The Priorities of Elementary and Secondary Principals for the Criteria Used in the Teacher Selection Process." *Journal of School Improvement.* (4)1: 87–93.

Shaten, Lewis N. (1983). "Merit Does Not Have to Be a Four Letter Word." *NASSP Bulletin.* 67: 56–63.

Steuteville-Brodinsky, Burbank, Russ, and Charles Harrison. (1989). *Selecting, Recruiting and Keeping Excellent Teachers.* AASA Critical Issues Report: Arlington, VA.

Thies-Sprinthall, Lois M. and Edwin Gerler, Jr. (1990) "Support Groups for Novice Teachers." *Journal of Staff Development.* 11(4): 18–22.

Tonnesen, Sandra and Susan Paterson. (1992). "Fighting First-Year Jitters." *The Executive Educator.* 14(1): 29–30.

Wise, Arthur E., Darling-Hammond, Linda, and Barry Barnett. (1987). *Effective Teacher Selection: From Recruitment to Retention—Case Studies.* Rand Corporation's Center for the Study of the Teaching Profession.

Young, I. P. and D. Ryerson. (1986). "Teacher Selection: Legal, Practical and Theoretical Analysis." *UCEA Monograph Series.* Tempe, AZ: UCEA Monograph Series.

CHAPTER 3

What Teachers Need To Know:
About Curriculum

What students will need to know and what they will be expected to do in order to be successful in the twenty-first century has been adequately debated by educators, business people, sociologists, politicians, and futurists. Those debates and the collective wisdom and the models that they have generated can be used to identify a relatively concise list of academic content, essential skills, and behaviors purported to be necessary for success in the future. Transforming these specifications, however, into a comprehensive curriculum deliverable at the classroom level, will require a major change in how we define, organize, and make our curriculum decisions.

What will students need to know? What will they be expected to do? Who will make the decisions about what they will be taught and expected to learn? These are fundamental questions in the transformation of our twentieth century curriculum. Those who control public education, as well as the professionals, clients, and recipients of the products of public education, will need to influence the answers. To ensure the quality of that influence they will need an understanding of current schools of thought on curriculum, a vision of the future, and a rational process by which a new curriculum for the future can be planned. Any curriculum for the future must be consistent with:

- what we know about teaching and learning
- the increasing diversity of the students attending our schools
- the demands the future will place upon them

CURRICULUM AND THE FORCES THAT SHAPE IT

The word curriculum defines a course of study that ideally guides a stu-

33

dent's education from preschool through graduation, teaching the intellectual habits of mind valued by the school's community. It is the stuff around which school days are structured and learning is measured (Cushman, 1993). From 1900 through the 1990s three distinct philosophies have dominated the debate as to what those intellectual habits should be. As the diversity of a school's population continues to grow and the demands of the future become more difficult to define, competition among the dominant philosophies has become more keen, and the inadequacies of our current curriculum to prepare students for that future are becoming more evident.

Intellectual traditionalists have held that the substance of the curriculum should be derived from what we have always expected students to know. It should be built around a background in the classics and a cultural literacy that comprises a common core of knowledge. Traditionalists argue that the student's interests and the interests of society are best served when all students are steeped in tradition (usually western tradition) and given a common access to the "best" ideas that the human race has achieved. Educators subscribing to this framework tend to view students as recipients of knowledge and support the organization of that knowledge into separate and discrete disciplines and units of study.

Three trends challenge the appropriateness of the traditionalist view:

- the increasing diversity of the growing student population, which raises questions about our reliance on predominantly western cultural traditions
- the explosion of knowledge and the rapidly expanding domain of what a student might be expected to know
- the increasing knowledge about teaching and learning and the questions it raises about how we learn and what it means to know

Social behaviorists believe in a more scientifically determined curriculum. Focusing on the behaviors of successful people, they suggest the use of that information as the basis for what students will need to know and be able to do. Their approach to curriculum views the student as a resource to be altered, and the substance of what might be taught has been heavily influenced by the politics and economics of the community that the school serves. Like the traditionalist view, the rapidly changing vision of the future, the increasing interdependence, and the complexity of the politics and economics of the future make the determination of what it may take to succeed increasingly difficult to define.

Experientalists suggest that any curriculum should be based on the interests and concerns of the learner, and from those the teachers should construct projects and activities to help the students understand the problems that comprise the common human experience. Learners are viewed as partners in the school experience. Emphasis is placed on process and the curriculum tends to be without a traditional organization or definition (Shubert, 1993). Although it is the most consistent with current learning theories, this constructivist approach is the least popular among those concerned with the perceived need for a quick and definitive reformation of public education. They presume that the imminent demands of the twenty-first century need to be met with a more deliberate prescription for how those demands will be addressed.

Among these competing philosophies perhaps a generic core curriculum may exist. Current schools of thought on curriculum design are constantly being influenced by the changing nature of society, the changing demographics of the learner, and by changes within each community. As a result, emphasis has been periodically placed on single issues such as a cultural literacy, a renewed emphasis on science and mathematics, a return to basics, or teaching for thinking. These initiatives, as well as other major influences in curriculum design (Figure 3.1), reflect a host of factors which weigh heavily in the decisions that need to be considered when planning a curriculum for the twenty-first century (Glatthorn, 1994).

Each of these issues must be considered as we attempt to redefine what an educated person will need to know and what schools of the twenty-first century will need to teach (Boyer, 1995).

Curriculum reform should then best develop as an eclectic endeavor borrowing from each of the many orientations available, responding to the uniqueness of the individual, and guiding each student toward an understanding of the many ways in which we are all connected.

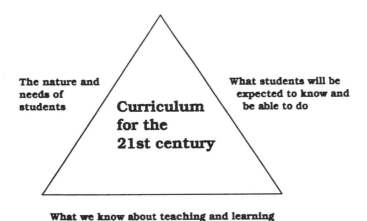

FIGURE 3.1. Factors influencing curriculum design.

CHARACTERISTICS OF A CURRICULUM FOR THE NEW MILLENNIUM

Several national commissions, comprised of educators and those outside the field of education, along with professional associations and educational pundits, have attempted to address the issue of what students will need to know and be able to do in order to thrive in the next century. Among them are the National Council of Teachers of English, the International Reading Association, the American Association for the Advancement of Science, the National Science Teachers Association, the National Council of Teachers of Mathematics, the National Association of Secondary School Principals, the Secretary's Commission on Achieving Necessary Skills (SCANS), and the New Standards Project. Most agree that the curriculum of the twenty-first century will address traditional core subjects, social skills, ethical behavior, employability, and personal fulfillment (Figure 3.2). Learning will take place beyond the classroom by using technology and combining classroom experiences with available workplace and community resources.

The Center for Education Management in the Netherlands conducted a study in 1993 to determine the characteristics of education for the year 2010 (Steffy and English, 1997). The study used a limited Delphi technique, and developed scenarios to describe the nature of education in the future in terms of content, technology, learning environment, and collaborative relationships

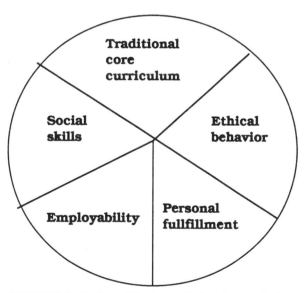

FIGURE 3.2. Content of the twenty-first century curriculum.

among the various stakeholders. Like many of the U.S.-based reports, this international perspective suggests that a curriculum be integrated across disciplines to show students the connections and interrelationships among disciplines. It should present students with experiences that cause them to think, reason, and apply their knowledge in situations approximating real life. In short, the curriculum for the new millennium must offer both substance and practicality, a combination of common core, requisite behaviors, and challenging experiences to prepare students for an unpredictable future.

This suggested synthesis of the dominant schools of thought is nothing new. In 1918, for example, in a National Education Association report, *The Seven Cardinal Principles,* guidelines were offered for what would have been then a modern curriculum. They included recommendations for instruction in:

- the command of fundamental processes
- worthy home membership
- vocational training
- citizenship
- use of leisure time
- the development of ethical character

The report stated that the educational process should be guided by "the needs of the society to be served, the character of the individual to be educated and the knowledge of educational theory and practice available" (Uchida et al., 1996).

This overview from 1918 can trace its roots back to the *Committee of Ten,* an earlier NEA report published in 1892, and its influence can be projected forward to more recent blueprints for curriculum reform such as Mortimer Adler's Paideia Proposal (Adler, 1984). Current prescriptions such as the SCANS report similarly reflect the influence of these earlier works in its identification of areas of competency and its three-part foundation of:

- basic skills
- thinking skills
- personal qualities

Yet despite this longstanding consensus on what students may need to learn and a plethora of additions to the "basics" that each school is now expected to teach, much of what is being taught in America's schools remains essentially the same as it was at the end of World War II (Figure 3.3) (Longstreet and Shane, 1995).

The resistance to redesigning the curriculum is deeply embedded in the conservative nature of educators, our cultural mind set against change, the constraints imposed by existing bureaucratic systems and the limited time available to meet the enormity of the task. In order to overcome these obstacles

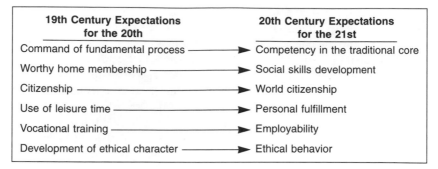

19th Century Expectations for the 20th	20th Century Expectations for the 21st
Command of fundamental process ⟶	Competency in the traditional core
Worthy home membership ⟶	Social skills development
Citizenship ⟶	World citizenship
Use of leisure time ⟶	Personal fulfillment
Vocational training ⟶	Employability
Development of ethical character ⟶	Ethical behavior

FIGURE 3.3. A comparison between curriculum prescriptions old and new.

the reorganization of the curriculum needs to be recognized as a priority and accomplished through a systematic and rational process.

At the *strategic level* it means making a paradigmatic shift from measuring learning by seat time to measuring learning by performance assessment.

At the *tactical level* it means redefining the curriculum in terms of what a student will be expected to know and be able to do and not in terms of what discrete content the student will cover.

The traditional curriculum, typically a series of required and elective courses, needs to be replaced by a curriculum that engages the students in activities designed to meet clearly delineated standards and increased expectations for every student.

A CURRICULUM FOR THE TWENTY-FIRST CENTURY

Schooling should provide students with the intellectual tools and the social skills they will need to cope with the complex human and technical problems they will face in the future. We can expect it will be a future that is fundamentally different from their past, reflective of their current needs, yet essentially disconnected from our present way of life.

The National Association of Secondary School Principals called upon the expertise and opinions of more than fifty leaders in education, business, and government. They were asked to address what students would need to know and be able to do in order to thrive during the next century. Their list of academic content, essential skills, and behaviors represents a comprehensive listing of the substance of a curriculum for the twenty-first century. Their report, *Breaking Ranks: Changing an American Institution* (NASSP, 1996), represents a guide for substantive discussion by teachers, administrators, parents, and community members engaging in curriculum reform. Figure 3.4 provides

Knowledge	Skills
Reading, writing, speaking, and listening	Communicate effectively
Math computation, concepts, and problem-solving skills	Think critically, reason, and solve problems
Using technology	Access and process information
Understanding history, government, geography, and related social sciences	Work in collaboration with others
Science and the scientific method	Conduct research
Multicultural understanding and knowledge of a foreign language	Participate productively in society
Self-discipline and ethical behavior	Be gainfully employed

FIGURE 3.4. What students will need to know and be able to do.

a summary of the most frequently listed outcomes for curriculums recommended for preparing students for the future.

State frameworks, exemplary curriculums, and commercially produced materials can all be used to guide decisions about what students may be expected to learn. Curriculum should be developed with some external criteria in order to measure the improvement of student performance relative to it, but curriculum development should also be governed by individual district's educational goals (Steffy and English, 1997). While it may not be necessary to reinvent a list of potential curriculum goals, each school community can better focus its curriculum by determining its emphasis among the basic goals of education, providing students with specific skills and knowledge, causing students to think critically about that knowledge, encouraging students to access information, solve problems, and think creatively about what they have learned, and developing in the students a positive self-image and a sense of responsibility for their relationships with others.

THE IMPORTANCE OF AN INTERDISCIPLINARY APPROACH

In addition to defining a curriculum in terms of what a student will need to know and be able to do, the curriculum of the future will need to be interdisciplinary in its structure. If we believe that students will need to figure out complex problems on their own some day, we begin to become less obsessed with discrete areas of knowledge and more focused on the student's ability to synthesize, analyze, and make solid intellectual connections. We cannot train people in specializations and then expect them to cope with the multifaceted nature of their work. The curriculum that achieves such an integration will focus more on the habits of mind and less on content coverage.

A critical attribute, therefore, of any curriculum for the future should be its integration across disciplines to show students the connections and interrelationships between the skills and knowledge they are expected to acquire and how they might apply those to their experience in the world. Current research on both learning and curriculum design indicates that teaching subjects in isolation from each other distorts knowledge. A curriculum that is integrated mirrors the real world and provides connections among subject areas so that students can better understand that their learning has application outside of school.

A curriculum that is discipline based makes learning artificially fragmented, and there is reason to be concerned that the fragments may never cohere. While disciplines can help to organize our thinking, they should not be the focus of instruction. Disciplines are an efficient vehicle for coverage but not for learning.

We have known for a long time that students learn more, remember more, and apply knowledge more when they are taught in an interdisciplinary mode. Students need to see the whole context of what they are learning (Wells, 1992). Drawing connections between subjects requires students to do more higher-level thinking, making for a richer learning experience. Retention is increased because information that has multiple connections is more easily remembered.

An interdisciplinary approach can also help to bring order to the chaotic curriculum being created by the knowledge explosion. It can lend coherence to the abundance of content by showing how the substance of what students are expected to learn is related.

Not everyone agrees that an interdisciplinary curriculum is entirely compelling. They argue that there are legitimate disciplines in the real world, and that what may be required is a more thoughtful approach to curriculum to make learning more contextualized and interesting. Most experts recommend striking a balance between integrated units and discipline-based work, suggesting that educators need to consider carefully which approach will best serve the students' needs regarding the content to be covered.

While content will remain an integral part of the curriculum for the twenty-first century, experts predict a shift toward a more process-oriented and skills-based performance criteria that will be less focused on specific disciplines or the acquisition by the student of discrete information. Such expectations and outcomes will more logically be served by a curriculum that is more thematic.

THE IMPORTANCE OF AN INTERACTIVE APPROACH
TO LEARNING

Along with the changes predicted for what students may be learning and how the curriculum can best be organized are issues about the learning environment and how we will integrate into any curriculum what we are learning about how the brain processes information and the implications that this has on instruction. Although the traditional classroom will not disappear as the predominate learning environment, we can expect that it will be supplemented by resources beyond the school site and that the dynamics between teachers and students and among students themselves will be dramatically different. Projected characteristics of education in the year 2010 (Kobus and Toenders, 1993) as summarized by Steffy and English (1997) describe a learning environment and a teacher/student relationship significantly different from the pattern of learning that is familiar to most students and teachers.

The curriculum for the twenty-first century will not be limited to the resources traditionally available. Curriculum design will be able to take advantage of an almost limitless scope as students and teachers acquire the skills and schools develop the resources to access more distant learning opportunities and develop electronic connections to colleges, libraries, and depositories of information around the globe. Opportunities for learning skills in practical situations will become increasingly common as the school site, the community, and the workplace become connected as learning environments for both students and adults.

Beyond the additional resources and expanded opportunities that may become available, the curriculum of the future will be shaped by the skills students will be required to learn. Many of the important behaviors will need to be taught in a much more interactive and participatory classroom. An expanded role for both the teacher and the student in the learning process will be required of the curriculum for the next century. The teacher will be less of a dispenser of knowledge and will be expected to lead students through learning activities, providing stimulation for the learning process, assessing student progress, and planning modifications in the student's program to ensure that performance outcomes can be met.

If students are to become problem solvers and collaborators and intelligent consumers and users of information, then the curriculum they will need is one that will require them to practice those skills and demonstrate those proficiencies through the activities and experiences that the curriculum provides for them. The curriculum for the twenty-first century will need to generate a learning environment that will encourage group learning activities, social interaction, and heterogeneity. It will need to be a curriculum that encourages the students to be active participants in the learning process in which they are guided through experiences where they construct the requisite knowledge for themselves. Students will be collaborative participants in a learning process in which they will interact with peers, teachers, adults outside the classroom, and with technology in an interactive process whereby they will be both the learner and, in some instances, the teacher of others.

Any curriculum for the twenty-first century must address a broad reconceptualization of not only what students should be expected to learn but also the increasing opportunities available to students and our best understanding of how they learn.

STEPS TOWARD DESIGNING A TWENTY-FIRST-CENTURY CURRICULUM

A curriculum for the twenty-first century must go beyond the acquisition of mere content and focus the students learning on useful generalizations and the attainment of universal concepts that cross disciplines. It should actively engage the students in structuring knowledge for themselves and be presented in such a way that it is practical and relevant to the world they will inherit.

In order to design a curriculum for the twenty-first century we must answer the question posed by almost every generation of curriculum reformers, "What knowledge and skills do we want our students to know and be able to use?" and then select the curriculum content that will support those learnings and skills. Reconceptualizing the curriculum should be a rational process, and the kind of studies to be pursued in schools ought to be determined by some reasoned analysis of our basic philosophy, the needs of the children in the present, and the most likely circumstances of the future.

Perhaps the most important aspect a school can consider in preparing a curriculum for the twenty-first century is determining what *not* to teach. Modern organizations have few procedures for conducting organized abandonment of anything. There are, however, numerous mechanisms that are in place at the state, district, and the building level that enable content to be added to the school curriculum. State legislators, textbook publishers, commercial test developers, curriculum committees, and special-interest groups all serve as instruments for adding to the list of things students should know. Confronted with a curriculum that is a mile long and one-half inch deep, teachers race to cover content with little attention to ensuring student mastery of the knowledge and skills that need to be acquired. One of the most meaningful first steps is developing a process that will identify significant curriculum and eliminate unessential material, thereby providing the time for the significant curriculum to be taught (DuFour and Eaker, 1992).

Teachers need to examine carefully what they are teaching and ask themselves

- What do the students need to know?
- What enrichment activities can be provided to broaden and deepen the students understanding of the essential concepts?
- What is currently being taught that may be dispensable?

Once these questions have been answered the curriculum can be more easily redesigned to emphasize the essential concepts to be mastered and those areas of enrichment that would logically follow. The remainder can be abandoned as unessential and dispensable.

As Chester Finn (1991) stated, "If we know what we want children to know and be able to do upon completion of their formal education, other decisions begin to fall into place. If we don' know, can't agree or won't say what the system would be producing if it were doing the job right, we will wander around aimlessly through the policy wilderness for years to come." A curriculum, therefore, must be designed to serve the larger scheme of things, the fundamental goals and how those goals are going to be assessed. Every curriculum decision should flow from a concrete vision of what the school's graduates should know and be able to do. If education for the future will require that students learn to gather and analyze information, communicate effectively, work cooperatively, and make connections between past, present, and future events, that vision must be articulated and supported by those responsible for implementing the school's curriculum and must be consistent with the wishes of those to whom the school is accountable.

We need to define the curriculum not in terms of the content to be covered but in terms of what students will be expected to know and to be able to do and then identify within the content the underlying generalizations or core concepts around which we will plan instruction and assessment. Currently, much of what we refer to as curriculum is driven by textbooks, content syllabi, or state or commercially produced tests (Figure 3.5). Instead, we need to identify what a student will need to know and be able to do in order to be successful in a competitive international marketplace and, after determining those skills and behaviors, choose from the content those ideas that best support those outcomes.

There are several models for curriculum development that can provide a framework for the systematic and rational process required. The following is a synthesis of the common characteristics of the most promising models.

Guiding Vision

A school hoping to develop a curriculum for the twenty-first century must first have the support and input of the key stakeholders in the school

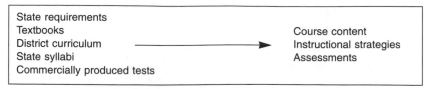

FIGURE 3.5. Traditional curriculum development.

community. From the initial development of a *guiding vision* of what students will learn, through the specific experiences to be planned, students, teachers, parents, administrators, and representatives of the community at large should be involved in making curricular decisions. The importance of these initially global discussions are sometimes dismissed as too far removed from the operational concerns about curriculum, but discussion focusing on the needs of children and the relative importance placed on particular knowledge and skills is critical to meaningful program development. The guiding vision should be written, widely disseminated, widely supported, and used as a constant reference point for the establishment of the goals, skills, knowledge, and core concepts of the curriculum. The vision need not be complex and is more practical if it can be stated clearly and concisely. An example of a guiding vision would be "to prepare students to function effectively in a global society."

Goal Statements

Discussions of a guiding vision must eventually lead to *goal statements* that are specific enough to give direction to curriculum development (see Figure 3.6). They are typically expressed as short declarative statements that operationalize the overall philosophy and vision of the school or district and provide a definition of what students will be expected to know and be able to do and how we might expect them to behave.

Schools do not have to reinvent the wheel, but each district must decide for itself those things that are most needed for their students, keeping in mind the eventual need for the students to compete and succeed in the larger society.

Skills, Knowledge, and Core Concepts

These goal statements can be compared with existing curriculum designed by professional associations, state and national standards, and commercially produced materials to identify the specific *skills and knowledge* that students

Students will be expected to
- speak and write effectively in various communication situations
- understand and use mathematical concepts and processes in practical situations
- understand and accept their rights and responsibilities as members of their families, communities, nation, and the world
- develop skills and understandings needed to pursue interests and use personal talents
- develop decision-making, planning, and organizational skills needed for sound judgments and personal problem solving
- investigate career and educational opportunities appropriate to their interests and abilities

FIGURE 3.6. Examples of goal statements.

will need to acquire to support the goal statements (Figure 3.7). Skills, knowledge, and core concepts specifically operationalize the goal statements by delineating what a student would need to know and be able to do—for example, in order to speak and write effectively in various communication situations. By comparing the resulting list of skills and knowledge you begin to identify the significant ideas or *core concepts* that will provide the foundation for the course outlines, instructional approaches, and assessment strategies that will constitute the district's curriculum.

Course Outlines, Instructional Approaches, and Assessment

A problem in developing curriculum is that we cannot meaningfully cover all the material that comprises most district curriculums. We are therefore left with only two choices. We either cover less and pick and choose what is to be left out, or we can identify the unifying skills and knowledge that we can agree students will need to know and plan *course outlines, instruction, and assessment* approaches to support that consensus (see Figure 3.8).

Speak and write effectively in various communication settings:
- adjusts style and tone to purpose and audience
- supports statements using facts, theories, and opinions
- reaches conclusions based on evidence
- clearly and concisely states key points
- organizes ideas
- uses correct grammar

FIGURE 3.7. Example of specific skills.

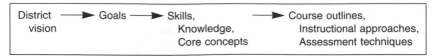

FIGURE 3.8. Curriculum development based on a vision, goals, skills, and concepts.

Teachers need to ask themselves what a student should understand or be able to do as a result of a particular course, seeking agreement with their colleagues, and then plan their instruction using available curriculum materials, textbooks, and primary sources as they relate to the chosen core ideas.

Kathleen Cushman (1993) writes, "Common sense and etymology tell us that a curriculum is a dynamic event and not an object—a river of experience that courses through student and teacher over the years of school; altering them both in a myriad of ways. Seen this way the first step to constituting a curriculum cannot be to decide what tiny packages of facts a school will pass on to its students. Rather a school must decide the direction in which the course of events will flow—the place where if the journey goes well the student will emerge" (p. 2).

A curriculum for the twenty-first century, therefore, must be designed to serve the larger scheme of things, namely, the fundamental issues we expect students will need to confront and the skills and knowledge they will need to succeed.

SUMMARY

An important first step in curriculum development for the twenty-first century is reaching consensus on a shared vision of the future. Only after we decide on what students need to know and be able to do can we approach the reorganization of the school's curriculum in a rational way. By focusing on the skills and knowledge that we believe the future will require, we set the stage to determine what content will be essential to a student's future success. The curriculum of the future will need to be derived from a clear definition of a community's expectations for its children and the nature of the children attending the school. From this philosophical statement or mission educational goals and fundamental outcomes can be developed. These desired learning outcomes and the standards derived from them should provide the guidance for the development of the curriculum framework that will constitute the district's curriculum.

REFERENCES

Adler, M. (1984). *The Paideia Program.* New York: MacMillan.

Boyer, Earnest. (1995). "The Educated Person." *Toward a Coherent Curriculum.* Alexandria, VA: The Association for Supervision and Curriculum Development: 16.

Cushman, Kathleen. (March, 1993). *Horace.* Providence, RI: The Coalition of Essential Schools, 6(9): 3.

Cushman, Kathleen. (March, 1996). *Horace.* Providence, RI: The Coalition of Essential Schools, 9(9): 2.

DuFour, Richard and Eaker, Robert (1992). *Creating the New American School: A Principal's Guide to School Improvement.* Bloomington, IN: National Education Service: 81–83.

Finn, Chester. (1991). *We Must Take Charge of Our Schools and Our Future.* New York: Free Press.

Glatthorn, Allen. (1994). *Developing a Quality Curriculum.* Alexandria, VA: The Association for Supervision and Curriculum Development: 24.

Kobus, Marc and Toenders, Liny (1993). *School 2010.* Arnhem, the Netherlands: Interstudie, Center for Education Management.

Longstreet, W. S. and Shane, H. G. (1995) *Curriculum for a New Millennium.* Boston, MA: Allyn & Bacon: 185–201.

The National Association of Secondary School Principals. (1996) *Breaking Ranks: Changing an American Institution.* Alexandria, VA.

Shubert, William H. (1993). "Curriculum Reform." *Challenges and Achievements of American Education.* Alexandria, VA: The Association for Supervision and Curriculum Development: 80–84.

Steffy, Betty and English, Fenwick W. (1997). *Curriculum and Assessment for World-Class Schools.* Lancaster, PA: Technomic Publishing Co., Inc.

Uchida, Donna, Cetron, Marvin, and McKenzie, Floretta. (1996). *Preparing Students for the 21st Century.* Alexandria, VA: American Association of School Administrators: 1–11.

Wells, Scott. (November, 1992). *Interdisciplinary Learning—Movement to Link Disciplines Gains Momentum.* Alexandria, VA: ASCD Curriculum Update.

CHAPTER 4

What Teachers Need To Know:
About Instruction

Fashioning instruction for the twenty-first century will not be about making America's schools as good as they once were. The challenge will be to create classrooms in which the vast majority of students will achieve levels of skills and competencies that were once thought to be needed by only a select few. As society continues to become more complex, knowledge based, and culturally diverse, its expectations for teaching and learning become more demanding. In meeting these new and higher expectations, teachers in the twenty-first century will face increasingly formidable social conditions that work against learning and impede student academic growth. More and more children will be coming to school less and less ready to learn. For the class of 2010, 23% of the students will have been born in poverty and 50% will have been born to single parents (Bracey, 1994). As Darling-Hammond (1996) writes, "To help diverse learners master more challenging content teachers must go far beyond dispensing information, giving a test and giving a grade. They must themselves know their subject areas deeply, and they must understand how students think if they are to create experiences that actually work to produce learning" (p. 194).

If we can agree that the goals for education that have guided instruction for the current century are inadequate for students to meet the challenge of the next century, then a rethinking of how we plan and deliver our instruction is clearly in order. Schools have traditionally emphasized rote learning, memorization of facts, and recall of information with little emphasis on conceptual understanding and reasoning. Methods deemed effective for those outcomes, however, will prove woefully inappropriate for preparing future graduates, all of whom will need to be knowledgeable, flexible thinkers capable of understanding complex ideas. The traditional view of learning, focused on knowledge and procedures of low cognitive challenge and superficial understanding, simply will not meet the demands of the present nor will it serve students in the future.

Workers in the twenty-first century will need to solve complex problems and be able to design more efficient ways to accomplish work. While they will need a mastery of basic knowledge, a deeper conceptual understanding of that knowledge will also be required. How they will acquire that knowledge and how they will process and develop a deeper understanding of that knowledge must be at the center of any model of teaching for the twenty-first century.

What teachers think about how students learn has a lot to do with the decisions they make about what they teach and how they teach it. A fundamental tenet, therefore, in developing an instructional model for the future should reflect what we know about teaching and learning.

There are aspects of classroom instruction that have been documented through empirical studies and theoretical research as leading to improved student learning. The origin of these ideas has been the effective teacher research conducted in the process–product and cognitive sciences. Popularized by Madeline Hunter and others, educators have come to believe that teaching is in part a science with practices and procedures that are demonstrably more effective than others.

Efforts to establish a "model" for teaching based on specific actions a teacher should take (popular in the 1980s) assumed that if the teacher performed the required elements, student achievement would increase. More recent conceptualizations of teaching recognize that while there may be a set of commonalities underlying a teacher's decisions and actions, those decisions and actions are mediated by the teacher, the student, and the context of the instruction (Danielson, 1996).

Two factors in particular about learning should shape our thinking about instruction for the future. They are the learner's need to understand the meaning of the material and the need of the learner to regulate to some degree their own learning. While constructing meaning and learning independently may not appear to be something new, it contrasts sharply with the understandings of traditional instructional strategies. Learning, as it will be required in the next century, will not be essentially a matter of responding to information as it is given. Learning, of necessity, will be thinking about, understanding, and applying the information in appropriate ways in authentic situations both inside and outside the classroom environment.

In order for teachers to be able to provide learning experiences that will effectively promote those types of educational outcomes, they will need to have:

- an understanding of how students learn
- facility with a repertoire of instructional strategies that actively engage the learner and sustain the student's motivation to learn

- a deep understanding of the learner's ability, prior knowledge, and preferences for learning
- a general content knowledge and how their instructional content is related to it
- specific knowledge in the content to be instructed and the materials and resources available to teach it
- designated outcomes to be achieved by the students and assessments to measure those outcomes

What teachers and students will be doing in the classroom of the future should be based on what we know about teaching and learning. It should reflect a new paradigm of learning based on constructivist approaches to curriculum, instruction, and assessment and should cultivate a community of learners engaging in activities and decision making that will lead to the learning of important content.

HOW STUDENTS LEARN

Research on learning is beginning to catch up with our curiosity about the human brain, but until very recently most of what we thought we knew about brain functioning was derived from the visible and measurable manifestations of cognition rather than from direct observation of the cognitive mechanisms and processes that we are rapidly learning so much more about. Learning and teaching have been separate acts related only through correlation and supposition that certain teacher actions increased the probability that learning would take place. For many classroom teachers learning was and is a covert act. While much of what we believed to be good instruction is now being validated through direct observation of the cognitive process, the practical base of teaching and learning has been described by Sylwester (1994) as being "closer to folklore knowledge than scientific knowledge."

Recent research and advances in medical technology, however, have provided us with a more complete understanding of brain functioning, and the educational implications for instruction are more frequently being discussed by researchers and practitioners alike. We currently believe that the human brain uses sensory/perceptual processes to take in events and objects from the environment. It then draws on memory and various problem-solving strategies to process the object or event and eventually translates that thought and decision into an action, behavior, or response (see Figure 4.1).

American thought on the process of learning has been influenced alternately throughout our history by British empiricists such as Locke and Hume, continental rationalists such as Descartes and Leibnitz, and early psychologists such as Thorndike, Skinner, and Piaget (Bracey, 1994). Empiricists

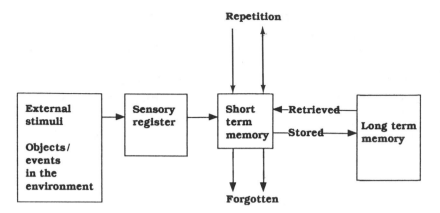

FIGURE 4.1. Information processing model.

believed that complex knowledge was no more than the simple accretion of basic skills and that all complicated knowledge could be broken down into building blocks corresponding to those basic skills. Rationalists, on the other hand, saw the mind as the ultimate analytical tool and emphasized its capacity for introspection and logic. Both ideas figured prominently into the early development of behaviorist psychology.

Skinner and Thorndike described human behavior essentially in terms of stimulus–response relationships coupled with reinforcement. Piaget, however, laid the foundation for the most promising understanding of human learning when he concluded that the growth of knowledge was the result of individual constructions made by the learner (Brooks and Brooks, 1993). Cognition, it would appear, is fueled by the learner's attempt to make sense of what is going on.

In addition to understanding that learning is an active and constructive process, it has also become clear that learning is more powerful when it is done as part of a group. Deborah Miere (1992) succinctly states the conventional wisdom inherent in this finding when she writes, "Human beings are by nature social, interactive learners. We check out our ideas, argue with authors, bounce issues back and forth, ask friends to read our early drafts, talk together after seeing a movie, pass on books, attend meetings and argue our ideas, share stories and gossip to extend our understanding of ourselves and others. Talk lies at the heart of our lives" (p. 264). Learning is not only situated in the physical environment of the classroom and dependent upon what the teacher and an individual student may do; it also occurs in a social context that can be more powerful and effective when conducted as a group.

To learn something a student must actively relate it to other knowledge in a way that either makes sense to him, based on what he already knows or in a way that modifies his current understanding so that the new information can be accommodated. This is a reflective process that takes time and is one that can be strengthened by the student's interaction with others. In order for learning to take place, teachers need to provide a learning environment that is both active and collaborative.

CONSTRUCTIVISM

The past decade of cognitive research has made it clear that learning is an active, constructive process. In *Toward a Thinking Curriculum: Current Cognitive Research,* Resnick and Klopfer (1989) write, "Before knowledge becomes truly generative—knowledge that can be used to interpret new situations, to solve problems, to think and reason, and to learn—students must elaborate and question what they are told, examine new information in relation to other information and build new information structures" (p. 208). According to Brooks and Brooks (1993), in order for learning to take place in schools, teachers must become familiar with this constructivist philosophy and provide within their classrooms learning environments that cause students to:

• search for meaning
• appreciate uncertainty
• inquire responsibly

Constructivism stems from a long and respected tradition in cognitive psychology. Since the early 1900s these cognitive approaches have competed for attention with the more popular behaviorist orientations supported by the process–product research, which many educators relied upon for making decisions about effective teaching. Constructivism implies that a learner's understanding of any concept depends entirely on his mental construction of that concept, which is derived from his own experience in constructing that concept for himself. Teachers can guide the process, but the students must undertake and manage the process of developing an understanding for themselves. This process is unique to the individual and is dependent upon their prior experience, knowledge, and existing cognitive structures. What students may gain and retain from a given presentation is dependent upon what their preexisting knowledge and cognitive structures allow them to absorb, regardless of the teacher's intention or the quality of the explanation.

Accepting a constructivist approach, a teacher recognizes that for students to "learn" a concept they must do the intellectual work themselves. This work must involve the active engagement of the learner and must allow for interactions between the student and the teacher and among students.

It is important to keep in mind that active learning in a constructivist sense is not the same as physical involvement with manipulative materials. Physical participation may or may not be constructivist. In a constructivist approach the student's mind is engaged in a cognitive process leading to an understanding of new information—what Danielson (1996) calls "minds on."

The constructivist approach to learning has an important implication for teaching and for the role the teacher plays in creating a conducive learning environment. A teacher's role in the constructivist class is no less important than in the traditional classroom, but it is dramatically different. The teacher's role is no longer simply to make presentations of information to be absorbed and stored by learners who are viewed as passive receivers of information nor simply to ask questions and direct students through exercises designed to reinforce skills. Teaching focuses instead on planning and conducting activities and assignments that present problems that engage the students in constructing important knowledge for themselves.

Constructivism emphasizes the importance of students taking responsibility for their own learning. It provides a rationale for moving away from instructional methods created to address now outmoded conceptualizations of how students learn, such as classrooms in which:

- Teacher talk dominated the lesson.
- Teachers relied heavily on textbook structure and resources.
- Students were discouraged from collaborating.
- Activities focused on low-level cognitive skills and devalued thinking.
- Assessments focused on the one right answer.

To embrace it as a model for teaching, educators must begin to make an important paradigmatic shift described as "abandoning the mimetic approach to learning and implementing practices that encourage students to think, demonstrate and exhibit" (Brooks and Brooks, 1993, p. v).

Teaching using a constructivist approach has implications that go beyond a shift in pedagogy (Figure 4.2). It affects:

- time—It requires more time for students to construct their own knowledge than it does to simply tell a student what they need to know.
- curriculum—Learning activities are structured around primary concepts instead of discrete pieces of information.
- assessment—Traditional assessment processes are replaced by observation, demonstration, and performance.

Constructivism is not a theory about teaching, it is a theory about knowledge and learning. However, it serves as a basis for many of the current

Traditional Classroom	Constructivist Classroom
Partial or whole presentation of material with emphasis on discrete skills and facts	Whole or partial presentation of material with emphasis on concepts and processes
Students viewed as empty, passive vessels	Students viewed as interactive participants and thinkers
Teacher disseminates information	Teacher facilitates learning
Focus is on a single correct answer	Focus is on points of view and problem-solving skills
Assessment is separate	Assessment is ongoing and integrated with learning
Student works alone or with the teacher	Students work alone, in pairs, in small and large groups, and with the teacher and other adults

FIGURE 4.2. Contrasting paradigms.

reforms in how we believe classrooms of the twenty-first century should be structured and operated. From this perspective learning is understood as being "a self-regulated process of resolving inner cognitive conflicts that often become apparent through experience, collaborative discourse and reflection" (Brooks and Brooks, 1993, p. vi). To bring this understanding of how we learn into the classroom, five principles of pedagogy are suggested:

- posing problems of emerging relevance to the learner
- structuring learning around primary concepts
- seeking and valuing student points of view
- adapting curriculum to address student suppositions
- assessing student learning in the context of the teaching

IMPLICATIONS FOR TEACHERS

A major obstacle to creating a constructivist classroom is that many teachers teach in only one way—the same way that they were taught—namely, a teacher-dominated classroom in which the teacher is the purveyor of knowledge, punctuating their dissemination of information with occasional questions and activities that leave the student unengaged. Teachers, if they are to be effective in developing the deeper and more complex understanding of content we believe will be required in the twenty-first century, must prepare themselves to take advantage of the methods that depend less on the teacher and more on what students can learn working together. Student-centered approaches suggested by our current understanding of how we learn are proving to be most effective. Research suggests that strategies that involve students directly in their own learning provide both deeper understanding and longer retention. With respect to specific strategies, including seminars, cooperative learning activities, debates and dialogues, field experiences, independent studies, and laboratory experiments, when levels of student engagement increases, academic achievement rises (Lee and Smith, 1994). While lecturing will always have its place and may remain as an appropriate method for some material, students who are exposed to only teacher-centered instruction are left with a narrow and superficial understanding of the content presented.

The teacher as facilitator, using a wider range of learning activities, can better guide the learning process for students with varying learning styles through creating what Ted Sizer calls "gaining skills through critiqued experience" (Sizer, 1984). While some may argue that good teachers have always infused their teaching with student activities, John Goodlad (1984) found in his studies a "low incidence of activities involving active modes of learning."

To create the kind of active engagement envisioned by a constructivist approach to learning, pedagogy must orient itself towards higher-order thinking skills such as drawing inferences, making judgments, engaging in logical reasoning, and solving problems. This transition can most easily be accomplished by embedding problems into the existing curriculum. Perhaps the best example of how that has been done can be found in the "Habits of Mind" model used by the Central Park East Secondary School in New York City. Students are deliberately taught to:

- weigh evidence
- consider varying points of view
- see connections and relationships
- speculate on possibilities
- assess value both for society and for themselves

Even with a well-intentioned constructivist curriculum, teachers resist adopting constructivist pedagogy because of:

- a commitment to their present instructional approaches
- concerns about student mastery of the content of the curriculum
- concerns about classroom control
- a limited understanding of cognitive development and recent findings about brain functioning

Becoming a teacher who helps students to learn for themselves rather than learn from the teacher is challenging and frightening in many ways. Teachers who resist, do so for understandable reasons. They were not taught that way nor were they trained to teach that way.

As Larry Cuban (Sizer, 1984) points out, "Schools that want teachers to shift their instructional emphasis must realize that change will require more of the time and energy of the teacher and that they will need help to put complex ideas into practice" (p. 186).

Describing constructivist teaching behaviors provides a usable framework within which teachers can take the complex ideas and begin to experiment with new approaches and modify strategies that they are familiar with so they can become more effective in actively engaging students. A summary of some behaviors is given in Figure 4.3. In a constructivist classroom teachers are mediators of students and the learning environment and not simply disseminators of information and managers of behavior. The constructivist classroom follows a learning cycle model that begins with open-ended consideration of an idea leading to concept formation, attainment, and application. In the traditional classroom concepts are typically introduced and applied without the opportunity for the students to construct the meaning for themselves.

To provide students with a classroom experience that will cause them to deepen their understanding and retain what they learn requires more than instructional behaviors. Teachers must have a thorough understanding of what it is they want students to learn and a more personal relationship with the students they are expected to teach.

---

1. Encourage and accept student autonomy and initiative.
2. Use raw data and primary sources, manipulatives, and interactive physical materials.
3. Frame tasks using cognitive terminology such as classify, analyze, predict, and create.
4. Allow student response to drive lessons, strategies, and sometimes content.
5. Inquire about student understanding before sharing your own.
6. Engage in dialogues beyond teacher to student.
7. Ask thoughtful open-ended questions and encourage students to question each other.
8. Elaborate students' responses to explore their thinking processes and to expand responses.
9. Involve students in experiences that engender contradictions and non-examples of concepts.
10. Provide wait time both before and after posing questions.
11. Provide time for students to construct relationships and create metaphors.

FIGURE 4.3. Constructivist teacher behaviors (adapted from Brooks and Brooks, 1993).

Knowledge of Content

A conceptual approach to teaching requires that the teacher have a sufficient command of their subject to expertly guide student learning. As Danielson (1996) writes, "A person cannot teach what he or she does not know." Constructivist teachers must not only know the factual information of the subject areas but the concepts, principles, relationships, methods of inquiry, and outstanding issues as well. They must be aware of the connections among different divisions of their discipline and between their discipline and the other disciplines that students are expected to learn.

Knowledge of Students

Knowing the student is equally important in preparing a constructivist learning environment. Research on cognition contends that understanding involves constructing meaning with respect to the students' experiences. Students vary enormously in their interests, talents, and preferred approaches to learning. A constructivist teacher helps students to build on their interests and talents while developing those areas that need additional competence. Using the social, cultural, and intellectual differences among students, adaptations are made both in the presentation of the curriculum and in the ways that students are permitted to demonstrate what they have learned.

Combining constructivist behaviors with thorough content preparation and an individualized understanding of the prospective learners should yield goal-directed lessons designed to engage the students in activities that have well-defined purposes and are compatible with accepted content standards and curriculum frameworks. A criteria for designing such a lesson appears in Figure 4.4.

Merrill Harm in *Inspiring Active Learning: A Handbook for Teachers* (1994) describes the need for lessons that are organized so that class periods

---

- Instructional goals should be clear and stated in terms of student learning instead of student activity.
- Instructional goals should be capable of assessment and appropriate to the diverse students in a teacher's charge.
- Instructional goals should be translated into learning experiences that progress from easy to hard, simple to complex, and from attention to one domain of learning to integration across several domains.
- Time allocations should be reasonable, with opportunities for students to engage in reflection and closure.

FIGURE 4.4. Criteria for lesson design (summarized from Danielson, 1996).

proceed smoothly, with interest and with high student involvement. To accomplish this, Harm suggests lessons that:

- are fast paced enough to keep all students actively involved
- return to topics from time to time rather than aiming for mastery at any one time so that learnings are reinforced over time and the risk of losing student involvement is minimized
- provide sufficient variety in the classroom to keep students involved, yet not so diverse as to threaten student security and the need for predictability

A CARING CLASSROOM

An outgrowth of providing interactive learning experiences is the concept of a community of learners. If the teacher is no longer the single source of knowledge, students and the teacher begin to interact in different ways and participate more fully in the learning process, both as student and teacher. The attitude of the teacher and the relationships between students and teacher affect the outcome of the lesson. Students do not try as hard if the teacher doesn't care. Research indicates that when students have a caring teacher they exhibit "academic, social and ethical benefits including greater enjoyment of the class, stronger motivation and stronger feelings of social competence" (NASSP, 1996). Caring affects the receptivity of the students to teaching and the acquisition of knowledge.

Teaching is a matter of relationships. Relationships that should be grounded in mutual respect between students and teachers. Teachers can cultivate this mutual respect by their own interactions with students and the type of interactions they encourage among the students. A classroom conducive to learning emphasizes high expectations where students and the teacher engage in activities of value and in such a way as to encourage students to take risks in a safe environment. Charlotte Danielson (1996) describes a "culture for learning" when she writes that classrooms should be "cognitively busy places with students and teachers setting high value on quality work" (p. 62).

Many students suffer anxiety in the classroom, but anxiety is inimical to the learning process. While some tension may need to exist in the classroom, too much tension can cause students to resist a learning activity. Some students worry about what the teacher thinks of them, whether they will understand what is being taught, and how their classmates will react to the mistakes they may make. Teachers who create interactive classrooms will need to have strategies for dealing with those anxieties.

G. H. Pilon (1991) suggests two simple techniques for creating a comfortable and respectful classroom. One suggestion is to post *truth signs* around

We each learn in our own ways.
It's okay to make mistakes.
It's intelligent to ask for help.
Everyone needs time to think and learn.
We learn more when we are willing to risk.

FIGURE 4.5. Truth signs.

the room. The signs do not tell students what to do, but they remind them of important truths about the learning process and life. Examples of truth signs are listed in Figure 4.5.

Posted truth signs alone do not guarantee that students will not feel anxious. A steady offering of support is also necessary. To reinforce the truth signs Pilon suggests a strategy called *cushioning,* which involves raising student awareness of the important ideas related to learning by reminding the students of the truths and inviting students to react to their applicability to learning. This can be done by asking students questions such as, "Is it okay to make mistakes?" and allow students to discuss briefly how making mistakes shows we are trying, taking risks, and learning from the mistakes we make.

In *Inspiring Active Learning: A Handbook for Teachers* (1994), Merrill Harm lists several factors that influence a student's willingness to participate, and gives direction for providing a caring learning environment. They include:

- providing opportunities for students to succeed
- making students feel important
- reducing student anxiety
- providing students with choices
- pacing instruction for the student's comfort
- providing both teacher and student-to-student support

A comfortable and respectful classroom is businesslike, where routines and procedures are well established, the teacher and the students have a mutual respect for one another, and they are engaged in activities that support the stated instructional purposes.

INSTRUCTIONAL STRATEGIES FOR THE TWENTY-FIRST CENTURY

Robert Sylwester in *A Celebration of Neurons: An Educators Guide to the Human Brain* (1995) describes the classroom of the future as one that will "focus more on drawing out existing abilities than on precisely measuring one's success with imposed skills, encourage personal construction of categories rather than impose existing categorical systems, and emphasize the individual personal solutions of an environmental challenge over the efficient group manipulation of the symbols that might represent the solution" (p. 139). Research overwhelmingly supports this personal engagement of the learner. When compared to traditional classrooms, ones where students are actively engaged in the learning process through interaction with the teacher and with each other have shown gains in the following areas (Cummings, 1990):

- academic motivation to learn
- understanding and retention
- attitudes towards peers (including multicultural)
- self-esteem and ethical behavior
- cooperation and problem-solving skills

These areas approximate those anticipated to be needed for success in the next century. If we accept Danielson's (1996) pronouncement that, "Engaging students in learning is the raison d'etre of education," then classrooms of the future will of necessity be built on instructional strategies that immerse the student in the process of learning and the active construction of their personal understanding of what they are expected to learn. Elements of student engagement are listed in Figure 4.6.

Several instructional strategies—some new, some old, and many revisited—can be used by teachers to create the community of learners who can achieve the more rigorous demands that the future will place upon them. At the core of many of these strategies is a cooperative classroom where students can be grouped in many ways for instruction: individually, in large groups led by the teacher or student, small groups working independently or with the

---

- presenting content in a way that connects new information to what a student may already know
- creating activities that cause the student to interact with the content by solving problems that are relevant or authentic to the student
- grouping students in different patterns to enhance engagement opportunities
- pacing lessons to allow for thinking, construction of meaning, and closure for the student
- providing feedback to students on how they are progressing as part of the instructional experience

FIGURE 4.6. Elements of student engagement.

teacher's guidance, homogeneous groups, heterogeneous groups, partners, triads, and other configurations conducive to the activity or consistent with the learner's preference.

Forming cooperative or collaborative groups is only a beginning for creating the kind of intellectual involvement required for the active construction of understanding. In addition to the now popular cooperative learning strategies and activities in use in many classrooms, teachers will need to think deliberately about the nature of the activities and interactions that comprise these cooperative endeavors.

A teacher's skill in questioning and leading discussions is critical to providing both individual and group interactions that truly engage the students in the process of learning. Both questioning and discussion become valuable as a constructivist strategy when they elicit student reflection and challenge deeper student engagement. The *Socratic seminar* is an effective strategy that provokes student thinking and dialogue and is a unique alternative to the traditional class discussion because students do almost all of the talking. In a Socratic seminar students are seated in a circle and are prompted by an open-ended question that encourages them to engage each other in a thoughtful dialogue. Unlike the traditional question and answer in which the teacher poses rapid-fire, short-answer, and low-level questions to individual students, the Socratic seminar focuses on carefully crafted questions that enable students to reflect on their understanding. Students are allowed time to think. They are expected to explain the thinking behind their responses, and other students are encouraged to elaborate on the responses given. Discussions are animated by important questions that engage all students. When run well,

- The teacher does not hold center stage.
- Students are encouraged to comment on each other's responses.
- Thinking is illuminated, and initial responses are probed and expanded.

Transforming a classroom from a traditional format to a constructivist one can begin by simply altering:

- the physical setup of our classroom—from rows of seats to a circle or circles
- the way we pose our questions—from single response to open ended
- the time we wait for a student's response—from 2–3 seconds to 8–12 seconds
- the ways we accept those responses—from teacher affirmation to affirmation from peers

Other constructivist approaches to learning include strategies adapted from *information processing models* such as those developed by Hilda Taba,

Bruce Joyce, and William Gordon (Canady and Rettig, 1996). A sampling of those techniques are summarized in Figure 4.7. Equally effective are time-proven methods such as simulations and learning centers. *Simulations* serve as active classroom experiences where participants are provided with life-like, problem-solving activities, which, when constructed well and implemented effectively, provide experiences that extend and deepen a student's understanding.

Learning centers can also be effective constructivist activities that provide individual students, pairs of students, or small groups of students the opportunity to

- practice skills learned in a larger group
- extend skills or knowledge beyond that acquired in the large group
- rehearse for an assessment
- improve skills not mastered earlier

Technology can also provide a significant vehicle for creating a more individualized and interactive learning environment and has an important role to play in assisting teachers in creating communities of learners. Teachers need to consider the many ways in which technology can be incorporated into their classrooms and consider the use of not only the computer but videodisc technology and CD-ROM. These technological tools can make the investigation of more complex tasks feasible and provide students with the opportunity to work at higher levels of cognition. By shifting the control for learning from the teacher to the student, a wide range of learning styles can be accommodated to meet individual needs.

A necessary outgrowth of raising student expectations and altering instructional strategies to meet that challenge will be the reconsideration of

Concept development	guides students through the process of categorizing and synthesizing information in order to make generalizations
Concept attainment	requires students to develop a definition of a selected concept by examining critical attributes and non-examples
Synectics	uses analogies and metaphors to encourage creative thought
Memory models	uses association techniques to link new information to familiar information

FIGURE 4.7. Summary of information processing models applicable to constructivist teaching.

the ways student achievement will be assessed. As instructional goals become increasingly complex and methods of classroom instruction become more diverse, so must our approaches to assessment. A minimum requirement for any constructivist learning outcome must be that it can be assessed in some way. A well-designed approach must include the specific ways in which the student's work will be evaluated; the student should know before hand the required standards against which his project or performance will be measured. Assessment methods should reflect real-world application of the skills and an understanding of the content being assessed. Their full power in the constructivist classroom is in providing feedback to the student's on what they have learned, reflection to the teacher on what he has taught, and usefulness in planning for the future. Assessment in the constructivist classroom should be an integral part of the instructional process, providing information to both the student and the teacher as they plan the next steps in the learning process.

SUMMARY

Changes in what we expect students to know and to be able to do and the increasing diversity of the students who comprise our student population require that we alter our instruction to meet both the increasing expectations and the individual differences among learners. Current brain research and the implications drawn from it suggest a new paradigm of teaching and learning that may prove critical as we plan for instruction for the twenty-first century. It would appear from what we are constantly learning that classrooms for the next century will need to be communities of learners where students are actively and cognitively engaged in the learning process in ways that allow them to construct their own understanding.

Through this constructivist approach to knowledge it is believed that the students' understanding will be deeper and more complex, that the knowledge they acquire will be retained longer, and that the probability of their transferring that knowledge to real-world situations in new and creative ways will be enhanced.

The classroom of the future will need to be a caring and interactive environment. Teachers will need to rethink both their instructional strategies and their classroom management to accommodate a wide variety of teaching methods and to encourage respect and rapport both among the students and between the students and themselves. Much of what teachers need to do can be accomplished by modifying traditional methods and by increasing their knowledge of what is constantly being discovered about how we learn.

REFERENCES

Adler, M. (1984) *The Paideia Program.* New York: Macmillan.

Bracey, Gerald (1994) *Transforming America's Schools: An Rx for Getting Past Blame.* Arlington, VA: American Association of School Administrators.

Brooks, J. G. and Brooks, M. G. (1993) *In Search of Understanding: The Case for Constructivist Classrooms.* Alexandria, VA: Association for Supervision and Curriculum Development.

Canady, Robert L. and Rettig, Michael D. (1996) *Teaching in the Block Strategies for Engaging Active Learners.* Princeton, NJ: Eye on Education.

Cummings, Carol (1990) *Managing a Cooperative Classroom: A Practical Guide for Teachers.* Edmonds, WA: Teaching Incorporated.

Danielson, Charlotte (1996) *Enhancing Professional Practice: A Framework for Teaching.* Alexandria, VA: Association for Supervision and Curriculum Development.

Darling-Hammond, Linda. (1996) "What Matters Most: A Competent Teacher for Every Child." *Phi Delta Kappan* (78) 3: 193–200.

Goodlad, John L. (1984) *A Place Called School.* New York: McGraw-Hill.

Harm, Merrill. (1994) *Inspiring Active Learning: A Handbook for Teachers.* Alexandria, VA: Association for Supervision and Curriculum Development.

Lee, Valerie E. and Smith, Julia B. (Fall, 1994) "High School Restructuring and Student Achievement." *Issues in Restructuring Schools.* Madison, WI: University of Wisconsin. 7: 4.

Miere, Deborah. (1992) "Reinventing Teaching in Central Park East School in Harlem." *Phi Delta Kappan* 74: 264–655.

The National Association of Secondary School Principals (1996) *Breaking Ranks: Changing an American Institution.* Alexandria, VA.

Pilon, G. H. (1991) *Workshop Way.* New Orleans, LA: Workshop Way Incorporated.

Resnick, L. and Klopfer, L. (1989) *Toward a Thinking Curriculum: Current Cognitive Research.* Alexandria, VA: Association for Supervision and Curriculum Development.

Sizer, Theodore R. (1996) *Horace's Compromise.* Boston: Houghton Mifflin.

Sylwester, Robert. (1995) *A Celebration of Neuron: An Educators Guide to the Human Brain.* Alexandria, VA: Association for Supervision and Curriculum Development.

CHAPTER 5

What Teachers Need To Know: About Assessment

The field of assessment is changing dramatically as we approach the end of the century. Assessment for documenting student achievement is being reexamined, and new and innovative alternatives to traditional testing are gaining in popularity. Traditional testing, which has dominated the landscape of assessment for the last 50 years, is being challenged by "new" methods of assessment generically referred to as alternative assessment. Almost every state is exploring alternative testing programs and many are gradually phasing in more open-ended response items and performance-based methods to replace or complement their standardized testing programs (Steffy, 1995).

Interest in redesigning how schools measure what students are learning has been prompted by both curriculum reform and changes in instructional design derived from current theories on learning and speculation about what students will need to know and be able to do in the future. As the curriculum becomes less dominated by the acquisition of specific information in a subject area, the usefulness of traditional assessment techniques such as multiple choice, true/false, and completion items diminishes. If knowledge is to become the ability to use information, then assessment strategies will need to reflect the application of what a student knows in multiple problem-solving situations.

As teachers broaden their approaches to teaching and curriculum and place more emphasis on purposes and meaning and less emphasis on specific, isolated subskills, the gap between instruction and curriculum and the appropriateness of traditional testing becomes wider.

Assessment strategies for the twenty-first century need to be reformed in terms of our changing educational goals, our understanding of the relationship

67

between instruction, learning, and assessment, and the limitations of traditional testing to address these new standards and outcomes.

PURPOSES OF ASSESSMENT

Schools should use assessment practices that are useful to students, teachers, and parents. Testing students solely for the purposes of simply reporting their scores or comparing their scores to some external benchmark is a waste of valuable time and money. The value of any assessment lies in what it is able to tell us about individual student progress, what evidence it provides in determining the educational system's accountability, and its usefulness in helping both educators and the public they serve to make educational decisions. In addition, well-designed assessment may be used to:

- help professionals make decisions about instruction
- screen students for readiness to move on
- determine remedial needs
- provide accountability to the public on its educational investment

Assessing the academic achievement of students should be an integral part of the educational process. If we want to measure the skills and knowledge we believe students will need to succeed in the next century, it will need to be done in a variety of ways. It should be individualized and ongoing as a student's progress towards performance criteria or graduation goals are measured and reported. Any single method of assessment will not capture the full range of information that should be available on each student. As the authors of *Breaking Ranks: Changing an American Institution* (NASSP, 1996) suggest, "Assessments of students should be a rich collection of information that reflects the students progress in moving through the curriculum" (p. 54).

It is similarly vital to disclose how a school as a whole fares. Both parents and the public need such information to make decisions about their child's education and the value of their investment in the local schools. However, assumptions about the quality of education cannot be made accurately on the basis of comparative scores on annual tests. A system of meaningful accountability, such as student assessment, needs to be ongoing, credible, and rich in useful information, including:

- student attendance
- teacher absenteeism
- student turnover
- state and local assessment results
- dropout rates
- graduation rates

- student participation in extracurricular activities
- failure rate and honor roll statistics
- college and postsecondary plans

Recent educational reform proposals have focused on using assessment to improve the quality of education. From the 1970s through today the role of educational assessment has been expanding dramatically in both its purpose and scope. Educational assessment is now considered to be a core component in school reform. However, if it is to have the desired effect, educators at the classroom level will need to increase their understanding and application of psychometrics and shift their perceptions about the relationships between teaching, curriculum, and assessment.

TYPES OF ASSESSMENT

Assessment in all its forms comprises a major portion of every student's life from grades K–12. As Dennis Cheek (1993) writes, "Assessments shadow us from cradle to grave and are often used to sort the population into convenient categories for the purposes of schooling, occupation, training, promotion and participation in sports, the performing arts and civic life" (p. 18). What typically forms the basis of these decisions is an overarching model of assessment built around a host of standardized tests that are not particularly close assessments of student learning and have not provided much information of genuine consequence. In many schools the effort to monitor student achievement begins and ends with the administration of these norm-referenced and standardized achievement tests. However, traditional assessments comprise a small portion of the full range of the assessment methods available. Assessments fall into two broad categories—traditional methods or alternative strategies (Figure 5.1).

Interest in the increasing range of assessment instruments has been prompted by changes in both curriculum and instruction. As teachers have broadened their approaches to instruction and increased their emphasis on process and performance, the gap between instruction and the appropriateness of more traditional testing practices has become wider. As schools attempt to become more results oriented, there is an increasing need to develop and use measurable indicators of their effectiveness. Traditional testing alone is clearly not the most appropriate method of assessment for increasingly complex school goals, such as the ability to communicate, to make responsible decisions, or to demonstrate tolerance, for example. To accurately assess these and other twenty-first century skills and knowledge, students will need to demonstrate their knowledge and perform tasks in situations that closely resemble the challenges of real life.

Traditional	Alternative
True/false	Set-performance task
Multiple choice	Open-performance task
Fill in the blank	Exhibition of work
Short open-ended answer	Reflective journal
Paragraph response, set question	Oral presentation
Paragraph response, open ended	Group project
Essay	Timed trial
Label	Video presentation
Label and explain	Debate
	Simulation
	Refereed article
	Interview

FIGURE 5.1. Range of assessment tools.

As a result, the entire field of assessment is changing dramatically. More *traditional or conventional methods* of testing are being replaced with what are generically referred to as *alternative assessment strategies* (see Figure 5.2 for comparison). The distinction between these two broad categories is that unlike traditional assessments where students answers come from ready-made lists or memorization, alternative assessments require that a student demonstrate their knowledge through the construction of a response or the completion of a task. The emphasis is on thinking and not on a mechanical response.

	Strengths	Weaknesses
Traditional	Assess specific skills/knowledge	Assess at the lowest levels
	More easily establishes reliability and validity	Does not require critical thinking or problem solving
	Easy to score	
	Allows for comparisons	
	Can be item analyzed	
Alternative	Requires application of a variety of skills	Takes more time to score
	Requires thinking and problem solving	Can be costly
	Allows for variations in performance	Validity and reliabilty are harder to establish
	Can assess behaviors	Requires more skill on the part of the evaluator
	Can measure growth over time	

FIGURE 5.2. Strengths and weaknesses of traditional and alternative assessments.

The terms *alternative, authentic,* or *performance assessment* apply to any assessment that differs from traditional or conventional methods (such as multiple choice, timed, and one-shot approaches) which characterize most standardized and teacher-made tests used for classroom assessments. The term was popularized by Grant Wiggins to convey the idea that assessment should engage students in applying the knowledge and skills they have acquired in the same way that they will be required to use that knowledge and those skills in the real world outside of school (Marzano, Pickering, and McTighe, 1993).

Not all of this is new. Some alternative assessment techniques have been used by many teachers for years. What is new is that what was once considered implicit and informal information about a student's performance must now be made explicit and formal so that substantive educational decisions can be made from the alternative assessments.

These *alternative* ways in which educators are beginning to look at assessment match more closely the emerging conceptions of learning and brain functioning that are being developed from recent research. They are more suited to current thinking about teaching and curriculum, and they provide teachers with an occasion to rethink their understanding of subject matter and their fundamental instructional goals. Although opponents to new assessments raise credible questions about costs, feasibility, objectivity, and fairness, educators need to embrace what promises to be a more useful and reliable view of assessment.

RETHINKING ASSESSMENT

Since mid-century there have been several studies of how testing is used in many schools. Walt Harvey (1991) summarizes several major themes from these studies:

- Most testing programs have no clear consequences and are not very useful.
- Educational professionals know little about the technology of testing.
- Standardized tests do not tell teachers anything they did not already know about their students.

Teachers do not need information about how their school is doing, they need information about how their students are doing. As a result, an increasing number of educators are questioning whether current traditional testing adequately assesses important goals for student performance in the twenty-first century. Their concerns include the:

- narrowness of traditional testing content
- mismatch between curriculum and testing content

- limited relevance to classroom and real-world learning
- too little instruction on complex thinking and problem-solving skills

Assessment is quickly becoming a cornerstone of educational reform, and the result has been an explosion of interest in alternative forms of assessment combined with attempts across the country by test makers and professional educators to create them. There is general agreement that traditional assessments reduce the decision-making potential of educators in schools and may very well be negatively influencing the direction of curricular and pedagogical practices.

When traditional testing determines what is taught, the correct response becomes the goal and the curriculum is narrowed. Children are given fewer opportunities to develop their strengths and spend more time in drill and practice for multiple-choice testing. Instructional strategies require less student participation, and the curriculum is dominated by isolated test-taking skills.

Skilled teachers, however, have always compiled a broader assessment of their students' performance. They have typically gone beyond what information the student has processed and have based student performance on a student's progress over time. They have informally formed opinions of a student's ability to think, create, inquire, and be responsible. They have observed a student's ability to use what he has learned as he makes judgments, draws conclusions, makes connections, and applies his skills and knowledge in thoughtful ways to new situations. Observations and performances of this kind are beginning to exert a powerful influence on the new models of assessment.

The idea that new tests may help to significantly improve our schools and raise student achievement deserves some scrutiny, but what proponents of assessment reform must consider is fitting the assessment model to the function that a particular assessment is to perform. We currently use different tests for program evaluation, college admission, and employment opportunities simply because tests for these very different purposes need very different characteristics. Common sense should therefore tell us that a single test cannot tell us everything we may need or want to know about a student's achievement. Any redesign, therefore, of a school's assessment strategy would have to include tests that can:

- provide students with information to help them improve their performance
- provide teachers with information to help them improve their instruction
- provide information to the public for the purpose of determining accountability

CURRICULUM, INSTRUCTION, AND ASSESSMENT

Changing educational goals, the relationships between teaching, learning, and assessment, and the limitations of the traditional methods of assessment have led to the growing recognition of the need for significant change in educational assessment. The back-to-basics movement of the 1970s led to an emphasis on low-level functioning skills and minimum-competency testing. The reform of the 1990s is directed toward more sophisticated goals and higher standards. The current emphasis on educational goals outside of traditional content requires more sophisticated assessments and new standards of performance, which current assessments do not adequately address.

Educational theories that characterized learning as the accumulation of discrete skills are giving way to a conception of learning and teaching based on cognitive psychology. This cognitive view calls for an active constructivist approach to learning in which the whole is greater than the sum of its parts (Marzano, Pickering, and McTighe, 1993). If learning occurs in this holistic fashion, then assessment should also be able to provide holistic information. Conventional selected-response test formats are by their very nature too narrow in their focus to fulfill this purpose. People often claim that testing helps students learn, but they rarely consider in detail exactly how it does so. As Harvey, (1991) writes, "Common sense, theories of learning and research on intrinsic motivation and feedback all indicate that the sort of standardized testing commonly done in schools. . . is simply not conducive to student learning" (p. 151).

Assessment and learning should be intimately linked together. How we structure our assessments directly affects learning in that it provides feedback and direction important to a student's motivation, understanding, and retention of what is being learned. It indirectly affects instruction in that what is taught and how it is taught is commonly geared toward what is assessed. Learning is not a one-way transmission. Meaningful instruction involves the active participation of the student, and effective teachers constantly use that participation to:

- assess how their students are doing
- gather evidence of progress and problems
- adjust their instructional planning

What the constructivists have introduced into discussions of teaching and learning is exactly what assessment reformers need to consider as they begin to formulate alternatives to traditional testing. How can we build assessments that are sensitive to and capable of documenting and measuring complex cognitive behaviors? Teachers cannot teach all students in the same way. They cannot rely on the same materials and strategies to teach all students, nor perhaps is the same assessment appropriate for all learners. Assessment reform is actually the introduction of the same flexibility in documenting what students learn as has been derived from learning theory about curriculum and pedagogy (Jorgenson, 1993).

Assessment reform can only meet its promise if it addresses some critical conditions:

- Does it represent significant outcomes and the important goals of classroom instruction?
- Does the knowledge, skills, and format match what the teachers are teaching and what the students are expected to learn?

Good assessment is an integral part of good instruction and ought to reflect the broad array of academic and non-academic goals for students. It should measure important classroom objectives, and its results should represent how students perform on the knowledge and skills reflected in those objectives. It is impossible to measure all the learning that takes place in school, but as Steffy and English (1997) point out, we must decide upon the most important learning and construct measures to determine that this learning is taking place. Good assessment provides accurate and useful information concerning the mastery of skills and knowledge and provides the data upon which significant decisions for improvement can be made.

ALTERNATIVE ASSESSMENT

Much of what is being described as new in alternative assessment has, in fact, a longer history. The types of documentation, portfolio, and performance we now call alternative assessment were common in the nineteenth century and were basic practices in numerous early progressive schools influenced by the works of Dewey and others (Jervis, 1991). Standardized testing has dominated educational assessment since it was first introduced in the 1920s to process military recruits. Over time considerable credibility as been given to standardized test scores as genuine measures of student learning, especially as attention has been focused on improved achievement and accountability. Only recently has the validity of traditional testing been questioned. Today, direct examination of student work is being touted as a more valid measure of assessment.

The concept of assessing what students produce is not new. Evaluating student learning and performance dates back to Socrates and has always been used by insightful teachers who kept running records and folders of student work. Through the 1930s until the middle of the twentieth century several studies conducted by Ralph Tyler and others demonstrated the connection between the necessity of this style of evaluation and educational objectives. Tyler maintained that because educational objectives are essentially changes in human behavior, it followed that the evaluation process must determine the degree to which these changes are actually taking place. He concluded that there are many ways of getting evidence about behavior besides a paper-and-pencil test, and that when thinking about assessment we are not talking about any single event or any particular method (Wraja, 1994).

Currently, alternative assessment is used to describe a broad range of evaluation techniques encompassing authentic and performance assessment activities. It refers to a variety of tasks and situations in which students are given an opportunity to demonstrate their understanding and to thoughtfully apply knowledge, skills, and habits of mind in a variety of contexts. These assessments often occur over time and result in tangible products or observable performances. They encourage self-evaluation and revision, require judgment to score, and reveal degrees of proficiency based on established criteria (Marzano, Pickering, and McTighe, 1993) The several types of alternative assessments all exhibit two central features; they are viewed as alternatives to traditional tests, and they involve direct examination of student performance on tasks of relevance to life outside of school.

Alternative assessments require students to actively accomplish complex and significant tasks while bringing to bear prior knowledge, recent learning, and relevant skills to solve realistic or authentic problems. They stress examining the process as well as the products of learning and attempt to capitalize on the actual work of the classroom. When structured properly they enhance student and teacher involvement in the assessment process and meet the accountability concerns of the various stakeholders about student achievement and district improvement.

Criteria for creating alternative assessment strategies from Herman, Aschbacher, and Winters (1992) is summarized in Figure 5.3. Putting alternative assessment into practice requires a profound shift of the roles and responsibilities of teachers, students, and administrators.

- They ask students to perform, create, or produce something.
- They tap higher-level thinking and problem-solving skills.
- They use tasks that are meaningful instructional activities.
- They invoke real-world applications.
- They are graded by people using human judgment.
- They require new instructional and assessment roles for teachers.

FIGURE 5.3. Common characteristics of alternative assessments.

DEVELOPING AN ALTERNATIVE ASSESSMENT PROGRAM

By embracing alternative assessments educators are beginning a complex process wherein many questions immediately arise. Which forms of assessment are most useful for which educational purposes (Figure 5.4)? How will teachers distinguish among assessments of differing quality and appropriateness? What will teachers need to know in order to design the required assessments? Although there is an abundance of literature on alternative assessment, there has been relatively little study of the specific steps to be taken and the potential problems faced by local educators who choose to develop and implement an alternative assessment program.

Use of alternative assessments implies new roles for teachers and implies a paradigmatic shift. Whereas traditional testing promotes the notion of the teacher-centered classroom, alternative assessment requires a student-centered classroom where students take center stage and the teacher becomes an accomplished guide in the process of self-assessment. Teachers become researchers in the classroom, posing critical questions to better inform their sense of a student's learning and their approach to teaching. The shift also involves moving away from an emphasis on covering desired content to an emphasis on achieving desired student learning goals.

The problems in trying to develop and use alternative assessments include:

- the lack of pre-service training in assessment
- the low level of assessment literacy among educators in general
- the need for professional development in order to implement alternative assessments (Aschbacher, 1994)

Even if teachers are not expected to create their own assessments, they need to be well acquainted with assessment so they can be wise consumers of

---

- teacher-made tests ensure that students are tested on what they are actually taught
- nationally-normed tests to ensure that the local definition of mastery is generally congruent with student achievement outside the district
- curriculum-based tests to emphasize the key concepts of the curriculum
- criterion-referenced tests to provide an assessment of each student in relation to the objectives established by the school
- standardized tests to provide a general assessment of the school as it compares to national norms

FIGURE 5.4. Matching assessment forms with purposes. (Summarized from Educational Research Service, 1983).

those large-scale, commercial assessments, which influence classroom practices. Training should include:

- the rationale for alternative assessment
- theories of teaching and learning that underlie constructivist instructional approaches and alternative assessment
- a process for developing alternative assessments
- alternative assessment models and materials (Aschbacher, 1994)

Workshops should include the development of prototype measures, opportunities to pilot them in the classroom, guided discussion of results, and refinement of the assessment instruments. The requisite training cannot be done in a one-day inservice but must be an ongoing process that is reinforced with classroom pilots, reflection, and revision.

Once a critical mass of teachers has been trained in the value of, appropriate use of, and development of alternative assessments, a few teams of dedicated volunteers can begin to experiment with assessment strategies. To begin that process, Herman et al. (1992) recommend the following series of steps:

(1) Specify the nature of the skills and the accomplishments the students are to develop.
(2) Specify tasks that would require students to demonstrate those skills and accomplishments.
(3) Specify the criteria and standards for judging student performance on the task.
(4) Develop a reliable rating system.
(5) Gather evidence of validity to show what kinds of inferences can be drawn from the assessment.
(6) Use the results to refine the assessment, improve curriculum and instruction, and to provide feedback to parents, students, and community.

QUALITY ISSUES AND ASSESSMENT

How to make quality decisions about assessments involves issues that are central to determining the value of the assessments. The Center for Research, Evaluation, Standards and Student Testing recommends several criteria, including the following (Bracey, 1993):

(1) Consequences of the test: Judgments about performance assessments are different depending upon the purposes they will serve. The technical

quality of an assessment must be much more stringent when an assessment is for accountability or for high-stakes decisions, such as high school graduation, than when assessment is used to give students and teachers a focus for improving teaching and learning.

(2) Issues of fairness: Assessments must be linguistically appropriate for all students and free from bias so that student performance is a true representation of student competency and is judged in an unbiased way.

(3) Instructional sensitivity: Some thought must be given to the relationship between assessment and instruction. A key criticism of assessment is that it often fails to test what is taught during instruction. We need to know that good instruction affects performance on the assessment and that the content, skills, and processes tested by the assessment are transferable and can be generalized to similar but untested topics.

(4) Meaningfulness: Each assessment task needs to be placed in a context in order to hold the student's attention and so that the student understands its purpose and makes sense of its content. It should adequately cover the content to be taught, demand thinking about complex tasks, and focus on important curricular concepts.

(5) Resulting data: In order for an assessment to be worth the time and effort, it should yield a rich array of data. Alternative assessments are best implemented as strategies to improve the teachers' understanding of the students in their classrooms. Good assessment provides information that teachers can use to help a particular student, rethink their instruction, redesign materials, and make them better teachers. The results should also serve as a way to communicate with parents and students about their individual performance and to meet the accountability demands of those with an interest in the quality of education (schools, districts, states, and programs).

As Bracey (1993) writes, "Unless proponents of alternative assessments are as tough minded in developing them as they as they have been in criticizing traditional practice, the newer tests may not be professionally credible, publicly acceptable or legally defensible" (p. 9). Psychometricians have been fine tuning the traditional technology of testing for 70 years, but until recently little attention has been paid to the reliability and validity of alternative testing. There are many issues that need to be considered and much to be cautious about when developing an alternative assessment system. Security of an assessment, its limited use, its administrative feasibility, and affordability are all factors to consider when selecting a commercially produced alternative or creating a locally developed measure of student performance.

The challenge for the immediate future is to assure that within the limits of our knowledge and the time available for implementation we develop alternative assessments that measure each student's performance.

GETTING STARTED

According to Aschbacher (1994), the shift to alternative assessments "requires a deeper level of conceptual involvement and intense reflection not only by students but also by teachers and other educators" (p. 217). Alternative assessment requires an integration of curriculum, instruction, and assessment. It involves articulating learning goals and analyzing student work through collegial networks within the school and perhaps across disciplines. Revising assessments goes beyond simply building better tests; it involves changing a school's culture, affecting pedagogical practice and curriculum, and influencing expectations and standards of performance.

Here again, The Center for Research, Evaluation, Standards and Student Assessment provides some guidance in how to start the process (Baker, 1993).

(1) Create a team or committee to agree on reasons for altering the current assessment practices. The best reason is to improve teaching and raise student performance. Traditional testing does not capture everything we need to know about student performance, particularly in the areas of thinking, learning by doing, and working with each other. Organize public support for a comprehensive assessment program through as wide and open a process as possible.

(2) Focus on getting a clear agreement on what students need to know and need to be able to do. Assessment needs to be a part of instruction. Think about artifacts and products as well as activities that would allow students to demonstrate what they know and are able to do.

(3) Don't revise everything at once. Begin by sampling students, and consider that every student need not be tested in every subject every year. Matrix sampling techniques can systematically sample grades, students, programs, and forms of assessment. Systematic sampling permits a wider range of assessment techniques than might otherwise be possible if all students were tested with the same instrument.

(4) Find a limited number of examples of alternative assessments that work and start with those. Don't reinvent assessments, adapt them.

(5) Monitor what you have done and how things are working, and keep everyone informed. Powerful assessment measures should reveal more than what students know. It can capture hidden aspects about both teaching and learning that can direct both students and teachers toward further improvement.

(6) Expect the process to take time.

What educators and policy makers are beginning to realize is that no single assessment can serve every assessment demand, and that there are assessments that work better than others for some purposes. This approach would appear to make sense. Alternative assessments may be superior to traditional assessments for instructional purposes, but demands for accountability might best be met by the data generated by standardized testing. Building a multiple-measure program recognizes the need for a variety of assessment data and an understanding of how that data might be used by the various stakeholders to whom the school is accountable. "At a time when public confidence in our schools is at an all time low," writes Michael Kean (1996), "it is not in our best interest to shun measurements that provide objective base-line data sought by educators, policy makers and the public" (p. 17). A school is effective when its standards are demanding, when high-quality work is required, and when a system of accountability can ensure that those conditions are met. You have it right, says Grant Wiggins (1994), when your assessments lead to improved performance.

SUMMARY

The promise of alternative assessment depends as much on how it is used as it does on the improved methodologies it employs. Changing assessment strategies without changing instruction, curriculum, and the way we use assessment results will not result in improvements in student achievement. Teachers, administrators, and the community must be involved in all of the stages of planning assessment, and it must be embedded in the curriculum and the teaching practices of the district. Its goal is to support more informed and student-centered teaching and to be intimately understood by teachers, students, and parents. In short, we must rethink assessment because we have entered an era when the goal of schooling is to educate all the children well, rather than selecting a talented tenth for knowledge work.

REFERENCES

Aschbacher, Pamela R. (June 1994). "Helping Educators to Develop and Use Alternative Assessments: Barriers and Facilitators." *Educational Policy* 8 (2): 202–223.

Baker, Eva L. (December 1993). "Questioning the Technical Quality of Performance Assessment." *The School Administrator.* Arlington, VA: American Association of School Administrators, 12–16.

Bracey, Gerald (December 1993). "Testing the Tests." *The School Administrator.* Arlington, VA: American Association of School Administrators, 8–11.

Cheek, Dennis W. (November 1993). "Plain Talk About Alternative Assessment." *Middle School Journal,* 16–21.

Educational Research Service (1983). *Effective Schools: A Summary of Research.* Arlington, VA.

Haney, Walt. (1991). "We Must Take Care: Fitting Assessments to Functions." *Expanding Student Assessment,* Vito Perrone, ed. Alexandria, VA: Association for Supervision and Curriculum Development, pp. 142–163.

Herman, John, Aschbacher, Pamela and Winters, Lynn (1992). *A Practical Guide to Alternative Assessment.* Alexandria, VA: Association for Supervision and Curriculum Development, 6–8.

Jervis, Kathe (1991). "Closed Gates in a New York City School." In: *Expanding Student Assessment,* Vito Perrone, ed. Alexandria, VA: Association for Supervision and Curriculum Development, 4.

Jorgensen, Margaret (December 1993). "The Promise of Alternative Assessment." *The School Administrator.* Arlington, VA: American Association of School Administrators, 17–23.

Kean, Michael (December 1996). "Multiple Measures." *The School Administrator.* Arlington, VA: American Association of School Administrators, 53 (11): 14–15.

Marzano, Robert, Pickering, Debra and McTighe, Jay (1993). *Assessing Student Outcomes.* Alexandria, VA: Association for Supervision and Curriculum Development, 11–13.

The National Association of Secondary School Principals (1996). *Breaking Ranks: Changing an American Institution.* Alexandria, VA.

Steffy, Betty E. (1995). *Authentic Assessment and Curriculum Alignment: Meeting the Challenge of National Standards.* Rockport, MA: Pro-Active Publications.

Steffy, Betty E. and English, Fenwick W. (1997). *Curriculum and Assessment for World-Class Schools.* Lancaster, PA: Technomic Publishing Co., Inc.

Wiggins, Grant (July 1994). "None of the Above." *Executive Educator,* Arlington, VA: American Association of School Administrators, 15.

Wraja, William G. (September 1994). *Performance Assessment: A Golden Opportunity to Improve the Future.* Alexandria, VA: National Association of Secondary School Principals, 71–79.

CHAPTER 6

What Teachers Need To Know: About Time

In *A Nation at Risk* (U.S. National Commission on Excellence in Education, 1983) it was suggested that school improvement was linked to the issue of time, in particular:

- more effective use of the existing school day
- a longer school day
- and an extended school year

However, time as an educational variable is only beginning to be viewed by educators as a significant catalyst in bringing about true and lasting change. Changing how we use the school day or school year requires more than simple modifications of the calendar and schedule. It requires rethinking how we teach and what we are teaching and a reexamination of the most important aspects of how educational programs are designed and implemented.

Attention to time has increased for a number of reasons, including:

- the establishment of national goals
- growing emphasis on the development of more interdisciplinary curriculums
- the use of more interactive learning strategies
- new assessment techniques

Our use of time needs to be more compatible with the emerging learner objectives of schools for the twenty-first century and our growing understanding of how the brain functions and how students learn. We know all students do not learn in the same way and at the same rate, and only through rethinking our organization of time and how we use it can we adequately pay attention to this reality.

As reported in *Prisoners of Time* (1984) *a report of the National Commission on Time and Learning,* "Unyielding and relentless, the time available in the uniform six hour day and a 180 day year is the unacknowledged flaw in American education" (p. 8). Organizing the school day is both a technical problem and one of the fundamental adaptive challenges in the quest to restructure schools. The available time and how students and teachers use that time is basic to the range of pedagogical and workplace issues faced by school reformers.

The typical school day involves shifting students from subject to subject and traveling from teacher to teacher (Figure 6.1), a process that has been adequately documented as being inimical to real learning (Miller, 1992). Our use of time has been labeled "the Procrustean Bed into which all instruction must fit" (Bowman and Kirkpatrick, 1995). It encourages a lecture style format that emphasizes coverage rather than comprehension.

Several new and emerging concerns are motivating educators to look for alternative ways to more effectively use school time. They include:

- fragmented approaches to instruction, which limit the development of deeper understanding
- impersonal school climates, which negatively effect student motivation
- exacerbated discipline problems resulting from frequent class movements

The traditional scheduling of the school day wastes both time and energy that could otherwise be focused on teaching and learning. For all of these reasons educators nationwide have turned their attention to the issue of how time is allocated during the school day and school year to discover

PERIOD	Monday thru Thursday	Friday
Tutorial/activity	7:30–8:05	7:30–8:05
Homeroom	8:09–8:19	8:09–8:19
One	8:23–9:07	8:23–9:03
Two	9:11–9:55	9:07–9:47
Three	9:59–10:43	9:51–10:31
Four	10:47–11:31	10:35–11:15
Five	11:35–12:19	11:19–11:59
Six	12:23–1:07	12:03–12:43
Seven	1:11–1:55	12:47–1:27
Eight	1:59–2:43	1:31–2:11

FIGURE 6.1. Sample traditional schedule.

ways to organize instruction more effectively and to improve the quality of learning.

The issue appears to be polarizing as the discussion of the relative benefits and deficiencies of traditional scheduling are compared to the growing number of alternatives. There is consensus only on the fact that careful examination of how time is used in school is a critical factor in our quest for qualitative improvement in our schools.

This quest reaches back as far as the 1890s but advances in technology have made possible an increasing number of ways in which the school day can be designed and structured. Principles of learning that have been previously ignored because of the scheduling nightmare they presented are no longer obstacles to creating a more conducive learning environment. Learning should be concentrated, free from distraction, facilitated by diversified teaching strategies, problem centered, and cooperative. To create such a learning environment requires a fundamental altering of the relationship between students and teachers and a change in each of their work loads. Through our use of time and how we structure the school day these fundamental changes can be made.

THE ORGANIZATION OF TIME

Using time as a focal point for educational reform has led to an increased demand for experimentation with the reorganization of time. Every aspect of how students and teachers use their time is coming under increasing scrutiny. Educators across the country are beginning to question the length of the school day, how time is used for learning academic subjects, increasing student achievement within the available instructional time, professional development opportunities for teachers, and how states might change regulations to facilitate innovative ways for schools to extend and make better use of their time. A rapidly growing number of schools are either considering or implementing some form of alternative scheduling.

The popular alternative uses of time can be grouped into four general categories. They include:

- **extended day:** a longer school day and/or before- and after-school programs with extended time for learning opportunities and support for local services
- **extended year:** a longer school year, usually in excess of 200 days for the reasons stated above
- **year-round school:** any redistribution of the traditional 180-day school year allowing for shortened summer breaks and several breaks during the school year

- **reorganized day:** varying the length of the learning experience within the traditional day based on student need or curriculum demand

The outcome of any decision to increase the amount of instructional time or to alter the use of existing instructional time should be to change fundamentally the relationship between students and teachers and the workload of each. The purpose should be to have students enrolled and teachers teaching fewer classes. In determining how this might best be done, attention must be paid to related issues such as:

- maintaining student motivation
- satisfying course requirements
- addressing issues of retention
- conforming to contractual obligations
- providing sufficient staff development for modifying instructional patterns to support the restructured use of time

The current standard use of time by most schools discourages teachers from using more interactive instructional methods, which are believed to be more effective in deepening a student's understanding of the material being covered and in aiding retention and transfer of that information for future application. Students subject to the so-called "shopping mall" schedules often do not have sufficient time to focus on in-depth learning because of the fragmented presentation of content and are often denied the opportunity to enroll in courses of special interest. Time to develop the personal relationships that have been deemed critical to a true learning community are similarly obstructed. As Canady and Rettig (1996) report, schools with alternative scheduling that allows for more active learning methods have significantly higher student achievement.

By rethinking our use of time we can find alternatives that better meet the needs of our current understanding of how students learn and the knowledge and skills they will need to be successful in the twenty-first century (Figure 6.2). Alternative uses of time will allow for and encourage cooperative learning teams of teachers and students in which students and teachers will get to know one another. They should provide time for students to explore concepts in depth and to discover the applicability and connections between the content areas. Students need time to put concepts into practice while teachers are present so that they can consult with the teacher to increase their understanding.

The reorganization of how we use our time will not be an overnight process but one that will take time, the commitment to a strong rationale, the involvement of all those concerned, and careful and extensive planning.

Traditional or classic schedule	6–10 periods with equal minutes per period offered within the context of the instructional day. Used by approximately 89% of schools.
Modified traditional schedule	Traditional or classical schedule with a variation provided to the day or week. Used by approximately 7% of schools.
Block schedule	Sets of extended classes, usually 3 or 4 per day, offered on an alternating day or semester basis. Used by approximately 1% of schools.
Modified block schedule	A block schedule with a variation provided to the day or week. Used by approximately 1% of schools.
Modular schedule	Dividing the instructional day into modules of 10–20 minutes each allowing for flexible class scheduling by the day and week. Used by approximately 2% of schools.

FIGURE 6.2. Scheduling practices: types and current use. (Summarized from Retooling the Instructional Day, 1994).

TIME, TEACHING, AND LEARNING

Scheduling should be compatible with learning outcomes. What students learn, not how long it takes them to learn it, is what is most important in education. Current scheduling practices have created a narrow view of human learning, focusing more on the student's ability to recognize and remember than on thinking about and using what has been learned (Kruse and Kruse, 1995). As a result, the curriculum has become a highly content-dominated dispensation of knowledge presented and assessed through predominantly linguistic methods. The flaw in this approach is that its reliance on the transmission and processing of knowledge through language develops recognition and familiarity with a concept, but it does not ensure comprehension or the ability to apply what is learned in a real-life situation.

We now have a substantial understanding of how human beings learn. Much has been learned in the past few years that suggests that student understanding and retention can be increased through the use of brain-compatible instruction and curriculum organization. How we use our academic time should reflect what we know about this process. The brain is a processor that constructs meaning through associative powers and systems of memory. Incoming information is constantly screened for its relationship to what is already known. As new information and experiences are gained they are linked to existing knowledge and stored in the brain for future retrieval.

The typical school day is not conducive to this associative process. As information is dispensed as facts, and drills of skills are segmented by subject and provided almost exclusively by linguistic means a student's ability to derive meaning and understanding becomes quite limited. Presenting knowledge as disassociated parts hinders the brain's natural ability to derive meaning from the whole-to-parts and parts-to-whole processing for which it was built (Kruse and Kruse, 1995). Students tend to be more interested and pay more attention when they can clearly see the usefulness of what it is they are expected to learn. Understanding an object, event, or relationship is derived or evoked when both the parts and the whole concept are linked in a student's mind and related to the student's experience.

Current school schedules isolate students by expecting them to work independently as they process information and artificially segregate curricular concepts that are naturally connected in the real world. An improved approach to school scheduling should provide greater flexibility, eliminate both student and curriculum isolation, and reflect how the brain processes information. All this implies a more flexible school day than currently exists.

Most uses of time in schools are based on assumptions about time and organization that are not directly applicable to the process of teaching and learning. The historical approach to school organization viewed the teacher as the worker, the student as the raw material, and the dispensation of knowledge as the end product. The result has been schools that look more like factories than the current paradigm of centers for thinking and learning where teachers guide students toward the construction of knowledge for themselves. Efforts to restructure our use of time reveal a great deal about how directly our organization of time is tied to these assumptions about how we believe learning occurs.

Successful change in how a school uses its time is invariably rooted to a conceptualization of teaching and learning that could not be accommodated by the more traditional scheduling options. Without such a commitment, any change becomes just another educational fad. The most common changes are those which introduce greater flexibility and the opportunity for teachers to work in greater depth with fewer students.

ALTERING OUR USE OF TIME

The models for altering the school day are many, and most ideas can trace their roots back several decades. Changing the schedule, however, should not be an end in itself but rather a means for achieving the more important goals of managing teacher and student workloads and for strengthening the relationship between teachers and students.

An early example of a progressive alternative to the current factory model is the Dalton plan developed by Helen Parkhurst in the early 1900s (Edwards,

1991). The plan involved a complete restructuring of the school day into subject labs for grades 5–12. The curriculum was student centered, self-paced and individualized by means of monthly contracts. Teachers guided students through educational experiences aided by paraprofessionals who handled most of the non-teaching duties. Assessments of this early alternative schedule reported that students learned responsibility and self-discipline. The flexibility it provided allowed students who needed to, to work slowly and thoroughly and provided the opportunity for those students who worked more quickly to advance. The laboratory structure required students to be actively involved in a non-threatening and noncompetitive environment that provided time for a high degree of individual help. Both students and teachers enjoyed long-term relationships with each other and their peers.

A more contemporary example of alternative use of time is the Copernican plan (Figure 6.3) introduced in the late 1980s by Joseph Carroll (1994). Primarily a block plan, this alternative schedule involves the scheduling of periods of varying length, almost always longer than the traditional 40–60-minute instructional periods used by most schools. Options in the Copernican plan include two periods per day with each period lasting 2½ hours and meeting for 9 weeks, three periods of 95 minutes each continuing for 12 weeks, and three 90-minute classes for 18 weeks.

Proponents of the plan point to its significant effectiveness as compared to more traditional scheduling and support the claim with better test scores, improved writing, the completion of more courses, and the rejuvenation of the teaching staff.

A number of issues may restrict schools from dramatically altering their use of time. Consideration must be given to and accommodations may need to be made for regulatory issues such as graduation requirements, the number of required and elective courses, state law, and district policy, as well as technical issues such as room availability, number of teachers, lunch requirements, transportation issues, and working conditions covered by negotiated contracts. An additional consideration for secondary schools is the Carnegie unit.

The Carnegie Standard has its roots in the industrial standardization reforms of the early twentieth century (Kruse and Kruse, 1995). Using the management philosophy of Frederick Taylor, who used time studies of factory workers to improve their efficiency at fixed stations, the Carnegie Commission assumed that a certain amount of time was directly related to content mastery. From this historical slant on time the modern master schedule has evolved and, until recently, remained unchallenged for decades. This allotment of what is typically an equal amount of time for every subject influences dramatically the school's use of space, often how students are grouped, and the dynamic of the instructional process. Assignments are often heavily influ-

Time	Schedule A	Schedule B Macroclass I (110 min) for 60 days
7:46		
9:36	Macroclass (226 min.) for 30 days	Passing (6 min.)
9:42		Macroclass II (110 min.) for 60 days
11:32		
11:38	Passing (6min.)	
12:13	First lunch (35 min.)	Seminar I/ Music/ Phys. Ed. (70 min.)
12:48	Seminar II/ Music/ Phys. Ed. (70 min.)	Second lunch (35 min.)
1:23		
1:29	Passing (6 min.)	
	Preparation/Help/Study/Phys. Ed./Music (70 min.)	
2:39		
2:45	Departure (6 min.)	
5:00	Activities/Sports (135 min.)	

FIGURE 6.3. The Copernican plan.

enced by the needs of the master schedule; therefore, teachers are arranged into departments of content specialists who are then assigned to rotating groups of students on a daily basis.

The standard schedule needs to be replaced so that schools will no longer equate seat time with learning. The amount of time devoted to a course of study should be based on how long it takes a student to accomplish the learning. To do that effectively requires better use of performance assessments and a more exact determination of which students are achieving the purported standards, which requires that teachers spend more time with fewer students.

Scheduling must be made more flexible. Traditional scheduling patterns are based on the needs of:

- current pedagogical practices
- the educational needs of an increasingly diverse student population
- the rising professional development needs of teachers

Among the most popular alternatives that provide this flexibility, or provide a significant variation to instructional time within the constraints with which most school districts operate, are the basic models of the block schedule.

BLOCK SCHEDULING

Block scheduling (Figure 6.4), or intensified scheduling as it is sometimes called, takes many forms but always involves longer class periods designed to improve instruction and to increase student learning. As Canady and Rettig write (1996), "Within the schedule resides power: power to address problems, the power to successful implementation of change and the power to make possible the institutionalization of effective instructional practices" (p. 9).

The block schedule and variations on it are built in much the same way as the traditional counterpart except that the variable of time is rearranged so that students take fewer classes, thereby spending a greater amount of time in each of those classes. This manipulation of time impacts positively on the teacher and student workload and many of the curricular and instructional concerns while fulfilling most seat time and statutory requirements. Supporters point out that by training teachers to vary their instructional strategies to capitalize on these longer classes, students will learn more. Critics argue that in reality, little actually changes, except for the longer class time.

Organizing the instructional program into extended blocks of time, typically 90 minutes in length and three to four blocks per day, makes class time available for a wider range of teaching strategies (see Figure 6.5 for sample). Changing the schedule can be a catalyst for classroom changes, which in turn create better interactions with students, allowances for a variety of learning styles, increases in student achievement, and improvement in school climate (O'Neil, 1995). Providing time for teachers to involve their students in activities that require more than reading and listening deepens the student's understanding and enriches the total learning experience.

The benefits of a less hectic and more authentic use of time, derived from the variety of block schedules now in use, are reported to be many (Figure 6.6). The increased available class time created by the longer class periods allows for qualitative improvements in instruction focusing more on critical thinking and problem-solving activities, which are more cooperative and interactive

4 X 4 Semesterized	Reorganizes the traditional 180-day year into two 90-day terms in which students take four 85-minute classes per day each semester.
Alternate day block	Students take eight classes that are 85 minutes in length and meet on alternating days for the entire school year.
75-75-30 Plan	Divides the school year into two 75-day terms and a 30-day intercession. The two 75-day terms include three or four blocks, while the 30-day term provides remediation and/or enrichment opportunities in two or three subjects.
Intensive scheduling	Offers semesterized or alternating blocks of 85 minutes, two in the morning and two in the afternoon, separated by a recess period, which has time for lunch and other activities such as extra-curricular programs and tutorials.

FIGURE 6.4. Variations on the block schedule.

than more traditional teaching methods. With students concentrating on fewer courses, they tend to prepare more thoroughly and experience more academic success. Teachers serving far fewer students are able to provide more individualized instruction and comprehensive feedback, getting to know individual students, their learning styles, and their strengths and weaknesses.

Schedule #1 Monday - Thursday		Schedule #2 Friday or Day Before a Teacher Holiday	
Teacher arr	7:20	Teacher arr	7:20
Homeroom	7:33–7:40	Homeroom	7:33–7:40
Block 1	7:44–9:08	Block 1	7:44–9:00
2	9:13–10:37	2	9:05–10:21
3	10:42–12:06	3	10:26–11:42
3C	10:42–11:12	3C	10:26–10:56
3D	11:16–11:46	3D	11:00–11:30
4	11:50–1:14	4	11:34–12:50
4C	12:10–12:40	4C	11:46–12:16
4D	12:44–1:14	4D	12:20–12:50
5	1:19–2:43	5	12:55–2:11
Teacher dismiss	2:48	Teacher dismiss	2:13
7 min homeroom		7 min homeroom	
84 min blocks		76 min blocks	
30 min lunch		30 min lunch	
30 min grade room		30 min grade room	

FIGURE 6.5. Sample block schedule.

- Students are able to focus on fewer courses at a time.
- Teachers have more time to focus teaching methods and strategies on cooperative and active learning activities.
- Teachers and students have more personal contact time and more individualized attention can be given.
- Students may be able to take more courses.
- Student achievement improves and the school climate becomes calmer.

FIGURE 6.6. Advantages to block scheduling.

Altering the master schedule to one that provides longer instructional periods can also create a climate in which teachers and students work as teams delving more deeply into concepts. Schools using some version of a more intensified schedule find themselves carefully reevaluating curriculum and course requirements. The school runs more smoothly, and a team spirit is fostered which pervades the entire school community.

The block schedule is not without its critics (see Figure 6.7) and the decision to change how a school will use its instructional time is a process that must be planned. Teachers, students, and parents have strong opinions. Parents and students have concerns about how altering the schedule may impact college admissions and how it may affect those students transferring in or out of the district.

A major concern for students and many parents is the assurance that teachers are prepared to use instructional strategies appropriate for the longer instructional periods. Teachers do make the necessary changes. Over time and with appropriate staff development, teachers lecture less and actively engage their students far more often than teachers who have more traditional periods.

Retention is also an issue with parents, students, and teachers as they anticipate the potential ill effects of longer breaks between levels of instruction. While some increased review may be needed in introductory lessons, teachers generally report that they find little difference in retention between students who have recently completed a prerequisite course and those with a greater lapse of time between courses. Canady and Rettig (1996) cite a June 1993 issue of *Journal of Educational Psychology,* which reports that students retain 85% of the major concepts they originally learn after 4 months and 80% after 11 months.

- extended absences due to illness, field trips, and school activities
- lapse of time between traditionally sequenced courses
- attention spans of special-education and lower-ability students
- advanced placement, performance, and production courses
- student mobility issues and transfer students

FIGURE 6.7. Concerns about the block schedule.

Parents, teachers, and production and performance students involved in programs such as band, chorus, and AP courses express concern about the negative consequences of semesterized classes on preparing students for tests and performances at established times. Schools using alternative scheduling, however, have typically found sensible accommodations.

Special-education teachers and teachers for low-ability students worry that the extended blocks of time will be too long for their students. However, teachers involved in the longer instructional periods have found that student attention is related more to the variety of active learning strategies in use than the actual length of the class period.

Undeniably, the restructuring of the school day poses some difficult problems and challenges, but they are not and should not be considered insurmountable. Serious rescheduling of a school depends upon how serious a school is about articulating priorities and accepting the necessary compromises.

IMPLEMENTING AN ALTERNATIVE

Changes in how we use our time, whether designed to impact the structure of the curriculum or to accommodate instructional strategies more aligned with how we know the brain functions, requires broad-base support from all those involved with and served by the scheduling process. An important first step in bringing about that change is creating a comfort level among all the members of the school community by providing opportunities for them to learn about and have input regarding the change before it is made. The support of students and parents is crucial, but the greatest challenge to successfully implementing any change is getting past the fear that many teachers have of radical change. Cunningham and Nogle (March/April, 1996) recommend six implementation steps designed to promote a successful change. The steps are summarized in Figure 6.8 and are discussed below:

(1) **Teacher input and ownership:** Changes to the master schedule and how a school or district uses its time must be derived from pedagogical or cur-

---

- Teacher input and ownership: research and visitations, contract issues
- Student and parent acceptance: visitations and communications
- Adequate staff development: instruction, curriculum and instruction
- Time for planning: anticipate problems, consider impact
- Implementation and monitoring
- Criteria for evaluation

FIGURE 6.8. Implementation steps.

ricular needs identified by those closest to the teaching and learning process. By involving professional staff in staff development activities that introduce them to innovative instructional strategies or current trends in curriculum development, the stage is set for exploration of alternative uses of time. This creates student/teacher workloads more conducive to contemporary thinking on both how students should be taught and what they might be expected to know and do.

(2) **Student and parent acceptance:** Students and parents, too, must come to understand and accept the need for the change, and their concerns about the change and its implications for them must be carefully articulated. Available mediums for communication such as school community newsletters, existing student and parent organization meetings, and other linkages the school may have with the community should be used early and regularly throughout the change process to communicate the need for and the reasons behind the decision to change. Both parents and students should be provided with background information on alternative uses of time and should be encouraged to voice their concerns and questions about the issues related to the change. Both parents and students should be included in committees established to study, recommend, and plan for the schedule change. Particularly useful are visits to other schools that have successfully implemented an alternative schedule.

(3) **Adequate staff development:** Staff development activities are important in the initial consideration of changing how we use our time and are increasingly important as the plan to make changes is developed and implemented. How teachers use the alternative schedule is a major concern of parents and students, and its eventual success and potential to effect long-range qualitative improvement to the educational process is linked to teacher implementation. Many teachers are not ready for the shift to a more active learning and interdisciplinary approach to teaching, and staff development on appropriate instructional strategies, materials, and equipment is needed. Successful classroom innovations, curriculum changes, collaborative planning with other teachers, and alternative assessment techniques that logically flow from the proposed changes in instructional time and methods all need to be addressed in a comprehensive and ongoing staff development program designed to train current staff, as well as an induction process for new staff as the restructuring of a district unfolds.

(4) **Time for planning:** One of the biggest challenges to implementing any change is finding time to research and plan for that change. Adequate time must be provided to establish the need for the change, to explore the available alternatives, to reach consensus on the chosen alternative, and then plan for and implement the alternative. One to two years may be

required to lay the proper foundation and provide the necessary training to successfully implement a change in how a school or district organizes its instructional time. Other initiatives should be delayed or postponed, and available resources should be focused on the single issue of the alternative schedule. In-service time and dollars should be committed to this single purpose. In-service time, staff meeting time, professional days, and using substitute teachers to make additional release time for teachers all need to be considered as options for creating time for professionals to study, plan, and implement any alternative use of time.

(5) **Implementation and monitoring:** Even after an alternative schedule has been implemented, a deliberate effort must be made to monitor and make adjustments. Forums should be scheduled regularly for discussion and feedback on the changes that have been made, as well as for adjustments that may need to be made immediately or in the future. Teachers need the opportunity to share both successes and concerns, and a systematic way to address the unanticipated must be established to ensure administrative responses to teachers, students, and parents.

(6) **Criteria for evaluation:** Early in the planning process it should be determined what quantitative results the school or district hopes to derive from the change in schedule. Typically, districts anticipate improvement in student achievement, discipline, and attendance. Less measurable outcomes might also be articulated related to school climate, improved student/teacher relationships, and increases in both student motivation and teacher morale. Whatever the anticipated outcomes, some measure of baseline data should be established against which the benefits of the alternative schedule can be measured. Projected improvements may or may not be established, but periodic assessment of measurable progress is required in order to document the value of the changes made. A clear idea of what will be measured and how it will be measured is a critical component to the planning process and will eventually be needed to validate any progress reported.

SUMMARY

Current schedules contribute to the impersonal nature of school, exacerbate problems, and result in hectic, fragmented school days, which limit instructional possibilities and do not meet the growing need to address increasingly diverse student learning needs. The growing research base on how the brain functions and how students learn, as well as the anticipated educational demands of the twenty-first century, require that educators serious about educational reform examine closely alternative ways to restructure our use of time.

Time is the key to providing both teachers and students with the opportunity to engage in learning activities that are less fragmented, less hurried, and more intensive. Though opinions differ on how time may best be used, there is a growing consensus that by reorganizing our day we can provide a more concentrated program, which will speed up and deepen the learning process and contribute to long-term retention.

Combined with restructuring the curriculum, innovative classroom techniques, and improvements in assessment strategies, the restructuring of time can be an important first step and catalyst for substantive educational reform.

REFERENCES

Bowman, Gerald and Kirkpatrick, Barbara. (May 1995). "The Hybrid Schedule: Scheduling to the Curriculum." *NASSP Bulletin.* Alexandria, VA: National Association of Secondary School Principals: 42–52.

Canady, Robert Lynn and Rettig, Michael D. (September 1996). "All Around the Block: The Benefits and Challenges of a Non-Traditional School Schedule." *The School Administrator.* Arlington, VA: American Association of School Administrators, 53 (8): 8–12.

Carroll, Joseph M. (1994). *The Copernican Plan Evaluated: The Evolution of a Revolution.* Topsfield, MA: Copernican Associates.

Cunningham, R. Daniel and Nogle, Sue Anne. (March/April 1996). "Implementing A Semesterized Block Schedule: Six Key Elements." *The High School Magazine for Principals, Assistant Principals and All High School Leaders.* Alexandria,VA: National Association of Secondary School Principals, 3(3): 28–33.

Edwards, June (January 1991). "To Teach Responsibility Bring Back the Dalton Plan" *Phi Delta Kappan.* Bloomington, IN: Phi Delta Kappa, 398–401.

Kasonovic, Gerald (1994). *Retooling the Instructional Day: A Collection of Scheduling Models.* Alexandria, VA: National Association of Secondary School Principals.

Kruse, C.A. and Kruse, G. K. (May 1995). "Reforming the Use of Time." *NASSP Bulletin.* Alexandria, VA: National Association of Secondary School Principals: 1–8.

Miller, Edward. (April 1992). "Breaking the Tyranny of the Schedule." *The Harvard Education Letter.* Cambridge, MA: Harvard Graduate School of Education.

O'Neil, John (November 1995). "Finding Time to Learn." *Educational Leadership.* Alexandria, VA: Association for Supervision and Curriculum Development, 53 (3): 11–15.

Prisoners of Time (1984) Report of the National Commission on Time and Learning. Washington, D.C.: U.S. Government Printing Office.

U.S. National Commission on Excellence in Education. (1983) *A Nation at Risk.* Washington, D.C.: U.S. Government Printing Office.

CHAPTER 7

What Teachers Need To Know: Technology as a Tool for Success

TECHNOLOGY

The integration of technology in education is not a new phenomenon. Beginning in 1900 with the lantern slides to present day microcomputer technology, educators have presented technology as a means to reform and improve education (Snider, 1992). While recognized as a necessary ingredient to improving schools and classroom practices, there is little evidence to indicate that technology has been infused into daily instructional delivery systems. The technological changes that have influenced society have left educational systems relatively unchanged. In the past 20 years, a dramatic rift has opened between the process of teaching and learning in schools and the ways of obtaining knowledge in society at large (David, 1990). Significant barriers, however, have slowed the integration of technology into the daily lives of school staff and students. The United States Office of Technology Assessment (1995) has identified the barriers as including teacher time, access and costs, vision or rationale, training and support, and current practices.

Teacher Time

Teachers need time to

- experiment with new technologies
- share experiences with other teachers
- plan and debug lessons using new methods that incorporate technologies
- attend workshops or training sessions

Access and Costs

In addition to limited hardware and software, other factors affect access:

- Costs are high for purchasing, connecting to, and training to use technologies.
- Technologies may not be located in or near the classroom.
- Hardware in schools today is old (50% of computers in schools are 8-bit machines) and cannot handle many newer applications.
- New or additional wiring or phone lines are necessary for telecommunications networks.

Vision or Rationale for Technology Use

- Schools must have plans, and teachers must have a clear understanding of curricular uses of technology.
- It is difficult to keep up with the rapid rate of technology development and changing messages of best use.
- Teachers lack models showing the value of technology for their own professional use.

Training and Support

- Overall, districts spend less than 15% of their technology budgets on training, but they spend 55% of the budget on hardware and 30% on software.
- Technology training today focuses primarily on the mechanics of operating equipment, not on integrating technology into the curriculum or selecting appropriate software.
- Only 6% of elementary and 3% of secondary schools have a full-time, school-level computer coordinator for technical support.

Current Assessment Practices

- Existing standardized measurements of student achievement may not reflect what has been learned with technology.
- Teachers are held immediately accountable for changes that take time to show results.

TECHNOLOGY AS AN ESSENTIAL LEARNING TOOL

The potential of technology has come to be recognized as an indispensable skill. The Secretary's Commission on Achieving Necessary Skills (SCANS) stated, "Those unable to use technology fail a lifetime of menial works" (U.S. Deptartment of Labor, 1991). Yet the importance of knowing about technology may be secondary to the impact technology has on the way students learn. While teaching students is very important, technology can be a guiding influence on how students not only find but create knowledge. Constructivism, a theory of cognitive growth and learning, underscores this concept (Piaget, 1973).

A basic premise of constructivist ideas is that children actively construct knowledge. Rather than being supplied with absorbing facts and ideas spoken by the teacher and repeating and practicing those facts and ideas, constructivist theory presumes that students actually invent their own ideas. They assimilate new information to simple, preexisting notions and modify their understanding in light of new data (Strommen and Lincoln, 1992). Constructivism emphasizes the careful study of processes by which children create and develop their ideas. Its educational applications lie in creating curricula that match and challenge children's understanding, fostering further growth and development of the mind (Strommen and Lincoln, 1992). Constructivism promotes the child as a self-initiated creator of knowledge. Learning activities are designed to nurture and facilitate a child's own active cognitive ability. Technology makes possible the instant access to information and the parameters to quickly and thoroughly analyze and evaluate that information.

While a definitive list of information literacy skills needed to facilitate constructivist philosophy does not exist, Ogden and Germinario (1995) suggest such a list might include:

(1) Students will be able to
- formulate questions and plan strategies for finding solutions
- find, collect, and analyze information from multiple sources to solve subject-specific and trans-curricular questions
- exchange, interpret, and develop information-based products cooperatively with other students within the school and through telecommunications with other students
- critique information in terms of validity and reliability of sources
- use research to propose solutions to everyday problems
- produce information-based products using multiple technologies
(2) Students will demonstrate the skills to use tools necessary for information literacy by
- finding information using print sources, video, computer databases, and telecommunications

- developing databases and spreadsheets using technology
- developing one-, two-, and three-dimensional and technology-generated visual representations of information
- using keyboarding, word processing, and desktop publishing skills to produce documents
- producing products incorporating multimedia

(3) Students will demonstrate the attitudes and habits of the mind necessary for continuous learning and problem solving by
- using multiple information sources to solve problems on a regular basis
- using the current tools of technology to gain and process information and showing confidence that they can and will learn to use emerging technologies to better solve problems
- selecting the appropriate technology resources for specific tasks
- working cooperatively with other students to develop multidimensional solutions and projects

As students learn to use technology and associated literacy skills, they will be much better able to take greater responsibility for their own learning and use resources that go far beyond textbooks. Technology tools will facilitate the completion of everyday tasks of learning such as writing, drawing, finding and accessing data, and sending and receiving messages. Finally, computers and associated technologies can be used to conduct investigations, solve problems, and complete assignments in all subject areas.

TECHNOLOGY AS AN ESSENTIAL TEACHING TOOL

In the past, even the most skilled teachers needed chalk, a chalkboard, pencils, paper and (maybe) technologies such as an audio-cassette player or overhead projector to ensure that students got the knowledge they needed to succeed in the society they were being prepared for. To succeed in the society of the twenty-first century, however, today's student must be able to assimilate, synthesize, and analyze information, not just memorize it.

The process of adopting new technologies into schools has been slow. Like other professions, educators have methods, styles, and working procedures that have (seemingly) served them well in the past and reflect their own professional preparedness. Moreover, the unique culture of schools and the expectations of the major stakeholders in the school create conditions that are substantially different from those of other workplaces. Yet despite its complexities, schools have increased staff accessibility to technology. Through this increased availability, teachers have been given access to wonderful learning tools (Office of Technology Assessment, 1993). The most commonly used modern technology includes:

(1) Computers: It is estimated that approximately 6 million computers are available in U.S. schools. This translates to approximately one computer for every nine students.

(2) Two-way communications: This technology allows teachers and students to share and receive ideas with others outside their immediate classroom. The primary tools for this technology are telephones and modems. About one in eight teachers have telephones; approximately 40% of schools have a modem that is accessible to teachers and students.

(3) Telecommunications networking: These networks include the Internet and other means of accessing shared communication systems. Local area networks (LANS) link computers and peripherals within a limited area, often a classroom or school building. Wide area networks (WANS) connect computers over greater distances, such as building to building or city to city. Approximately 75% of public schools have computers with some networking capabilities (U.S. Department of Education, 1995).

(4) Internet: The Internet is an intellectual collection of interconnected electronic networks and a set of protocols for communicating between computers on these networks. Approximately 35% of schools in the United States have access to the internet. Very few (approximately 3%) have access to instructional classrooms.

(5) Television and video: Nearly every school in the country has a television for instructional use. The vast majority of those schools have access to broadcast television. Nearly 74% have access to cable television and 25% of schools have the availability of closed circuit television (in-house transmission on noncommercial lines).

Access to the technologies described above provides a wealth of opportunities for teachers. Specifically, these technologies can improve teaching and learning, assist in daily tasks, and enhance professional development. The understanding and application of these technologies has the potential to transform teaching and teachers so that they may

- become classroom facilitators helping students solve problems and create knowledge
- tailor learning to individual student learning styles and needs
- use multimedia workstations to present curriculum to students using a display system
- communicate with colleagues across the school, the state, and the nation
- exchange administrative data such as grades, attendance, and student schedules
- use software tools to prepare teaching and complete administrative tasks
- use most of the above-mentioned functions from home through dial-up access

PREPARING TEACHERS TO USE TECHNOLOGY

In a general sense, the potential for effective classroom use of technology exists in many schools. Yet this technology has not changed the way most classrooms operate. Far too often, teachers do not have the appropriate training to effectively know about and use technology in their classrooms. In a nationwide survey, Siegel (1995) used an in-depth questionnaire to determine the nature of technology staff development programs in schools across the country. Several findings stand out:

- Despite the lip service paid to the importance of technology staff development, 28% of the respondents spend not one penny on it; on average, staff development makes up only 8% of technology budgets.
- Even though nearly everyone talks about the importance of integrating technology into the curriculum, when asked to describe their most recent offering, 66% of respondents said they gave straight workshops on specific software titles or hardware, rather than on how to use the technology as a tool to expand and enrich the curriculum.
- Technology trainers and the teachers they instruct often differ tremendously in their satisfaction about the technology training.
- Both participants and trainers said that not enough time, inadequate hands-on practice, and insufficient follow-up were weaknesses of the programs offered. Yet only 6% of the respondents said their schools or districts give or loan technology equipment to teachers or offer a discount for teachers to buy their own equipment following their training—all of which can address these weaknesses.
- Though principals are considered gatekeepers for buying technology for their schools, 41% of the respondents said their schools or districts do not offer technology staff development for principals.

To be effective, technology training must be a systemic process that not only teaches how we may more efficiently accomplish tasks, it should also enable teachers to set new goals for teaching–learning and create ways of achieving those goals. Additionally, the focus of the training must be differentiated. That is, it must be directed at the skill level of the participants and be applicable to their responsibilities.

The following guidelines should be used in the development of technology training for teachers:

- Begin with a skills assessment that determines an individual knowledge of technology and technology applications.
- Analyze the results of the skills assessment to develop appropriate content and grouping patterns.

- Align training with the curricular goals of the school.
- Each training session should build upon the previous one; if a session introduces teachers to tools for science, the next session should provide science-oriented applications or projects.
- Focus on teaching and learning applications, not hardware and software.
- All training should be hands-on, where staff learn by doing, not watching.
- Schedule training sessions well in advance and accept few excuses for not attending (especially for administrators).
- Evaluate each training session to gather necessary feedback to determine the content, scope, and pace of subsequent sessions.
- Repeat the skills assessment at the end of the training experience to determine the relative growth of each participant.
- Provide support at the school level so that teachers can continue to use the skills they have learned.

A MODEL FOR TECHNOLOGY TRAINING

The Moorestown Township Public Schools, Moorestown, New Jersey has developed a technology training program that introduces the guiding principles stated above. This program teaches about technology, teaches about the research on educational technology, teaches about the development of new technologies, and teaches about the integration of subject content into daily lessons. Originally funded through a federal Goals 2000 grant, the program involves a partnership between the Moorestown Township Public Schools and two local colleges—Burlington County College and The College of New Jersey (formerly Trenton State College). Partnerships were built around spending principles inherent to school–college collaborations. These include

- Proper goals should be jointly conceived and agreed upon (Allum, 1991).
- The college must be committed to the collaborative ideal and provide financial support if necessary, including stipends or credit for faculty members (Allum, 1991).
- School teachers must be actively involved, not just passive recipients (Allum, 1991).
- Education must be mutual; each party must develop an appreciation of the other's contribution (Wiske, 1989).
- Outcomes should be mutually owned (Wiske, 1989).

Following a number of collaborative planning meetings, a skills assessment was designed to determine the degree to which teachers (and other staff) knew about and used technology (see survey at end of chapter). An analysis of the results of the assessment survey was used to place teachers into one of three training clusters: awareness, skill development, or application.

Awareness

Faculty who are at the level of "awareness" need to be exposed to word processing and spreadsheet software packages. The awareness model will take the form of a 12-hour workshop or course that builds word processing and spreadsheet skills. This will allow participants to experience the technology first hand and facilitate the participants in moving to the next staff development training cluster. This module could be expanded, based upon the response and needs of awareness-level participants.

Skill Development

When faculty have completed the awareness level, they will have an understanding of word processing and spreadsheet technology. The next level of proficiency will be "skill development." This module will take the form of 12 or more hours of concentrated study in database software and telecommunications applications. The skill development module will include instruction on accessing the Internet, using gopher to collect information on the World Wide Web, e-mail, etc. The participants will be encouraged to create authentic content-specific lessons that incorporate database, telecommunications, and Internet applications. Collaboration will be encouraged and participants will be expected to share their work with other members of their group to increase the level of peer interaction.

Application

The final stage of achievement will be the "application" level. This workshop will include 12–36 hours of instruction in multimedia. In this module, Moorestown staff will demonstrate understanding of the skills acquired in the previous workshops by developing technology-based lessons and incorporating them into their daily classroom activities. Various multimedia software packages will be presented for use by the participants in the development of content-specific lessons. Use of the New Jersey Content Standards will be the basis for the development of content-specific lessons.

Figure 7.1 illustrates how participants in each group would be trained (or provided a review) on personal productivity enhancers such as word processing, developing databases, etc. Additionally, Figure 7.1 illustrates how training is then differentiated by the participants' skill levels and by the subjects they teach.

Figure 7.2 illustrates the structure of each of the five training days each staff member is responsible for attending. In addition to the five off-campus training sessions (at the Burlington County College Technology Center), the entire staff

DELIVERY OF THE NEW JERSEY CONTENT STANDARDS THROUGH TECHNOLOGY

DIFFERENTIATED TRAINING

	Business Careers & Family/Consumer Sciences	Science	Mathematics	Social Studies	Foreign Language	Health & Physical Ed.	Industrial Tech	English	Fine & Performing Arts
Application	Application	Application	Application	Application	Application	Application	Application	Application	Application
Skill Development	Skill Development	Skill Development	Skill Development	Skill Development	Skill Development	Skill Development	Skill Development	Skill Development	Skill Development
Awareness	Awareness	Awareness	Awareness	Awareness	Awareness	Awareness	Awareness	Awareness	Awareness

PROFESSIONAL STAFF'S DIFFERENTIATED TRAINING GOALS

Word Processing
Spreadsheets

Database
Telecommunications

Multimedia

Reprinted with the permission of the Moorestown Public Schools

FIGURE 7.1. Goals 2000 staff development plan (Moorestown Township Public Schools in partnership with The College of New Jersey and Burlington County College).

Course Level*	Day 1	Day 2	Day 3 Content Concentration	Day 4	Day 5
I **Awareness** (entry)	Intro to: Computers Windows MSOffice MSWord disk & file mgt.	MSWord	Curriculum Content Stnds. & Content App. Power Point Concepts	Excel	Word, Excel- Integration Access Intro
IIA **Skill Devel.** (progressive)	Intro to: MSOffice Word review Excel review	Object linking and embedding (Word/Excel) Access, intro	Content Stnds. & Content App. Power Point Concepts	Access	Power Point, progressive
IIB **Skill Devel.** (progressive)	MSOffice intro Word review Excel review Object linking and embedding	Object linking and embedding (Word, Excel) Access	Content Stnds. & Content App. Power Point Concepts	Object linking and embedding (Word, Excel, Access)	Power Point, progressive
III **Application** (proficient)	MSOffice- review Word review Excel review Access-brief review Object linking and embedding	Object linking and embedding (Word, Excel, Access) MSOffice, integrating	Content Stnds. & Content App. Power Point Concepts	Power Point adv'd Multimedia authoring software	Multimedia authoring software
	6.25 Hours Sept./Oct. **2.5 Hours-** District-wide Inservice October 31 **(Internet)**	**6.25 Hours Oct./Nov.**	**6.25 Hours Nov./Dec.**	**6.25 Hours January** **2.5 Hours-** District-wide Inservice March 20 **(System design & Ethical/legal aspects)**	**6.25 Hours Jan./Feb.**

Total Hours = 36.25

*Curriculum content standards and electronic portfolio will be discussed in each lesson.
Reprinted with the permission of the Moorestown Township Public Schools, Moorestown, New Jersey.

FIGURE 7.2. Goals 2000 course structure ("Instructional Technology for the Learning Environment").

participated in two large group presentations, one involving the use of the Internet and another on legal and ethical issues involving technology.

A large group of substitute teachers were hired and trained to provide continuity in classroom instruction for the days the teachers received training. Additionally, technologies such as laptop computers and LCD plates were presented to each school so that teachers could practice the skills they had learned and demonstrate those skills in their classrooms.

An important part of the project was the ongoing assessments that guided and adjusted training sessions. Figure 7.3 illustrates the evaluation form com-

---

Date _____   Your Group Number _____   Instructor _____

Directions: The following are statements about the session that you attended today. Please indicate the extent to which each statement reflects your opinion by filling in the appropriate response in the circles. Your feedback will be used to improve the quality of instruction that you receive in this course. Before you leave class today, please return the completed form to your instructor. Thank you for your cooperation.

1=Strongly Disagree   2=Mildly Disagree   3=Mildly Agree   4=Strongly Agree

	1	2	3	4
1. The instructor was knowledgeable and helpful.	o	o	o	o
2. The material was presented in a clear and organized manner.	o	o	o	o
3. The pace of the presentation was appropriate.	o	o	o	o
4. The supplemental materials (i.e., text, overheads, handouts) were helpful.	o	o	o	o
5. The content (i.e., grade level, subject manner) was relevant to my classroom needs.	o	o	o	o
6. The content was applicable to my professional needs.	o	o	o	o
7. The time allowed to practice was sufficient.	o	o	o	o
8. I have a clear understanding of the applications presented.	o	o	o	o
9. The instructor-to-student ratio was favorable.	o	o	o	o
10. I would have preferred to work cooperatively with another person.	o	o	o	o

We welcome your additional comments.

Reprinted with permission of the Moorestown Township Public Schools.

FIGURE 7.3. Moorestown Township Public Schools instructional technology course evaluation.

pleted by participants following each training session. Additionally, a questionnaire was given to students both before and after the teacher training to assess the impact of the training on daily classroom instructional practices (see Technology Survey at end of chapter). Finally, the skills assessment survey (Computer Usage Survey) was administered again as a post test to gauge the relative success of the training in terms of teacher knowledge and the extent of teacher use of technology in classroom instruction.

A final and critical feature of the project involves access to computers and related technologies in each school so that teachers could independently (and collegially) apply and practice their newly acquired skills.

Computers and other technologies are now an integral part of most efforts toward school reform and improvement. McKenzie (1992) stated, "Mastery of new technologies is a fundamental rite of passage for young people who will do their problem solving, learning and living in the next millennium . . . any school that fails to blend such mastery throughout the day and the curriculum is failing to achieve its fundamental mission at a very basic level" (p. 2).

Training staff to understand and use technology is critical to their individual and collective success. Of course, the ultimate benefactors of these successes will be the students, who will be better prepared to live and learn in the highly technical, information-rich world in which they live.

SUMMARY

This chapter provided a conceptual framework of how technology has and can influence classroom practices. Additionally, it described technologies commonly used in classrooms and barriers that often impede the integration of computers and other innovations into daily classroom life.

Finally, a staff training model was described that provided differentiated skill-based instruction aimed at enriching teachers' abilities to use technology in their respective subject disciplines.

INDIVIDUAL TEACHER COMPUTER USAGE SURVEY[1]

D E M O G R A P H I C S

Name _____

School _____ Survey Control Number _____

I. This section is designed to obtain general information. Please complete the following regarding your use of computers and computer-related technologies.

Subject area specialty(ies) _____ Grade Levels _____

1. Have you received any graduate credits for courses you have taken in the past 5 years relating to the use of computers in education?   Yes   No

2. Have you received any inservice credits for courses you have taken in the past 5 years relating to the use of computers in education?   Yes   No

Please circle the estimated hours   **Hours per Week**
per week for the following questions:

3. Estimated time using computers for administrative work (grades/record keeping, parent/staff memos, e-mail).   Not used   0–5   6–10   11–15   16–20   21+

4. Estimated time using computers in the classroom or computer center (with students).   Not used   0–5   6–10   11–15   16–20   21+

5. Estimated time using computers for planning (worksheets, tutorials, previewing software).   Not used   0–5   6–10   11–15   16–20   21+

6. Estimated time using a computer at home.   Not used   0–5   6–10   11–15   16–20   21+

Please circle all platforms used and how they apply:

None

Apple II series	In my classroom	Use never/infrequently	Use frequently
Macintosh	In my classroom	Use never/infrequently	Use frequently
IBM PC	In my classroom	Use never/infrequently	Use frequently

[1]Reprinted with the permission of Ellen Willoughby and June Lane, Moorestown Township Public Schools.

Technologies I use regularly (more than once a month): Circle all that apply.

1. Computer productivity tools (word processing, spreadsheet, graphics)
2. CD-ROM information/multimedia
3. Videodisk experiential audio or video tapes
4. Educational television programming
5. Instructional and/or tutorial computer software
6. Inter-school e-mail
7. Internet resources
8. Other on-line resources
9. Other:_____

Individual Teacher Computer Usage Survey

Please answer as many of the following questions as honestly as you can by circling a response. If you are unfamiliar with an item, circle "5."

II. Please circle the appropriate number to indicate your familiarity with each computer related activity:

	Very Familiar	Familiar; Can do this without help	Can do this, but need help	Do not know how to do this	Unfamiliar
1. Formatting a disk	1	2	3	4	5
2. Saving, copying, moving files	1	2	3	4	5
3. Loading and running software	1	2	3	4	5
4. Printing (local, remote)	1	2	3	4	5
5. Customizing the toolbar	1	2	3	4	5
6. Organizing icon groups, files	1	2	3	4	5
7. Using word processing software	1	2	3	4	5
8. Using paint/draw software	1	2	3	4	5

	Very Familiar	Familiar; Can do this without help	Can do this, but need help	Do not know how to do this	Unfamiliar
9. Using spreadsheet software	1	2	3	4	5
10. Using presentation software	1	2	3	4	5
11. Using database software	1	2	3	4	5
12. Loading/using CD-ROM programs	1	2	3	4	5
13. Using graph creation software	1	2	3	4	5
14. Using on-line services/Internet	1	2	3	4	5
15. Using multimedia creation software (i.e., Hypercard, Linkway)	1	2	3	4	5
16. Troubleshooting a malfunctioning computer	1	2	3	4	5

If you circled 5 to all the questions above, go to section V.

Individual Teacher Computer Usage Survey

III. Please circle the appropriate number to indicate your level of experience in performing each task on the computer.

	Often help others	Need help now and then	Seldom need help	Often need help	Unfamiliar
1. Word processing	1	2	3	4	5

	Often help others	Need help now and then	Seldom need help	Often need help	Unfamiliar
2. Knowing when/when not to use	1	2	3	4	5
3. Text styles, editing, placement	1	2	3	4	5
4. Paragraph styles, columns, tables	1	2	3	4	5
5. Header, footer, footnotes	1	2	3	4	5
6. Spell check, thesaurus	1	2	3	4	5
7. Envelopes, mail merge	1	2	3	4	5
8. Spreadsheet	1	2	3	4	5
9. Knowing when/when not to use	1	2	3	4	5
10. Entering data (text/numbers)	1	2	3	4	5
11. Formula creation	1	2	3	4	5
12. Cell formatting	1	2	3	4	5
13. Importing/exporting data	1	2	3	4	5
14. Sorting data	1	2	3	4	5
15. Creating graphs	1	2	3	4	5
16. Printing	1	2	3	4	5
17. Creating/using macros	1	2	3	4	5
18. Database	1	2	3	4	5

	Often help others	Need help now and then	Seldom need help	Often need help	Unfamiliar
19. Knowing when/when not to use	1	2	3	4	5
20. Creating forms	1	2	3	4	5
21. Creating tables	1	2	3	4	5
22. Defining fields, keys	1	2	3	4	5
23. Creating and printing reports	1	2	3	4	5
24. Creating queries	1	2	3	4	5
25. Presentation	1	2	3	4	5
26. Knowing when/when not to use	1	2	3	4	5
27. Creating screens/slides	1	2	3	4	5
28. Formatting slides	1	2	3	4	5
29. Formatting text	1	2	3	4	5
30. Drawing and graphics	1	2	3	4	5
31. Importing objects	1	2	3	4	5
32. Rearranging, sorting slides	1	2	3	4	5
33. Instructional software (drill and practice, tutorial)	1	2	3	4	5
34. Knowing when/when not to use	1	2	3	4	5
35. Evaluation prior to purchase	1	2	3	4	5

	Often help others	Need help now and then	Seldom need help	Often need help	Unfamiliar
36. Installation and setup for class use	1	2	3	4	5
37. Evaluating student learning	1	2	3	4	5
38. Customization	1	2	3	4	5
39. On-line services/Internet	1	2	3	4	5
40. Knowing when/when not to use	1	2	3	4	5
41. Navigating on-line services	1	2	3	4	5
42. Conducting searches	1	2	3	4	5
43. FTP download	1	2	3	4	5
44. Joining Listservs	1	2	3	4	5
45. Posting to Usenet	1	2	3	4	5
46. Locating useful Web sites	1	2	3	4	5
47. Access/send e-mail	1	2	3	4	5
48. CD-ROM/reference	1	2	3	4	5
49. Knowing when/when not to use	1	2	3	4	5
50. Evaluation prior to purchase	1	2	3	4	5
51. Installation and setup for class use	1	2	3	4	5
52. Evaluating student learning	1	2	3	4	5

	Often help others	Need help now and then	Seldom need help	Often need help	Unfamiliar
53. Access information from	1	2	3	4	5
54. Run software from	1	2	3	4	5
55. Multimedia creation software	1	2	3	4	5
56. Form creation	1	2	3	4	5
57. Inserting buttons	1	2	3	4	5
58. Linking buttons to functions	1	2	3	4	5
59. Audio/video capture	1	2	3	4	5
60. Importing different image formats	1	2	3	4	5
61. Creating stand along show	1	2	3	4	5

If you answered 4 or 5 to all the questions above, go to section V.

Individual Teacher Computer Usage Survey

IV. This section applies to your overall computer experience. Please circle the appropriate number to indicate how comfortable you are with the software you use.

	Often help others	Need help now and then	Seldom need help	Often need help	Unfamiliar
1. I feel confident enough about my basic computer operation knowledge to use technology regularly in my classroom and teach others about it.	1	2	3	4	5

	Often help others	Need help now and then	Seldom need help	Often need help	Unfamiliar
2. I regularly perform maintenance on important files and servers to ensure I back up important data and optimize hard-disk space available.	1	2	3	4	5
3. I use the word processor for nearly all my written professional work and have used it with students for all stages of writing as a process.	1	2	3	4	5
4. I encourage students to use a word processor for their written reports and accept their work in printed or electronic format.	1	2	3	4	5
5. I use spreadsheets for several applications and employ them with students to help them improve their own data-keeping and analysis skills, showing them how to explore questions and the power of mathematical relationships.	1	2	3	4	5
6. I use databases for personal applications and can create them from scratch.	1	2	3	4	5
7. I can use formulas with my database information to create summations of numerical data and provide useful statistical information.	1	2	3	4	5

	Often help others	Need help now and then	Seldom need help	Often need help	Unfamiliar
8. I have used databases with students to help them improve their own data-keeping and analysis skills.	1	2	3	4	5
9. I use clip art and graphics not only on my own work but have used them to help students improve their own written communication skills.	1	2	3	4	5
10. I involve my students in using e-mail to communicate with other students and various kinds of experts from other states and nations.	1	2	3	4	5
11. I subscribe to several educational Listservs to stay current with developments in my educational specialty and with uses of technology in my field.	1	2	3	4	5
12. I encourage and help students to locate relevant resources on the Internet as a routine part of research assignments.	1	2	3	4	5
13. I have experience using the computer with monitoring sensors, robotic devices and/ or other peripheral equipment (scanners, laser disks, etc.) and feel competent with the installation and setup of these devices.	1	2	3	4	5

	Often help others	Need help now and then	Seldom need help	Often need help	Unfamiliar
14. I encourage my students to employ new technologies to support communicating, data analysis, and problem solving outlined in the district technology plan.	1	2	3	4	5

To be answered by all respondents

V. This section is to be answered by all respondents.

A. What type of computer training would be most helpful to you?

	Most Helpful . . . . Least Helpful			
1. Word processing	1	2	3	4
2. Spreadsheet	1	2	3	4
3. Database	1	2	3	4
4. Desktop publishing	1	2	3	4
5. On-line research	1	2	3	4
6. Presentation software	1	2	3	4
7. Content-specific software	1	2	3	4
8. Basic programming	1	2	3	4
9. Internet and on-line services	1	2	3	4
10. Gradebook software	1	2	3	4
11. CD-ROM software	1	2	3	4

12. Creating Web pages	1	2	3	4
13. Publishing on the Internet	1	2	3	4
14. Basic file management	1	2	3	4
15. Advanced file management	1	2	3	4
16. Laserdisc software to show video	1	2	3	4
17. Other:	1	2	3	4

B. Regarding the software you use, how would you answer the following?

Knowledgeable . . . . No Knowledge

1. I clearly understand the difference between freeware, shareware, and commercial software and the fees involved in the use of each.

   1   2   3   4

2. I know the programs for which the district or my building holds a license and understand the school board policy on the use of copyrighted materials.

   1   2   3   4

3. I demonstrate ethical usage of all software and let my students know my personal stand on this issue.

   1   2   3   4

THANK YOU FOR YOUR TIME AND HELP.

Please return this questionnaire to your building principal by

_____
    (Date)

MOORESTOWN SCHOOL DISTRICT—TECHNOLOGY SURVEY[2]
STUDENT OPINIONS

Directions: We would like to know what you think about the following statements. Answer each question and use a pencil to fill in the bubbles on the scanning sheet. Please use #2 pencil. Darken circles completely, but do not stray into other circles. Please completely erase any stray marks.

1. Which school do you attend?
   0 = Baker   1 = Roberts   2 = South Valley   3 = Middle School
   4 = High School

2. In which grade are you?
   0 = 3rd   1 = 4th   2 = 5th   3 = 6th   4 = 7th   5 = 8th
   6 = 9th   7 = 10th   8 = 11th   9 = 12th

---

0 = Never True   1 = Not Usually True   2 = Sometimes True
3 = Very Often True   4 = I'm Not Sure

3. In my school, we use computer technology.
4. In my school, we think that computer technology is important.
5. In my school, we learn how to use computer technology.
6. In my school, we use computer technology for math lessons.
7. In my school, we use computer technology for science lessons.
8. In my school, we use computer technology for English/language arts lessons.
9. In my school, we use computer technology for social studies lessons.
10. In my school, we use computer technology for reading lessons.
11. In my school, we use computer technology for art lessons.
12. We work in groups when we use computer technology.
13. I can use computer technology without any help.
14. In my school, assignments are accepted on disk.
15. In my school, we use computers in the computer lab.
16. In my school, we use computers in the classroom.
17. I use a word processor for almost all my written work.
18. Use of a word processor encourages me to revise and edit my work.
19. I can use the spell-check.
20. I can use the thesaurus.
21. I use the spell-check regularly.

[2]Reprinted with permission of Moorestown Public Township Schools.

22. I use the thesaurus regularly.
23. Using spell check helps me produce better work.
24. Using the thesaurus helps me produce better work.
25. I use a spreadsheet for my work.
26. I can create graphs from a spreadsheet.
27. I can insert a graph into a word processing document.
28. Spreadsheets are used to explore mathematics in my classroom.
29. I know how to use e-mail.
30. I know how to use the Internet.
31. I can locate a useful web site on any topic that interests me.
32. I know how to use CD-ROMs.
33. I can capture audio and video clips to use in a multimedia presentation.
34. I use a computer to play computer games.
35. I know how to use a computer for reference.
36. I use a computer for class projects and reports.
37. I use a computer for homework.

---

0 = False   1 = True

38. I have a computer at home.
39. I have a printer at home.
40. How often do you use a computer?

0 = Never   1 = Once every 2 months   2 = Once a month
3 = Once a week   4 = Every 2-3 days   5 = Every day

REFERENCES

Allum, K. F. (1991). "Partners in Innovation: School–College Collaborations." *EDUCOM Review,* 26(3–4): 29–33.

David, J. L. (1990). "Restructuring and Technology: Partners in Change." In K. Shangold and M. S. Ticker (Eds.) *Restructuring for Learning with Technology* (pp. 75–89). New York: Center for Technology in Education, Bank Street College, and the National Center on Education and the Economy.

McKenzie, J. "Taming the Minotaur," *Now On,* April, 1992.

Ogden, Evelyn H. and Vito Germinario (1995). *The Nation's Best Schools: Blueprints for Excellence, Volume II—Middle and Secondary Schools.* Lancaster, PA: Technomic Publishing Company, Inc.

Office of Technology Assessment (1995). *Teachers and Technology: Making the Connection.* Washington D.C.: United States Government Printing Office.

Piaget, J. (1973). *To Understand Is to Invent.* New York: Grossman.

Siegel, Jessica (1995). "The State of Teacher Training." *Electronic Learning:* 14(8): 43–53.

Snider, Robert C. (1992). "The Machine in the Classroom." *Phi Delta Kappa,* 74(4): 316–323.

Strommen, Erik F. and Bruce Lincoln (1992). "Constructivism, Technology, and the Future of Classroom Learning." *Education in Urban Society,* 24(4): 466–476.

United States Department of Education, "Advanced Telecommunications in U.S. Public Schools, K–12" (Washington, D.C.: United States Department of Education, OERI, February 1995).

U.S. Department of Labor (June 1991). *What Work Required of Schools: A SCANS Report for America 2000,* Secretary's Commission on Achieving Necessary Skills. Washington, D.C., p. 15.

Wiske, M. S. (1989). A Cultural Perspective on School–University Collaborative Research. Report No. ETC-TP-89-3. Topical paper. Cambridge, MA: Educational Technology Center.

CHAPTER 8

What Teachers Need To Know:
About Collaboration

If schools for the twenty-first century are going to be different, the role of the teacher will need to be transformed from the relatively independent and isolated position it currently is to one that will involve teachers in working relationships with other professionals, parents, and the full range of community members, many of whom may not have been traditionally expected to be involved with schools. In *A Place Called School,* Goodlad (1984) describes schools as having no "infrastructures designed to encourage or support either communications among teachers in improving their teaching or collaborating in attacking school wide problems" (p. 188). Little has changed. The traditional school organization generally is not conducive to collegial behavior on the part of either teachers, administrators, or paraprofessionals and provides few incentives for school employees to collaborate with the communities they serve. Yet recent studies of effective business and industry practices and studies of effective schools have taught us much about the importance of teamwork, shared decision making, and client orientation to both restructuring and maintenance of qualitative service. Schools for the twenty-first century will need to use those lessons to cultivate new connections among teachers and other school employees working together, working with students, and working more closely with the home and the community to support student learning.

The nature and scope of this new collaboration will encompass new relationships:

- among teachers
- between teachers and administrators
- between the school and the students' homes

125

- among the workplaces and service providers throughout the community

Teachers just emerging from their relatively autonomous classrooms will not be anxious nor ready to assume their new responsibilities. To encourage and to implement this broad conceptualization of the teacher as collaborator, professionals within the school, and more than likely their partners throughout the community, will need specific training in how to assume these very different responsibilities as partnerships evolve and the opportunities for working together are established. Without a clear understanding of the need for this new role and without preparation for it, teachers and administrators, students and parents, and community members alike will find their initial attempts at collaboration clumsy, inefficient, and unrewarding.

WHY COLLABORATE

When schools work as learning communities involving students, teachers, and administrators and establish genuine partnerships with parents and the communities they serve, they perform better. The reasons might be considered self-evident. First, we know that problems are best resolved by those most closely associated with the problem, and that the implementation of the solution to a problem is more effectively carried out when those responsible for the implementation have ownership of the solution. Stakeholders in the educational process are better prepared to identify what needs to be fixed and are more likely to fix it when they are directly involved and not just acting on the ideas of others. Second, the nature and complexity of the challenges facing most schools can no longer simply be met by the school working independently from the other resources available throughout the community. By working as a focused team, teachers, administrators, parents, and the community can:

- improve the quality of education
- develop better solutions to the problems they face
- increase confidence among all school community members
- address the social and emotional needs of students which influence their potential for learning

At the very least, such a collaboration will serve as a model for what we hope all students will learn. As Richardson et al. (1995) write, " If we want students who will learn to make decisions, to work with other adults and to solve problems, then teachers must be heavily involved in making the decisions that affect their work and the life of the school" (p. 117). If we want children to learn to be fully functioning adults, then we must teach them in a school community environment that models the type of responsible participatory adult behaviors we hope they will learn. According to Susan Moore Johnson (1990), "A lone teacher can impart phonics, fractions . . . or the periodic table, but only through teachers' collaborative efforts will a school produce educational graduates who can . . . conduct themselves responsibly as citizens" (p. 149).

COLLABORATION WITHIN THE SCHOOL

There is overwhelming evidence that the nature of the relationships among the adults who live and work in a school community has a tremendous influence upon the school's climate, its effectiveness, and the level of student performance (Smith and Scott, 1990). Collaboration among teachers and between teachers and administrators and among the primary stakeholders within the organization has demonstrable benefits over more bureaucratic, isolated relationships more typical among school professionals. Collaborative environments, however, are not easily created, nor are they simple to maintain. They require a change in policy and more often a shift in the dominant management philosophy and the beliefs and values that support it.

Collaboration is a management process borrowed from what has been learned about effective business practices. It is defined as it relates to school organizations by Richardson et al., (1995) as "a process or philosophy to improve education by increasing the autonomy of those operating within the educational system to make decisions and sharing the responsibility for those decisions with everyone who has an interes t in the educational process" (p. 119). It represents a fundamental change in the policies and practices of many schools. It transforms operational procedures by creating the opportunity for increased participation by the various stakeholders within and outside the school in making decisions and in setting policy. Collaboration, if it is to be effective, involves specific training in problem solving, group process, and shared decision making and requires a commitment of time and energy on the part of all those involved.

Collaboration takes time for participants to identify those things to be improved, to debate the alternative ways in which those improvements can best be made, to plan and implement the improvement process, and to acquire and practice the skills required in working together to improve instruction or to solve school-wide problems. There are several strategies for dealing with the issue of time:

- **freeing teachers during the school day** to train and/or participate in collaborative activities by using substitute coverage or having teachers volunteer to meet over lunch can provide a limited amount of time:

Bringing teachers together when their classes are engaged in other activities such as assemblies, health screenings, or meetings with guidance or other ancillary staff can also create additional in-school time for collaborative activities.

- **lengthening the day or year** through contractual agreements can create more professional development time in which teachers can meet and arrange to meet with community members to address school improvement issues: Professional days can be used for specific training and collaborative activities, and after-school and evening meeting times could be used for training of and meetings with parents and other community partners.

- **making better use of existing planning time** within the school day can often yield opportunities for teachers to work together during the regular work day: By scheduling common planning among those teachers who can benefit most from being available at the same time, collaborative efforts to improve instruction and to work toward resolution of school-wide problems can begin to emerge.

- **making better use of existing professional time** such as in-service and faculty meeting time can also encourage collaboration: A well-planned staff development program to make staff aware of the need for collaboration and to provide them with the skills they will need to work together effectively may prove to be more valuable than the typical eclectic offerings of workshops and seminars on innovations that often comprise most in-service programs. Faculty meetings and department meetings also offer opportunities in which staff can learn about, practice, and even meaningfully engage in collaborative activities.

- **purchasing the time required** beyond or before the traditional school day or yearly calendar: Teachers can be paid for the time it will take to train for and participate in collaborative activities, but offering direct financial incentives should be used sparingly or, if at all possible, be avoided. Working together as professionals, and especially working cooperatively with members of the school community, should be its own reward. While offering incentives for training may be necessary to draw participants into the process, the benefits of working as a professional in a community group should eventually be an intrinsic motivation.

The philosophy behind collaboration makes sense for schools. If we accept the premise that effective organizations are client centered, then those closest to the students (teachers and administrators) must be involved in the process of making those decisions that affect students. If we further believe that ownership is an important motivation to put policy and practice effectively into operation, then teachers and administrators must have a genuine opportunity to influence the decisions determining the policies and practices they will be expected to implement. Collaboration within the school and even between the school and its community then becomes a viable process for concentrating the collective energy of the school community toward the accomplishment of school goals and objectives.

Models of collaboration are numerous and can be found across the country as districts aware of the potential encourage teachers to work together to:

- develop and implement new instructional programs
- evaluate school outcomes
- identify areas for improvement
- select alternative ways to bring about improvement
- improve their own professional skills and plan staff development
- establish partnerships with community groups

Local councils and other forms of site-based management, whereby individual schools are given the authority to make decisions about priorities, programs, and the utilization of resources, are the most common vehicles to involve staff and community in decision making, the determination of policy issues, increasing ownership, and working in a common direction. As the authors of *Preparing Students for the 21st Century* (Uchida et. al., 1996) suggest, "Adoption of site-based management could be the single most important reform that school districts can adopt. . . . It is the most effective way to foster the adoption of significant innovations" (p. 7). To make it work, training and information need to be provided, and expectations for teacher involvement need to be changed.

Teachers, in particular, and parents and students, where applicable, must all take greater responsibility for making the educational process work. As stated, governance issues should be carried out largely by those associated with the particular school, operating, however, within the parameters set down and monitored by the district and, where applicable, guidelines established by state regulatory agencies. Through governance councils at the school level educational needs specific to the school or ancillary to district needs should be identified so that those most knowledgeable about the students and the local community can:

- set performance goals to meet *their needs*
- consider alternatives and reach consensus on a plan best suited to accomplish the goal at *their school*
- take responsibility for implementing plans to improve *their students'* performance

The transition to the collaborative management model, regardless of the specific process used, involves an extensive change in how professional staff view their relationships with each other, with administrators at the building and district level, and with parents and other community members, and it must be accompanied by deliberate development of new skills and abilities for each of them.

Teachers and administrators need to view each other as partners with each having the ability to define and work toward solving classroom and school-wide problems. They need to respect each other's role in finding and allocating resources and their ability to work together in removing the barriers to collaboration within the school and between the school and the stakeholders within the community. Generally, this means empowering teachers, which in its simplest form might involve modifying school structures such as principal-directed faculty meetings and replacing them in whole or part with faculty advisory committees. At its optimal level, it may involve complex collegial structures such as site-based councils with the authority to make decisions about program, budget, and personnel. Regardless of its extent, collaborative efforts only work if they represent genuine opportunities for meaningful involvement and are a part of an overall plan for school improvement.

School improvement more readily succeeds in situations where teachers work in a collegial manner (NASSP, 1996). However, working cooperatively, sharing ideas, and engaging in professional dialogue with colleagues are activities unfamiliar to many professionals accustomed to working in a traditional setting of isolation. Many teachers are comfortable with their isolation, and many schools are structured to promote it. Isolation, however, tacitly implies that practitioners have nothing to learn from each other, and it ignores the fact that in schools where teachers work in supportive teams, students perform better. This is because the nature and complexity of teaching diverse students what they will need to know for success in the next century cannot be accomplished by even the most knowledgeable individuals working alone.

The transition from the traditional isolation within which many teachers work to the collaborative environment required by modern management practices is described by Richardson et al. (1995) as, "a complex social structure with many complicated tasks." Professionals and community participants alike need to understand clearly what they are now expected to do and why these new responsibilities are important. They must also be provided with the skills to accomplish the task.

Participants in the collaborative process need to understand or receive training in the following areas:

- group dynamics and group efficacy: Both school personnel and the community representatives they will be expected to work with will need some guidance and practice with working in groups. Organizing and planning meetings and conducting productive meetings are skills that both professionals and non-professionals are very often unfamiliar with, but they are essential to successful collaborative efforts.

- consensus building: Collaboration is not majority ruling. The process of gaining broad-based support and agreement on what needs to be done and how to do it is one that may be unfamiliar to individuals unaccustomed to working with groups.
- effectively working with adults: Teachers spend much of their time interacting with children, and many community members have very limited experience in working with other adults and can be easily intimidated by the experience of working with school professionals. Special attention needs to be paid to preparing participants for these new roles.

Most importantly, as stated earlier, those expected to work collaboratively need to be provided with both the time to train and the time to participate in the collaborative process. Professionals within the organization must begin to see themselves as responsible for more than the supervision of students and the transmission of the curriculum. All participants in the collaborative process will need to understand the process of analyzing issues, debating differences of opinion, compromise, and group dynamics and have a sensitivity to issues of diversity as they might apply to the groups they will be working with.

Where a school is on the continuum from isolation to collaboration is important in determining both the extent and nature of the training that may be required to accomplish this transition. A school's prior experience with professional staff involvement will determine how much energy will be required to establish the need for collaboration and how much time will be needed for skill training. A school with a tradition of staff involvement will need only to add to and refine those skills that staff members have acquired through their experiences with involvement. However, a school that has had a tradition of administrative control may find it necessary to train extensively both teachers and administrators in the need for and in the background required to establish a productive process for collaboration.

Collaboration within the school requires communication between participants, and the attitudes within the organization about the process and the history of communications between the participants influences heavily the probability for success. Equally important with respect to a climate for collaboration are issues related to:

- the participants' willingness to work beyond the school day
- the availability of time for professionals to meet within the school day

- the incentives available to those who participate in activities beyond the school day

Creating a collaborative school and empowering professionals requires school personnel to perceive and accept a new role, and in most instances an expanded role in the school's operation—a concept not readily accepted by some. For teachers it means compromising their autonomy as they engage in activities outside their classroom to work with other adults, colleagues, administrators, and community members. It means sharing responsibility for instructional decisions and assuming a greater accountability for the results of those decisions. It means engaging in activities that are in addition to, and may even take them away from, their customary role of direct instruction. Failure to recognize these role changes and not prepare staff for such a fundamental change can doom any attempt to foster collaboration.

Converting to a collaborative school and empowering teachers rests heavily on fostering teacher engagement (Figure 8.1). Several strategies for initiating productive teacher engagement include:

- selecting volunteers who are motivated and have some background in collaborative endeavors or the skills to ensure success
- involving participants in planning the implementation of the collaborative process (i.e., finding the time to meet)
- focusing initial collaborative efforts on school-wide concerns that directly affect classroom problems and on problems that can be addressed successfully at the school level

---

Round Table Discussion

WHAT: Proactive round table discussion of an isolated topic each month . . . the goal of each meeting will be to formulate solutions and strategies to alleviate problems

WHY: To open lines of communication, increase communication among staff and between staff and administration, share concerns and problems, and find and implement solutions to staff and administration concerns

WHO: All interested faculty, staff, administration, and students

WHEN: Wednesday 3:00 p.m.

WHERE: Cafeteria

TOPIC FOR JANUARY: TUTORIALS

Suggestions for topics for future meetings are welcome and can be placed in the suggestion box in the main office.

FIGURE 8.1. Sample flyer to staff for collaborative activity.

Once a structure is in place the next steps are to define a problem to be addressed, generate alternative solutions to be assessed, choose an alternative to be implemented, evaluate the implementation, and celebrate and make public your success.

Collaboration for each school community is a unique process. It is a long-term process that requires commitment from all those involved and can serve as a valuable model for students who can also learn the value of working collaboratively.

COLLABORATION WITH PARENTS

Parental involvement in schools is also generally recognized as being vital to a child's education, yet many educators cite a lack of parent involvement as a serious problem in many schools. According to recent studies by the National Center for Education Statistics (Uchida et al., 1996), 25% of the public teachers surveyed listed the absence of parental involvement as the major obstacle to student success in school.

To begin to work with parents more collaboratively schools need to recognize that today's parents:

* have limited time to work with teachers
* are unclear as to what they are expected to do
* find schools intimidating to approach

Modern family structures, including single parents, dual-income families, culturally diverse families, and non-nuclear families, are often unable to provide the same level of support that families in the past have provided without some deliberate intervention, assistance, and initiative on the part of the schools their children attend.

To capitalize on the potential of this valuable and generally underutilized resource of teacher/parent collaboration, the school must clearly define the purposes of parental involvement and must prepare teachers to reach out and work with parents in new or additional ways. At the least, children whose parents demonstrate that they care about education need to get encouragement. It is therefore important for schools to reach out to help parents to express and act on their interest in their child's education.

Many teachers and administrators are fearful of parental involvement. They often express concern that an emphasis on parent involvement and collaboration in decision making can lead to demands for unsound practices (Zeichner, 1991), and they believe that many parents are unconcerned about their child's performance in school. They interpret the fact that parents need information and guidance on how to support education at home as proof of a lack of interest in their children's education. Parents, for their part, see the school as disinterested in their particular child and base their perceptions of the school on what was often their own experiences with learning and school, which may or may not have left them with positive attitudes about or confidence in education.

To bridge these misunderstandings, schools for the twenty-first century will need to take the initiative in seeking ways to work with parents to better define their role as partners in their child's education. This initiative should minimally involve:

- helping parents to understand the home and the community as learning environments
- explaining programs and services available through the school and community and their relationship to the child's education
- building parent confidence and comfort with working with the school

By working collaboratively with parents, school personnel come to better understand the parents' needs and frustrations, and parents come to understand the complexity of the teacher's task. Teachers often gain insight into an individual student's strengths and weaknesses, and a bond develops within the community that builds parental support for school programs. Students benefit as well. The consistent message from home and school that learning is important has been found to be critical to student achievement. Student achievement has been directly related to relatively simple parent involvement, such as how much parents talk to their children about how they are doing in school (Uchida et al., 1996).

School/parent collaboration can take many forms, from meeting minimum parental responsibilities such as sending a child to school ready to learn to a parent's active participation as a member of a site-based council or candidate for school board. Schools in the next century will need to aggressively cultivate parental involvement in all of its forms by working with the community to overcome the obstacles of time constraints, language, and cultural barriers where they exist and the multitude of negative experiences parents may already have had as students and parents.

Parent involvement in schools is important, but parent involvement must have a purpose and should offer a range of involvement opportunities that meet the needs and expertise of all the potential participants within the community (see Figure 8.2). Such roles might include:

(1) Parents as partners: In its simplest form parents should work with the school in enrolling the student, ensuring regular attendance, and making sure that the student comes to school prepared to learn, that is, rested, well-fed, and healthy. Schools need to provide parents with information and guidance regarding the schools expectations and the importance of

Name _____

Address _____

Phone Number _____Sending District _____

Child(ren) at RV and Grade _____

Comments _____

The RV School and Community Committee has openings for parents who would like to become involved in the RVRHS experience. Our committee has reorganized and refocused since last year. We're ready to start working, but we need your help. Please indicate your area(s) of interest and have your child give the completed form to his/her homeroom teacher (or send the completed form to the RVRHS office, Attention: [name]). You will be contacted shortly.

Committees in place for the 1996–97 school year:

☐ **Chaperones for:**
___ **Field Trips**—[name], Parent Co-Chair; [name], Administration—Parents are needed who would be available during the day to accompany students on field trip excursions. A faculty advisor will always be present to run the trip. Trip lengths vary from a couple of hours to a full school day and, in some cases, longer than a school day. Parent volunteers would be contacted ahead of time for availability.
___ **Dances**—[name], Staff Co-Chair; [name], Parent Co-Chair—Parent volunteers are needed to attend school-sponsored dances along with faculty and staff. Parents would help supervise student behavior; monitor entrances, exits, restrooms, and refreshment stand.

☐ **Career Mentors**—[name], Staff Co-Chair; [name], Parent Co-Chair—___(a) Parents are needed who would be willing to share their expertise in a career field on either an informal or formal basis: as a guest speaker for a class; as a guest speaker for Junior/Senior Career Day (3/14/96); as a contact for students interested in that particular career; for possible on-site visitation; or ___(b) Parents are needed who would be willing to solicit business and professional people for the above; or ___(c) Parent surrogates/advocates for the Student: occasionally an adult is needed to stand in for an absent parent in discipline conferences to supervise fairness on behalf of the student.

☐ **Image Committee**—[name], BOE; [name], Staff Co-Chair; [name], Parent Co-Chair—Parents are needed who have a positive attitude about RVRHS and are willing to work toward publicizing the positive aspects of the school's image.

☐ **Booster Parents**—[name], Staff Co-Chair; [name], Parent Co-Chair—___(a) Parents volunteers are needed to support specific school activities to provide activity and fund-raiser support. Active booster clubs in existence: Choir, Band, Wrestling, Baseball, Football, Cheerleading. ___(b) Other group that you wish to start:_____

☐ **Outreach Committee**—[name], Staff Co-Chair; [name], Parent Co-Chair—Parents are needed to help with various projects, such as the Burlington County Mall Projects, letters to prospective executive board members, contacting and trying to involve more community members in school activities.

☐ **Guidance Office/Library Volunteers**—[name], Guidance; [name], Librarian; [name], Parent Chair—Parents are needed who can volunteer a specified time each week to assist as a guidance aide or library aide.

☐ **Overview**—[name], Advisor; [name], Parent Chair—Newsletter published monthly for parents by parents. Parents are needed to help collect information and/or write articles for the newsletter.

☐ **Homeroom Parent Coordinating Committee**—[name] and [name], Parent Co-Chairs—Volunteers are needed to make phone calls encouraging parents to register to vote and to promote school budget awareness. ___(a) Volunteers are needed to man a voter registration table at specified school functions. ___(b) Parent volunteers are needed to organize a phone calling chair for homerooms for voter registration and other important events.

☐ **RV Foundation**—[name] and [name], Co-Chairs—Parents are needed to help organize and promote alumni affairs and events, to administer the School and Community V.I.P. recognition program, and to help establish ways to solicit funds for necessary school programs.

FIGURE 8.2. Sample flier for parents for collaborative opportunities.

parental support in eliminating potential obstacles to the child's education. Parents need to come to understand the importance that nurturing,
love, safety, and routines at home can have on a child's achievement in
school.

(2) Parents as supporters: Parents can play a significant role as supporters of
the school by getting involved with and assisting in the performance of
direct and supplemental services to students. Parents can serve as chaperones for school and after-school activities such as field trips or dances.
They can function as career mentors or assist in publicizing the positive
aspects of the school's image. Booster clubs, outreach activities, and vol-
unteering to aid in offices or with special projects are all legitimate ways
to involve not only parents but members of the community in ways that
assist in the school's operation and build linkages between the school and
the communities they serve. Procedures to solicit parent involvement
need to be developed, and, where applicable, special training as a school
volunteer needs to be provided.

(3) Parents as collaborators: The parent role can also be a more proactive role
as parents can be encouraged to create within the home a learning environment and model practices that have been found to contribute to the
child's performance in school. Providing reading materials, taking children to educational resources within the community, traveling, involving
students in family decisions, decorating rooms with educational materials, talking with their children about school, modeling academic behaviors such as reading and using the library, monitoring schoolwork, and
maintaining school as a priority will help make the home and family
experience a rich and stable intellectual environment. Schools can again
provide information, but they should also supplement their encouragement for a more proactive parent involvement with seminars and activities to provide the parents with skills and guidance they may need to fulfill their role.

Parents need to know that study after study confirms that parental involvement is an important factor in determining a child's success in school. The
opportunities for that involvement can range from simple support by attending school activities to a major commitment as members of a school board or
site-based management committees.

Schools often pay too little attention to parental involvement. Sometimes
this neglect is a lack of interest, but more commonly it is a lack of understanding of how to form and maintain productive ties with parents. Schools
need to actively tighten the bonds to the community so that both students and
parents understand the importance of their working together. Schools need to
send parents information, hold seminars about parental involvement, and pro-

vide opportunities for genuine participation. *Working with Parents* (1994), a publication of The Teacher Institute, gives the following recommendations for working with parents:

- Keep communications clear and simple, and whenever possible, make them as personalized as practical.
- Recognize and positively reinforce those parental involvement activities already in place.
- Provide the necessary resources to make sure that parent involvement activities are successful.
- Have parental involvement opportunities on a frequent and regular basis.
- Structure parent involvement around realistic tasks and reasonable expectations.
- Where necessary, provide training for both parents and staff in working together.

The major issue for many schools when working with parents is developing strategies to address the issues and potential obstacles presented by a community which is diverse. In these instances it is important that the efforts to engage the parents are planned to reflect a sensitivity to the special issues of single and/or working parents, families that are culturally diverse, and parents with limited literacy and/or language skills. It is important that particular attention be paid to:

- scheduling meetings at convenient times
- holding meetings at convenient community sites
- enlisting the assistance of community leaders to contact hard-to-reach parents
- offering topical meetings of particular interest to special groups
- using active parents to establish contacts with groups within the community

An additional consideration in planning for and increasing opportunities for parents to work more closely with the school is the application of technology as a communication tool. With the availability of fax machines and the increasing availability of Internet access, schools for the twenty-first century will need to look for new ways to both send and receive communications with parents. Web sites and homepages offer exciting alternative mediums for making information about the school available to an ever-growing audience of Internet users. Likewise, innovations such as e-mail create the opportunity for teachers, students, and parents to have an effective way to exchange information at convenient times for all participants virtually 24 hours a day and

7 days a week. Telecommunications, computers, and the use of local cable access are only beginning to be appreciated as mediums for improving both the volume and quality of school communications, and schools for the twenty-first century will need to consider them carefully as they plan to increase their connections to the communities they serve.

COLLABORATION WITH THE COMMUNITY

Students have always learned from experiences they have had apart from school. There are a variety of places throughout the community where both children and adults are learning, and schools for the twenty-first century will need to work more collaboratively with them. The need to share resources and the potential to link a variety of learning venues electronically throughout the community should serve as the catalyst for schools and communities to work more closely together in providing a comprehensive response to all of the student needs related to success in school. Schools in the next century will find themselves increasingly in the position of identifying resources within the community to meet the range of social, economic, and psychological factors that affect a student's ability to learn. There are two important reasons why this community–school collaboration is a legitimate and potentially powerful partnership to improve education. First, the community is a stakeholder in the public education system with a direct interest in the quality of education being provided to its children and a vested interest in how local tax dollars are being used. Second, the community has at its disposal an extensive pool of resources which can be both directly and indirectly used by the school (Richardson et al., 1995).

Like other types of collaboration, schools can work with the community they serve in a variety of ways and to varying degrees. The options include more traditional linkages to service clubs and small businesses within the community who traditionally provide occasional supplemental services and programs to full-service schools, in which both educational and comprehensive social services are provided under one roof. At a minimum, schools planning for community collaboration should think about and deliberately plan for school–community linkages in terms of businesses, community services, and service learning opportunities.

Working with business has been a major initiative for many schools, and rightly so. Establishing true partnerships and long-term commitments designed to prepare students for gainful employment ought to rank among the highest priorities for schools of the next century. To establish productive long-range partnerships with either local businesses or national corporations, school personnel must be prepared to listen to and respond to what businesses expect. They must develop an awareness of economic trends and must be prepared to provide opportunities that are mutually beneficial to both the school and its business partners. Some activities of mutual benefit to schools and businesses appear in Figure 8.3. Faculty can gain a valuable understanding of the application of knowledge in the real world, and business people can serve as career counselors, mentors, and models so desperately needed as part of the precollegiate education envisioned for the twenty-first century. Education is a recipient for businesses' philanthropy, and schools should endeavor to create projects and programs worthy of businesses' support.

Another area of community collaboration that is often overlooked is the articulation between the school and other health and social-service providers in the community. Schools simply cannot afford to maintain the required specialized staff to meet the social and health needs of every student. They can, however, work more closely to establish linkages with the health and social services that students may require access to. There exist in most communities a sufficient array of services to assist schools in addressing health issues, the need for economic support, and resource allocation to intervene and prevent at-risk behaviors. Welfare services, child advocacy agencies, the judicial system, health services, and counseling services throughout a community share the student population with the schools but only infrequently act in concert with the school to provide services or resolve problems.

Research confirms that combing prevention services with schools creates stronger and more effective institutions (Dryfoos, 1996). So-called full-service schools report better school attendance, higher academic achievement, greater parental involvement, and generally a more positive school climate

Benefits to Schools	Benefits to Businesses
Sharing of equipment and facility resources for technology/labs	Sharing of classroom facilities for training and recreational programs for fitness and entertainment
Career guidance and job-shadowing experiences for students	Teachers providing literacy, second-language and basic-skills training to unskilled workers
Work–study, part-time, and summer work opportunities for students and teachers	Local access to qualified workers for part-time and temporary employment needs

FIGURE 8.3. Benefits of community collaboration.

and attitude toward school. Such a collaborative effort requires a designated facilitator and the provision of space, with the school being the focal point to connect students and families with service providers. However, like most innovations there are a number of points to be considered and addressed in order to ensure success. With the concept of full-service schools, consensus needs to be reached on the following issues:

- Governance issues between the school and the service providers with which it intends to work need to be stipulated.
- Procedures for sharing student time between classroom activities and related support activities such as counseling need to be established.
- Required confidentiality and a teacher's need to know must be carefully balanced.
- Parochial loyalties need to be abandoned.

Despite the potential obstacles, full-service schools may be the most effective way for achieving school, family, and societal goals.

Many of the organizations within a community that schools collaborate with are businesses or service providers. Among them are youth service organizations, service clubs, public and private citizen organizations, and churches, which often share with the school common interests and most often deal with the very same students. By thinking about and creating linkages between students' activities at school and those they already have or might have through linkages to these community agencies, the school and community can generate a genuine sense of belonging for both the student and community members (Figure 8.4).

COMMUNITY ORGANIZATIONS

By sharing and better coordinating resources each might have, the potential exists to improve and expand the services provided by both, and the opportunity is created to generate even more and higher quality programs. By promoting organizations in the community and by linking them to school-sponsored activities, a more productive day and a broader range of experiences are provided for both the student and the community organization participant. The range of collaborative efforts could be from academic assistance for students to service learning opportunities that would benefit specific organizations or the community at large.

School community partnerships with agencies and organizations throughout the community yield several benefits. For students it builds self-esteem and provides authentic opportunities in which they can explore and use what they have learned. For the community it offers an opportunity to act on a

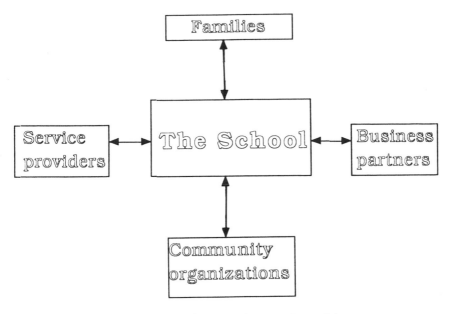

FIGURE 8.4. School and community model.

sense of caring. For the school it creates a process to raise its image throughout the community.

SUMMARY

There is a gap between schools and the communities they serve, which can only be bridged by school personnel building partnerships, first within the learning community, and then by reaching out to parents, businesses, service providers, and social organizations throughout the community. Doing so has a great many benefits for improving student achievement, enhancing professionalism among educators, strengthening bonds with parents and the community, and more effectively and efficiently preparing students for their roles in the next century.

But collaboration means advocating participatory decision making and new leadership from the school and from educators in establishing and working with partners in planning and providing the educational services to the community. To begin the process requires overcoming the enormous inertia of indifference to the cooperative process that exists and the selection of a few carefully chosen examples of how this new cooperation might work. By expanding the arena of participants in the educational process to include stakeholders beyond teachers and parents, schools can access additional resources available in the community and help students to see connections between what they do in school and the world outside.

REFERENCES

Dryfoos, Joy G. (April 1996). "Full Service Schools." *Educational Leadership.* Alexandria, VA: Association for Supervision and Curriculum Development. 53 (7): 18–23.

Fowler, R. Clarke, Corley, Kathy Klebs (April 1996). *Educational Leadership.* Alexandria, VA: Association for Supervision and Curriculum Development. 53 (7): 24–26.

Goodlad, John L. (1984) *A Place Called School.* New York: McGraw-Hill.

Johnson, Susan Moore (1990) *Teachers at Work.* New York: Basic Books.

The National Association of Secondary School Principals (1996) *Breaking Ranks: Changing an American Institution.* Alexandria, VA., p. 90.

Smith, Stuart C. and Scott, Janis J. (1990) *A Work Environment for Effective Instruction.* Alexandria, VA: National Association of Secondary School Principals.

Richardson, Michael D., Lane, Kenneth E., and Flanagan, Jackson L. (1995). *School Empowerment.* Lancaster, PA: Technomic Publishing Co., Inc.

The Teacher Institute (1994) *Working with Parents.* Fairfax Station, VA.

Uchida, Donna L., Cetron, Marvin, and McKenzie, Floretta. (1996). *Preparing Students for the 21st Century.* Alexandria, VA: American Association of School Administrators.

Zeichner, Kenneth M. (Spring, 1991) "Contradictions and Tensions in the Professionalization of Teaching and the Democratization of Schools." *Teachers College Record.* New York: Teachers College Columbia University.

CHAPTER 9

Professional Development for the Twenty-First Century

"The reform of elementary and secondary education depends first and foremost on restructuring its foundation—the teaching profession" (The National Commission on Teaching and America's Future, 1996, p. 2). According to the report, more than 50,000 people who lack adequate preparation enter teaching annually on emergency or substandard licenses. Nearly one-fourth of all secondary teachers do not have even a minor in their main teaching field.

Issues related to meaningful preparation and development are not limited to teachers entering the profession. All too often, professional development and training activities comprise a very small portion of school budgets. Additionally, many schools have not developed an ongoing mechanism and culture to sustain professional growth.

The designation of teacher education and professional development as one of the National Education Goals (added to the original six in mid-1994) is genuine recognition that well-prepared teachers are essential to all education reform efforts *(National Education Goals Report, 1995)*. Specifically, the goal states: "By the year 2000, the nation's teaching force will have access to programs for continued improvement of their professional skills and the opportunity to acquire the knowledge and skills needed to instruct and prepare all American students for the next century" (p. 11).

BARRIERS TO EFFECTIVE PROFESSIONAL DEVELOPMENT

While most would agree that ongoing teacher staff development is at the heart of any effort to improve education, conventional professional develop-

143

ment is sorely inadequate (Sykes, 1996). The shortcomings of current practices in professional development are complex and multidimensional. Yet several common elements act as barriers to effective professional development.

The initiation of professional development is often centralized at the district level. The school, not the district, should be the focus for change and improved professional practice. In a very real sense, districts improve school by school. Similarly, teachers improve in each of their respective classrooms. Those who have a stake in student learning must be involved in the selection of professional development goals and programs. This school collaboration for improvement in classroom practices must also include parents and community, since their resistance to change will significantly decrease a program's potential for success (Wood and Thompson, 1993).

Professional development is often a "one-shot" approach. Meaningful professional development takes time and must be conducted over several years before change in classroom practices can occur. All educators must be involved in professional development throughout their careers. As Rubin (1971) states, the minute educators stop their education, they start down the road to incompetence.

Little recognition is given to the norms, beliefs, and culture of the school. Professional development efforts must address the complex values, norms, and beliefs that shape school practice. If the school culture is one that believes that teachers are powerless to impact on student learning, then teachers are unlikely to embrace improvement efforts. Similarly, if the school culture values autonomy and professional isolation, collegial learning activities would prove ineffective.

Professional development activities don't utilize adult learning theory. Speck (1996) cites key points that should be reviewed when designing professional development plans:

- Adults will commit to learning when the goals and objectives are considered realistic and important to them. Application in the real world is important and relevant to the adult learner's personal and professional needs.
- Adults want to be the origin of their own learning and will resist learning activities they believe are an attack on their competence. Thus, professional development needs to give participants some control over the what, who, how, why, when, and where of their learning.
- Adult learners need to see that professional development learning and their day-to-day activities and problems are related and relevant.

- Adult learners need direct, concrete experiences where they apply the learning in real work.
- Adult learning has ego involved. Professional development must be structured to provide support from peers and to reduce the fear of judgment during learning.
- Adults need to receive feedback on how they are doing and on the results of their efforts. Opportunities must be built into professional development activities that allow the learner to practice the learning and receive structured, helpful feedback.
- Adults need to participate in small-group activities during the learning to move them beyond understanding to application, analysis, synthesis, and evaluation. Small-group activities provide an opportunity to share, reflect, and generalize their learning and experiences.
- Adult learners come to learning with a wide range of previous experiences, knowledge, self-direction, interests, and competencies. This diversity must be accommodated in the professional development planning.
- Transfer of learning for adults is not automatic and must be facilitated. Coaching and other kinds of follow-up support are needed to help adult learners transfer learning into daily practice so that it is sustained.

Insufficient resources and investments are made toward systemic professional development. Professional development activities often make up a very small portion of a school's budget. Yet to provide meaningful, ongoing learning opportunities for teachers, significant financial investments must be made at all levels of the school system. The investment must also include the opportunity for sustained periods of time for teachers to receive training and for collaboration within the school. Increasingly, schools will have to look to sources outside the traditional school budget. State and federal grants, collaborations with colleges and universities, and support from local businesses and foundations should be explored as potential partners in professional development (see Chapter 7 for a description of such a partnership).

School-based support is inadequate. Effective professional development programs are characterized by a healthy degree of "pressure" within the school culture to improve professional practices and collegial "support" to discuss, reflect, and collaborate on new knowledge and skills. Teachers must be collectively (as well as individually) involved in the acquisition, development, and implementation of new ideas and strategies. This can be done in a variety of ways: by building new roles such as teacher leader, peer coach, teacher researchers; by creating new structures such as problem-solving groups, school-based research teams, peer review; by working on new tasks such as proposal writing, alternative assessments, written case studies of practice; and by creating a culture of inquiry (Speck, 1996).

Recognition and rewards are lacking for professional growth. The traditional reward structure in the school places significantly more monetary reward on years of service than on professional growth. While incremental monetary rewards may be awarded for completion of formal college/university courses, little recognition is given to the "applied scholarship" developed as a result of professional development activities. Teachers need and deserve recognition for the implementation of improved classroom practices. While these initiatives may not be reflected in the traditional salary guide, recognition can be reflected in opportunities for leadership in the school (and through outside professional organizations) by mentoring other staff members and through the teacher evaluation system. Regardless of the approach, schools need to develop both a culture and specific mechanism to support attempts by teachers to improve daily practices.

MODELS OF STAFF DEVELOPMENT FOR TEACHERS

Nearly all research relevant to teacher training has been conducted in the past 25 years. In the 1970s growing concern about the effectiveness of in-service education resulted in a new interest in the impact of such programs on teacher change and staff development and, more importantly, student learning. The findings indicated nearly unanimous dissatisfaction with current efforts but a strong consensus as to the critical importance of staff development and school improvement (Wood and Kleine, 1987).

Staff development came of age in the 1980s as teachers, administrators, and state legislators began to see it as a prerequisite for school improvement. From the research during this time, Sparks and Loucks-Horsley (1987) identified and described what is known about effective staff development into five currently utilized models:

(1) In individually guided staff development the teacher determines his or her own goals and selects activities that will result in the achievement of those goals. The model holds that individuals will be most motivated when they make their own personal assessment of their needs.

(2) Observation/assessment is most commonly implemented with a supervisor directly observing the teaching act using predetermined criteria. A basic assumption underlying this approach is that reflection by an individual on his or her own practice can be enhanced by another's observations. Peer coaching, where fellow teachers visit one another's classroom, gather objective data about student performance or teacher behavior, and

give feedback in a follow-up conference, is an increasingly common form of observation/assessment.

(3) Involvement in a development/improvement process is a combination of learnings thatresult from the involvement of teachers in committees that have as their goals the improvement of classroom instruction or curriculum. Teachers often serve on school improvement committees where they may be required to conduct research on priority goals for the school, learn group and interpersonal skills, or develop new content knowledge. In each instance, the teachers' learning is driven by the demands of problem solving. Teacher involvement and ownership in organic school improvement initiatives provide a strong motivational foundation for this approach.

(4) Inquiry strategies result in an individual or a group of teachers using their basic research techniques to formulate research questions and appropriate studies to improve instruction in their classrooms. Inquiry reflects a basic belief in teachers' abilities to formulate valid questions about their own practices and pursue objective answers to those questions.

(5) Training or workshop-type sessions are given by an expert who establishes the content and flow of activities inherent to this strategy in the hope that teachers' decision-making and thinking skills can be enriched through awareness, knowledge, and skill development. The basic assumption that guides this strategy is that teachers can change their behaviors and learn to replicate in their classrooms skill that were not previously in their repertoire.

Within these models, considerable research exists as to the common characteristics that facilitate successful staff development. Glickman (1990) provides a summary list of characteristics embodied in these activities:

(1) Training was concrete, continual, and tied to the world of the teachers.

(2) Local resource personnel provided direct follow-up assistance to teachers after the learning experience.

(3) Peer observation and peer discussion provided teachers with reinforcement and encouragement.

(4) The school leader participated in the activity.

(5) Regular project meetings were held with the teachers for problem solving and adapting techniques and skills of the innovations that were not working as expected.

(6) Release time was used for teachers instead of monetary payment for after-school work.

(7) Activities were planned with teachers prior to and during the project.

FROM STAFF TO PROFESSIONAL DEVELOPMENT

Much has been written as to the types, benefits, and shortcomings of how schools typically organize staff development. Traditionally, these systems are aimed at developing three kinds of efforts (Joyce and Showers, 1989):

- an individual component to enrich an individual's knowledge or clinical competence as a instructor, principal, etc.
- a collective component requiring the cooperative enterprise of the entire staff
- a systematic component embodying a district-wide initiative requiring a coordinated effort among all branches of the school district organization

Recently, emphasis has been shifted to the individual teacher to initiate, design and implement his or her own path to improve classroom practices. To this end, teachers are more frequently asked to take control of their own development using the school or district as a support vehicle. Commonly referred to as professional development, the nature of these improvement efforts is quite different from traditional staff development programs. Duke (1990) highlights the basic differences inherent in two themes of teacher improvement:

(1) Staff development:
   - is designed for groups
   - encourages collective growth in a common direction
   - focuses on similarities
   - is guided by school and district goals
   - leads to an enhanced repertoire of skills and concepts
(2) Professional development:
   - is designed for individuals
   - fosters the cultivation of uniqueness and virtuosity
   - focuses on differences
   - is guided by individual judgment
   - leads to increased personal understanding and awareness

While both types of teacher development vehicles have their appropriate place in improving professional skills, professional development has distinct advantages for those teachers who are at an appropriate stage of their career. Specifically,

- teachers focus less on the transfer of predetermined knowledge and strategy and more on analytical and reflective learning.
- teachers should shift away from dependency on external sources for the solution to their problems and toward professional growth and self-reliance in instructional decision-making.

- teachers are jointly responsible for their work in classrooms, and their wisdom and experiences are perceived as professional resources.
- a shift in the central administrator's role from organizing teacher development activities to supporting and facilitating those activities that school staff have determined are important and necessary (Dilworth and Imig, 1995).

This process begins with teachers reflecting on their own classroom practices, including questioning the utility of those practices, and results in change (presumably improvement). In this way teachers are empowered to have greater responsibility for their own professional development. The focus of this development often revolves around teacher research and the application of research findings to improve learning for their own students. Johnson (1993) found that classroom teachers derived a number of benefits from participating in self-initiated professional development. These benefits included an enhanced sense of professionalism, improved relationships with administrators and parents, and an increased sensitivity to the affective concerns of students.

While some instructional issues such as technology are so pervasive that every staff member must engage in focused training, self-initiated professional development activities have shown to have a wide variety of benefits for teachers at the appropriate stage of readiness.

DIFFERENTIATED PROFESSIONAL DEVELOPMENT

In many respects, teacher training and development must be reconceptualized to meet the needs of the teachers from entry into the profession, to advanced stages of development, and finally to a point where they are recognized as competent and proficient. Each teacher has different needs relating to professional growth and development. Each brings a different set of expectations of the usefulness of staff and professional development activities. Finally, each derives different benefits from generic in-service and training, as well as from self-initiated classroom problem-solving research.

While teachers at every level of professional life stage could benefit from opportunities to improve their skills, the real benefit occurs when the teachers are afforded opportunities for learning experiences that are consistent with their respective needs. The National Association of Secondary School Principals (1991) provided a practical rationale for individualizing teacher development opportunities. These include

(1) Lock-step learning does not serve the needs of classrooms of students, nor does it serve well as a model for staff development. Just as with the

students they serve, the adults in schools have a diversity of needs, interests, and learning styles. Some of these differences are related to curriculum and some to the students served. Still others are affected by career phases; for example, contemporary research has shown very different needs for novice and for veteran teachers. Factors outside the school such as family, other employment, or approaching retirement also affect staff development needs and interests. Whole-staff and whole-district in-service is likely to miss the mark for a good portion of any staff.

(2) Every major report on school reform in recent years has concluded that for schools to be effective students must be actively involved in the learning process. The adults in schools are learners, too. They must participate in selecting goals and determining learning strategies. Individualized staff development is very much walking the path of school reform.

(3) Traditional in-service delivery cannot keep up with all that school staff members need to know. There are not enough in-service days to cover all the material. An individualized program recognizes that theoretical and practical knowledge are more effective when vested in individuals who then work in teams and address problems and needs as they arise.

(4) Limited resources must be adapted and targeted for maximum effect. Given so few dollars and so little time for staff development, resources should not be diffused among less-than-priority issues and concerns. Scarce resources tend to stretch when individuals are motivated to use them.

(5) The primary aim of school restructuring is to move instructional and curricular decisions closer to the student. This shift brings with it a changing role for school staff that demands more individualizing and personalizing of staff development.

The following discussion will focus on training and other professional development activities that are aimed at three distinct levels of teacher expertise and readiness. Additionally, practical examples of strategies appropriate to each of these levels will be explored.

THE BEGINNER TEACHER

Few things in education are more difficult than one's first year as a teacher. The research on new teacher attrition is disturbing:

- Almost 15% of new teachers leave teaching after 1 year.
- Between 40% and 50% of new teachers leave after fewer than 7 years.
- As a group, the most academically talented teachers are the least likely to stay in the profession.

- Young teachers, when compared to more experienced teachers, report more emotional exhaustion and a greater degree of depersonalization (Tonnesen and Paterson, 1992).

Beginner teachers are expected to come into the classroom equipped with the skills that can promote classroom management and active student learning. To facilitate these skills, novice teachers must internalize a set of skills that are basic to effective teaching and are reinforced through reflection, discussions with experienced teachers (mentors), and formal supervisory practice. This instructional model can serve as the framework for learning more about the teaching–learning process and provide a common vocabulary for discussing classroom practices. An example of such a model is provided in Figure 9.1.

Within the context of such a model, novice teachers need to implement routines and procedures that help keep students productively on track, minimize student disturbances, and maximize teaching time. To a large degree, beginning teachers should devote considerable time to actively teaching students about these procedures (Everton and Harrison, 1992). A common list of routines and procedures would include

(1) Effective means for establishing classroom procedures and routines during the first weeks of school
(2) A work-oriented but relaxed classroom climate
(3) Clear and reasonable expectations, standards, and tasks
(4) A predictable, consistent environment
(5) Established consequences and rewards
(6) Rationale for rules and procedures
(7) Manageable activities organized to minimize confusion with clear directions and smooth transition from one activity to the next
(8) Quick, quiet, and calm behavior monitoring
(9) Student input in selected classroom discussions
(10) Accountability for assignments, tasks, and behavior
(11) Use of feedback and praise
(12) Use of a variety of class activities
(13) Attempts by the teacher to encourage and motivate students by taking a personal interest in each student
(14) Teacher enthusiasm and love of the subject

All too often, little recognition is given to the quality and quantity of classroom assignments, worksheets, projects, and homework given to students. While a significant amount of student learning time is devoted to such

---

Teaching is both a science and an art. The *science* is characterized by a process of deliberate decision-making and action that have both an empirical and common sense relationship to student learning. The *art* is the individual teacher's application of effective teaching behaviors based on the best match of teaching styles, methods, content, and students.

Class climate: A class in which teachers make a conscientious effort to promote student emotional well-being and self-esteem. These classrooms are characterized by teacher behaviors that promote an enthusiastic commitment toward task, a success orientation, a high degree of active student participation, and a positive feeling tone.

Class
management: Maintenance of a proactive management style aimed at handling students' misbehavior in a way that: takes the least amount of time, takes the least amount of effort, creates the least unpleasant feelings, and creates the least disruption to the learning environment.

Planning: Teaching behaviors related to the effective, sequential delivery of subject content at the appropriate level of cognition and the efficient use of instructional time.

Instructional
management: The development and delivery of instructional lessons and activities that are characterized by a diagnosis of student prerequisite skills; the establishment of a student mental set; a clear statement of objectives; instructional input with emphasis on the teaching to an objective and checking for understanding; and closure activities to review expected lesson outcomes and to evaluate the extent of student learning.

Curriculum
management: Instructional planning and teaching behaviors that ensure curriculum alignment by providing the appropriate match between the written, taught, and tested curriculums.

Reprinted with the permission of the Moorestown Township Public Schools, Moorestown, New Jersey.

FIGURE 9.1. District instructional model.

activities, little is done to analyze its effects on student learning. In addition to the issue of the amount of time spent on "seat work," teachers need to examine the nature of the seat work itself. Of the seat work and homework assigned, most are commercially produce and accompany a textbook. While it would be comforting to assume that these materials have been carefully selected to match the intended objectives, such is not always the case. It is important that novice teachers have the opportunity to share and discuss the quality and quantity of *teaching artifacts* they routinely distribute.

As part of a novice teacher's professional development, they should have an ongoing vehicle to ensure that they are using appropriate learning supplements. An effective strategy would include having the novice teacher leave a box in his or her desk. As they distribute a learning worksheet, assignment, etc. to students, they simply drop a copy in the box. Periodically, the contents of the box could be reviewed with a mentor or supervisor or within a discussion group. Regardless of the method, artifact collection and analysis must be an active part of the ongoing training of novice teachers.

It is widely accepted that teachers (and most other professionals) need time to analyze the outcomes of daily activities and events. This self-reflection provides a way for teachers to "sort out" their work day, reinforcing what they felt went well and developing strategies to improve those areas that did not go well. A simple way to do this reflection is to have novice teachers keep a *professional journal*. This diary may or may not be shared with fellow teachers or administrators and would serve as a record of a novice teacher's strategies and feelings about his or her workday.

A novice teacher must have frequent *classroom observations* by both the mentor and immediate supervisor. These observations should focus around the development and retention of those skills outlined in the accepted instructional model. Further, these observations must serve to reinforce those skills needed for success and quickly identify and rectify behaviors that do not lead to student learning. Finally, through ongoing classroom observations and related discussions, the beginning teacher will get the necessary feedback to model appropriate behaviors and avoid what would otherwise be undetected "bad habits."

The needs of novice teachers are both complex and quite different from the needs of experienced teachers. Their professional development should emphasize the skills associated with effective classroom management and instructional delivery. Specifically, ongoing opportunities for training and discussion in areas related to (1) instructional modeling, (2) the development of classroom routine and procedures, (3) an analysis of teaching artifacts, (4) time for self-reflection through the keeping of a journal, and (5) direct classroom observations should provide the foundation for successful induction into the teaching profession.

THE COMPETENT, ADVANCED TEACHER

As new teachers begin to conceptualize and effectively utilize basic models of instruction, their need for professional growth become increasingly more sophisticated. No longer do they need to direct their efforts toward the comprehension and application of teaching strategies and behavior, but, instead, considerable time must now be spent on evaluating the appropriateness of those strategies as they affect student learning and well-being. Each strategy needs to be carefully analyzed to ensure that it is modeled and transferred at the right time and to the right students. Thus, consistent follow-up and support is needed to foster professional development.

Joyce and Showers (1988) identified five essential elements of the successful transfer of a new teaching strategy. Teachers need

- to study the theory and rationale for the new practice
- an opportunity to see the new strategy demonstrated
- an opportunity to practice under simulated conditions
- feedback about performance
- coaching by colleagues to provide support, technical feedback, and mutual problem-solving opportunities as the new strategy is implemented

Joyce and Showers (1988) go on to state that when the goal is transfer of training, the coaching element is by far the most important.

The concept and utility of *peer coaching* is not new. Simply stated, "peer coaching is teams of teachers regularly observing one another and providing support, companionship, feedback, and assistance" (Valencia and Killion, 1988, p. 170). Identified as a major component of staff development, Joyce and Showers (1981) outlined the four functions of the coaching process as (1) the provision for companionship, (2) the provision of technical feedback, (3) the analysis of application (attaining "deep" meaning), and (4) adaptation to students.

There are a variety of approaches to peer coaching, yet most have three common characteristics (Ackland, 1991):

(1) Peer coaching is distinct from evaluation. By not being part of a formal evaluation system, teachers are provided a non-threatening environment to experiment with and perfect new strategies. Additionally, opportunities for reflection and discussion become productive substitutes for summary analysis of what is right or wrong.

(2) Peer coaching includes observation followed by feedback. Whether a teacher is experimenting with a new strategy or examining existing practices, all peer coaching includes observation of classroom teaching followed by feedback. This feature of peer coaching emphasizes the need for formal training in both qualitative and quantitative observation techniques. Glickman (1990) suggests that this training should also include training in pre-conferencing techniques, focused classroom observation methods, and post-conference techniques using non-directive and collaborative approaches. Thus, the observation is purposeful;

the peer teachers are skilled in data collection techniques and share a common understanding (and vocabulary) of the instructional phenomenon being observed.

(3) Peer coaching focuses on improving instructional techniques. Regardless of the format of peer coaching or the models of teaching being observed, the goal is to improve instructional delivery skills to enhance student learning.

Peer coaching is a viable strategy for improving teachers' instructional skills. Through professional collaboration, teachers who have an operational understanding of effective instruction can solidify those skills and experiment with more complex strategies in a safe, non-evaluative environment. This process empowers teaching professionals by enabling them to develop their own criteria for classroom observation and places internal emphasis on improving classroom performance. If effectively used, peer coaching, with competent teachers, can have a very positive effect on the transfer of training skills, including: more frequent practice of strategies; more appropriate use of strategies; longer retention of knowledge of coached strategies; and a clearer understanding of the teaching–learning process.

THE SKILLED, EXPERIENCED TEACHER

Most studies indicate that staff and professional development programs have some effect on teacher behavior and initial teacher enthusiasm. As previously stated, though, it appears that real change must be experienced teacher by teacher, classroom by classroom, and student by student. Traditionally, teachers have been the realities of their work. Although most teachers become skilled and develop a genuine caring for their students, they rarely refer to research findings as a primary information source to guide their practice. Teacher research has emerged in the last decade as a potential source for improving education. Teachers who work with students on a daily basis have a unique perspective on educational problems, which can be a ready source of hypothesis formation and testing.

Skilled, experienced teachers need to make their own decisions as to the direction and scope of their professional development. In this new role, they need to initiate investigations that are aimed at solving problems related to their classrooms and students. There is growing support that research by teachers about their own classrooms and practices can function as a powerful means of professional development and can also contribute to the knowledge base in education (Goswani and Stillman, 1987).

Commonly called *action research,* it is a solution-oriented investigation that is conducted by individual or groups of teachers. It is characterized by spiraling cycles of problem identification, systematic data collection, reflection, analysis, data-driven action, and finally, problem redefinition. The linking of the terms "action" and "research" highlights the essential features of this method: trying out ideas in practice as a means of increasing knowledge about and improving curriculum, teaching, and learning (Kemmis and McTaggart, 1982). Because action research is conducted by practitioners, it provides a way for teachers to investigate issues of interest or concern in their classrooms and to incorporate the results into future teaching. This process, which begins with teacher's questions and aims at influencing practice, affords the opportunity for teachers to have greater responsibility for directing their own professional development. "Action research is based around a practical problem and is planned and carried out by the person most likely to be interested in and affected by the findings—the teacher" (Sardo-Brown, 1994, p. 458).

Action research as a means for solving school problems has its roots in the 1950s (Corey, 1953). It was Corey's belief that the lack of linkage between educational research and classroom practice could be reduced when teachers engage in forms of classroom research aimed at improving their daily practices and their decision making.

Action research is often a collaborative activity where practitioners help one another design and carry out investigations in their classrooms. When conducted by teams of teachers, the process enables them to: (1) improve student learning, (2) improve their own practice, (3) contribute to their own profession, and (4) overcome the isolation commonly experienced by classroom teachers (Sagor, 1992).

While action research takes several forms, McKay (1992) identifies the salient features in this process:

(1) Identify an issue, area of interest, or idea.
(2) Define the problem or issue related to the area of interest.
(3) Review related information from journal articles, books, or workshops.
(4) Identify the questions to be dealt with in the action research project.
(5) Develop a plan or procedure to answer the question.
(6) Make a recommendation based on the results of the project.

While recognizing that collaborative research has both successes and failures, Liberman (1986) reports that the process can

- facilitate reflection about teaching
- unite teachers and promote collegial interaction
- close the gap between doing research and implementing research findings
- give teachers an opportunity to assume new roles and gain a sense of empowerment
- legitimate teachers' practical understanding and professional concerns

Similarly, Goswani and Stillman (1987) cite six important changes that occur when teachers conduct action research. The authors assert that teachers who do research find connections between their theoretical perspective and their practice. These teachers' self-perceptions are enhanced, and they become professionally more active. These teachers begin to observe students more closely and learn about new ways to promote success. They become users of current literature and research, becoming more evaluative of curricular material and methods. They are able to study learning and report their findings in practical, inexpensive ways. Finally, they believe that teachers who collaborate with students in classroom research help learners achieve at higher levels.

The benefits of action research for skilled, experienced teachers have been reported by teachers from kindergarten through twelfth grade (Johnson, 1993), and several key considerations must be recognized in the implementation of such a project. Caro-Bruce and McCreadie (1994) have identified six issues that are critical to the implementation of action research.

It takes time and effort for a district to embrace action research. Some teachers (and principals) are reluctant to support research because they believe that it is not helpful in dealing with the daily realities of teaching.

Finding a meaningful context for action research is critical. Teachers need to know that what they will be doing will make a difference to their growth and the growth of their students.

Moving action research from the initiative of individuals to a district commitment is essential. The district needs to accept the value of action research and commit resources to its success.

Funding release time for teachers to do action research results in teachers feeling valued and renewed. There is significant importance to giving teachers time away from their classrooms to talk with colleagues about issues that are important to them.

Sharing the costs among schools leads to increased commitments by principals. Principals supported action research when schools started sharing the cost of release time with the district. Through this process principals also developed a sense of ownership and commitment to action research.

Action research is more likely to succeed if it has many different sources of support. Given the uniqueness and complexities of teachers as researchers, support should be engendered from a variety of sources inside the school, inside the district, through professional organizations, and through local colleges and universities.

Research emerging from practice has a natural place in schools. When conducted by skilled, trained teachers the research questions are more relevant, the investigation more natural, and the findings more credible and practical for classroom practice. It can be said that teachers often leave a mark on their students. Through action research teachers can also influence their profession.

SUMMARY

This chapter characterized the importance of teacher professional growth as the key ingredient to school improvement and reform. Additionally, it emphasized the need for differential professional growth opportunities based on a teacher's degree of readiness and expertise. Asayesh (1993) has summarized what the research has concluded about professional development:

(1) It is one of three essential ingredients of successful school improvement. The two others are a supportive institutional context and strong content.

(2) It employs strategies that are research based, meaning they have been proven to be effective.

(3) It is an ongoing process beginning with intensive training but continuing in the job site. Follow-up and support activities should be built into the school system's institutional structure.

(4) It will make a difference in student learning, improving outcomes ranging from attendance to grades.

(5) It will include an evaluation component that measures effectiveness in terms of both implementation and student outcomes. This information can demonstrate progress and serve as a blueprint for modifications.

(6) The staff developers practice what they preach, maintaining an attitude of openness to change and personal growth.

(7) Opportunities for collaboration and joint planning are built in.

(8) Teachers and other staff are involved in their own growth and take ownership of the program.

REFERENCES

Ackland, Robert (1991). "A Review of the Peer Coaching Literature." *Journal of Staff Development*. 12(1): 22–27.

Asayesh, Gelareh (1993). "Staff Development for Improving Student Outcomes." *Journal of Staff Development*. 14(3): 24–27.

Caro-Bruce, Cathy and Jennifer McCreadie (1996). "Educational Action Reserach." *Practically Critical: An Invitation to Action Research in Education.* ed. Sue Noffke. New York: Teachers College Press.

Corey, Stephen M. (1953). *Action Research to Improve School Practices.* New York: Teachers College Press.

Dilworth, Mary E. and David G. Imig (1995). "Professional Teacher Development." *ERIC Review,* 3(3): 5–11.

Duke, Daniel L. (1990). "Setting Goals for Professional Development." *Educational Leadership,* (47): 71–75.

Everston C. and A. Harrison (1992). "What We Know About Managing Classrooms." *Educational Leadership,* 49(7): 74–78.

Glickman, Carl D. (1990). *Supervision of Instruction: A Developmental Approach.* Second edition. Boston, MA: Allyn & Bacon.

Goswani, Dixie and Peter Stillman (1987). *Reclaiming the Classroom: Teacher Research as an Agency for Change.* Upper Montclair, NJ: Boynton Cook.

Johnson, R. W. (1993). "Where Can Teacher Research Lead? One Teacher's Daydream." *Educational Leadership.* 50(9): 66–68.

Joyce, Bruce and Beverly Showers (1981). "Transfer of Training: The Contribution of Coaching." *Boston University Journal of Education.* 1(2): 163–172.

Joyce, Bruce and Beverly Showers (1988). *Student Achievement Through Staff Development.* White Plains, NY: Longman.

Joyce, Bruce and Beverly Showers (1989). *Student Achievement Through Staff Development.* White Plains, NY: Longman, Inc.

Kemmis, S. and R. McTaggart (1982). *The Action Research Planner.* Victoria, Australia: Deakin University Press.

Liberman, A. (1986). "Collaborative Research: Working With, Not Working On. . . ." *Educational Leadership.* 41: 4–9.

McKay, Jack A. (1992). "Professional Development Through Action Research." *Journal of Staff Development.* 13(1): 18–21.

National Association of Secondary School Principals (1991). "Individual Staff Development for School Renewal." *The Practitioner.* 17(4): 1–6.

The National Commission on Teaching and America's Future (1956). *What Matters Most: Teaching for America's Future.* Woodbridge, VA.

National Education Goals Report. (1995). Washington, D.C.: U.S. Government Printing Office.

Rubin, L. J. (1971). *Inservice Education of Teachers: Trends, Processes, and Prescriptions.* Boston: Allyn & Bacon.

Sagor, Richard (1992). *How to Conduct Collaborative Action Research.* Alexandria, VA: Association for Supervision and Curriculum Development.

Sardo-Brown, Deborah (1994). "Description of Six Classroom Teachers' Action Research." *People and Education.* 2(4): 458–467.

Sparks, Dennis and Susan Loucks-Horsley (1987). "Five Models of Staff Development for Teachers." *Journal of Staff Development,* 10(4): 40–57.

Speck, Marsha (1996). "Best Practices in Professional Development for Sustained Educational Change." *ERS Spectrum.* 14(2): 33–41.

Sykes, Gary (1996). "Reform of and as Professional Development." *Phi Delta Kappan,* March: 465–467.

Tonnesen, Sandra and Susan Patterson (1992). "Fighting First-Year Jitters." *The Executive Educator,* 14(1): 29–30.

Valencia, S. W. and J. P. Killion (1988). "Overcoming Obstacles to Teacher Change: Direction From School-Based Efforts." *Journal of Staff Development.* 9(2): 168–174.

Wood F. and P. Kleine (1987). "Staff Development Research and Rural Schools: A Critical Appraisal." Unpublished paper, University of Oklahoma, Norman, OK.

Wood, F. H. and S. R. Thompson (1993). "Assumptions About Staff Development Based on Research and Practices." *Journal of Staff Development,* 14(4): 52–56.

CHAPTER 10

Supervision for the Twenty-First Century: A Developmental Model for Professional Collaboration

The movement toward accountability in education has touched virtually every aspect of educational delivery systems. In this regard, monitoring and evaluation of teacher competence has increasingly become a point of focus. Many believe that the key to educational improvement lies in upgrading the quality of teachers. Prompted by both an empirical and commonsense perspective, teacher evaluation and accompanying professional development have become an important element of school improvement efforts; however, developing effective systems for assessing teacher competence has proven extremely difficult. For decades, researchers and practitioners have searched for ways to accurately assess teacher performance. The search for a categorical system that meets the needs of both the teacher and the evaluator seems forever elusive because the issues embodied in teacher evaluation and improvement are much too complicated to be reduced to checklists or annual narrative statements.

The most frequently used technique to evaluate all teachers and to attempt to improve instruction involves a classroom observation followed by a post-observation (interpretative) conference. Occasionally, a conference preceding the observation is held to establish broad frameworks that will guide the classroom observation. Some researchers have suggested that through classroom observation supervisors can increase teacher effectiveness by identifying the techniques and behaviors that are not enhancing instruction and by giving the teacher alternative approaches and strategies that might accomplish lesson objectives. While this is a widely held belief, and for most a standard practice, teachers believe they learn little from this process (Blumberg, 1980).

161

SUPERVISION: A HISTORICAL PERSPECTIVE

Early school supervisors were inspectors assigned to ascertain the tone and spirit of the school, the conduct of the students, the management and methods of the teachers, and the conditions of the school. At the turn of the twentieth century, instructional supervision was institutionalized as a form of social control over teachers. Supervision, in most instances, was a deliberate attempt to centrally control and to regulate the pedagogy, knowledge, and behavior of teachers through elaborate systems of prescription, inspection, and evaluation (Glanz, 1991).

From the controlling perspective that dominated the turn of the century, supervision in the late 1950s began to be influenced by a redirection to a more scientific model often termed *neotraditionalism,* which finds it origins within behavioral psychology (Tracy and MacNaughton, 1989). The purpose of supervision was to change teachers' behavior so that they would use theory and accepted practice more effectively. While this movement was considered to be based on knowledge of behavioral sciences, much of the orientation and application continued to be toward fulfilling bureaucratic organizational goals of control, efficiency, and uniformity (Siens and Ebmeier, 1996).

Since the 1980s, the research (but not necessarily practice) seems to have shifted toward a more teacher-centered supervisory process that focuses on the need for increased collaboration to facilitate professional growth. Through individual and collective reflection teachers and supervisors analyze teaching practices in an attempt to identify successful behaviors and eliminate those that (presumably) lessen student learning. Common to this movement is the notion of clinical supervision (Cogan, 1973).

Although many variations of the model are used, the supervisory cycle in a clinical relationship revolves around eight phases:

(1) Establish the supervisory relationship: Build a relationship of trust and support and induct the teacher into the role of co-supervisor.
(2) Plan lessons and units with the teacher: Determine objectives, concepts, teaching, learning techniques, materials, and assessment methods.
(3) Plan the observation strategy: Teacher and supervisor discuss the data to be gathered and the methods for gathering the data.
(4) Observe in-class instruction.
(5) Analyze the observational data to determine patterns of behavior and critical incidents.
(6) Plan the conference strategy: Set tentative conference objectives and processes.
(7) Confer to analyze data.

(8) Resume the planning: Complete the cycle by determining future directions for growth and planning the next unit or lesson.

Recently, researchers have maintained that there is no one best approach to the evaluation of classroom teachers but, rather, that the process should be tailored to the background, needs, and the developmental readiness of the individual teacher (Marczely, 1992). The basic premise for teacher improvement is based on the belief that everyone has the potential to improve and that the challenge for the supervisor is to treat teachers as individual adult learners to enable them to use their potential.

Glickman (1990) identifies two propositions for supervision that emerge from adult and generic teacher development:

- Proposition 1: Supervision, to be effective, must be a function that responds to the developmental stages of teachers. Teachers are not all alike in their thinking or their motivation for teaching; thus, they should not be treated as a homogeneous group.
- Proposition 2: Supervision, to be effective, must be a function that responds to adult life transitions of teachers. Initial enthusiasm should be sustained by gradually increasing responsibilities through mid-career. Late in their careers, teachers should be given reduced responsibilities so they may pursue their remaining educational goals.

This *developmental or differentiated* approach provides for a variety of strategies tailored to the interest and professional growth stage of the individual teacher. Emphasis is placed on a continuum of reflective strategies and practices ranging from directive supervisory actions to non-directive practices, which capitalize on the teacher's self-interest and willingness for self-improvement.

THE TEACHER PERFORMANCE CYCLE

To provide a conceptual framework to discuss teacher evaluation, a brief description of standard methods of teacher evaluation would seem appropriate. Basically, teacher evaluation in America has two separate functions. The first centers on the improvement of teachers' skills so that they can perform their roles more effectively. This type of evaluation is frequently described as *formative teacher evaluation,* for its mission is to help modify (form) the teacher's classroom behaviors.

The second function of teacher evaluation centers around decisions such as whether to dismiss a teacher, whether to grant tenure to a teacher, whether to place a teacher on probation, or whether a teacher should advance on a career ladder. This type of evaluation is typically called *summative teacher evaluation* because it deals more with final, summary decisions about teachers. Summative evaluation is not improvement oriented; instead, it is aimed at making judgments about how teacher performance relates to a district's standards for continued employment.

In a more general sense, many writers (Denham, 1987; Harris, 1986; McGreal, 1983) seem to agree that the major purposes of an evaluation are to:

(1) Provide a process that allows and encourages supervisors and teachers to work together to improve and enhance classroom instructional practices.

(2) Provide a process for bringing structured assistance to marginal teachers.

(3) Provide a basis for making more rational decisions about the retention, transfer, or dismissal of staff members.

(4) Provide a basis for making more informed judgments about different performance levels for use in compensation programs such as merit pay plans or career ladder programs.

(5) Provide information for determining the extent of implementation of knowledge and skills gained during staff development activities and for use in judging the degree of maintenance of the acquired knowledge and skills.

The supervision and evaluation of teachers has had a significant role in a teacher's perception of his or her teaching environment. Bureaucratic systems have long been associated with close organizational environments that tend to inhibit teacher creativity and growth and actually negatively impact on teacher performance. Conversely, laissez-faire or permissive systems tend to communicate misleading information and promote continuation of poor teaching behaviors. Ogden and Germinario (1994) have identified practices that are embodied in effective supervisory systems:

(1) The supervision/evaluation takes place within a professional context of collegiality and collaboration.

(2) A clear understanding exists between the supervisor and teacher as to the common language describing good teaching.

(3) Data collection methods that are used in the classroom are clearly understood by both the teacher and the evaluator.

(4) Data collected through classroom observation are valid (in terms of measuring what they are intended to measure) and reliable (in terms of their intended consistency from one application to another).

(5) Conferences are held by the teacher and evaluator to share data collection and exchange perceptions of lesson outcomes.

(6) Consideration is given to differentiated systems of evaluation for beginning, advanced, and expert teachers.

It is clear that issues embodied in the evaluation and professional development of teachers are much too complicated to be reduced to checklists or annual narrative statements. In a real way, the value of evaluation is in its use as a tool for school and teacher renewal. This collegial activity by the teacher and the supervisor helps them develop a greater understanding of their roles and performances as it relates to the mission of their school. Supervision, evaluation, and its associated professional growth work best when they become a part of the culture of the school, a culture that values constructive feedback, individual reflection, collegial dialogue, and a commitment to use the process to improve the quality of education for students.

SUPERVISORY MODEL FOR THE TWENTY-FIRST CENTURY

Many believe that supervision in public schools is in a state of transition from a traditional view of supervision as a hierarchical construct, focusing on control and maintenance of current practice, to a more horizontal, collegial process (Glickman, 1992). In a powerful representation of this transition, Gitlin and Price (1992) describe the process as movement away from a traditional model of "administrative supervision" toward one of "horizontal supervision." Administrative supervision views the purpose of supervision to be quality control, in which "teachers are treated as if administrative supervision is necessary to ensure proper behavior." Horizontal supervision, on the other hand, is an "empowerment approach" to supervision. Teachers start out by collaboratively analyzing the relationship between their teaching intentions and their practices in ways that point to "living contradictions."

Glickman (1990) expands the collaborative teacher assistant model by adding a dimension concerned with human development and differences. This dimension encourages supervisors to select the method of supervision that will allow the greatest growth potential for each teacher. This developmental approach is based on three general propositions (Glickman, 1990).

First, teachers operate at different levels of professional development. They vary in how they view and relate to themselves, students, and others. Teachers differ in their abilities to analyze instructional problems, to use a repertoire of problem-solving strategies, and to match appropriate strategies to particular situations. Furthermore, the same teacher may vary depending upon the particular instructional topic or timing of life and work events.

Second, teachers need to be supervised in different ways because they operate at differing levels of conceptual understanding, ability, and effectiveness. Teachers at lower developmental levels need less structure and a more active role in decision making.

Third, the long-range goal of supervision should be to increase every teacher's ability to grow into higher stages of thought. Glickman suggests that more reflective, self-directed teachers will be better ale to solve their own instructional problems and meet their students' educational needs.

An essential component of this type of model is that through appropriate activities and professional opportunities at each developmental level, teachers would be able to think in a reflective manner and become increasingly more responsible for their own supervision and professional growth. Figure 10.1 illustrates the nature of the developmental (differentiated) model for supervisory practices and provides specific activities that are appropriate for professional development within each teacher developmental stage.

This model provides for a differential treatment of supervisory/evaluation behaviors based on the individual needs of the teacher and the organizational demands of the school. Unlike existing systems, differentiated practices discriminate between the need for knowledge acquisition and detailed accountability of probationary teachers and the need to stimulate professional development for experienced teachers. The model moves from direct supervisory assistance and monitoring toward increasing non-directive applications emphasizing self-initiated growth through reflection and problem solving.

Beginner	**Competent/Advanced**	**Skilled/Experienced**
1–3 Years	**3–5 Years**	**Career**
Probationary	Developmental	Self-Initiated Growth
Induction		
1. Induction	1. 2 classroom observations focused around pre-determined instructional phenomenon	1. Classroom observations, if required by state law or district policy
2. Knowledge instructional model		2. Action research
3. 4–6 classroom observations	2. Instructional innovations, cooperative learning, technology, etc.	
4. Mentor/coach	3. Peer coaching	
5. Artifact collection		
6. Journal (diary)		
7. Discussion groups: ongoing reflective activities		

FIGURE 10.1.

As described in Chapter 9 (Professional Development), the probationary teacher must be equipped with a set of classroom skills and techniques that promote classroom harmony and ultimately student learning. Thus, supervisory activities and teacher evaluation systems must be set up to assess the nature of teacher competence in this area. Figure 10.1 identifies both the type of data that should be collected and collegial support vehicles to assist in the judgment about the success potential of the probationary teacher.

The most common mechanism to collect such data is through classroom observation. The observation should be focused on an accepted, understood model for effective instruction. (Chapter 9 describes such a model, which includes elements associated with class climate, planning, instructional management, pupil management, and curriculum management.) Frequent visits to the teacher's classroom for both formal (summative) and informal (formative) assessments must be made. It is advisable that different supervisory personnel observe the probationary teacher. This will help provide for different strategies aimed at helping the probationary teacher reach success and promote accountability into the ultimate employment decisions concerning probationary teachers.

Additionally, at least once a semester the probationary teacher should submit all student assignments, worksheets, etc. to the supervisor for his or her review and for the basis of discussion as to the appropriateness of such "artifacts." McGreal et al. (1984) provide a framework for analyzing the artifacts of teaching:

Content

The quality of artifacts should be determined by their content or essential meaning. Some considerations related to quality of content are

(1) Validity: Is the artifact materially accurate and authoritative?
(2) Appropriateness: Is the content appropriate to the level of the intended learner?
(3) Relevance: Is the content relevant to the purpose of the lesson?
(4) Motivation: Does the artifact stimulate interest to learn more about the subject? Does it encourage ideas for using the material?
(5) Application: Does the artifact serve as a model for applying learning outside the instructional situation?
(6) Clarity: Is the content free of words, expressions, and graphics that would limit its comprehension?
(7) Conciseness: Is the artifact free of superfluous material? Does it stick to the point?

Design

Analysis of artifact design should also focus on the content of the lesson or instructional unit. The quality of an artifact is the product of its design characteristics, relevance to instructional objectives, and application to content.

(1) Medium selection: Is the most appropriate medium used for meeting each objective and presenting each item of content (films, textbook, teacher-prepared handout, and so on)?

(2) Meaningfulness: Does the artifact clearly support learning objectives? If so, is this apparent to the learner?

(3) Appropriateness: Is the design appropriate to the needs and skill levels of the intended learner? Are time constraints considered in the artifact's design?

(4) Sequencing: Is the artifact itself sequenced logically? Is it employed at the appropriate point in the presentation?

(5) Instructional strategies: Is the artifact format appropriate to the teaching approach? Does its construction incorporate sound learning principles?

(6) Engagement: Does the artifact actively engage the learner? Does it reinforce the content with appropriate practice and feedback questions?

(7) Evaluation: Is there a plan for evaluating the artifact's effectiveness when used by the intended learner? Can the success rate for the artifact be easily determined?

Presentation

Presentation includes the physical and aesthetic aspects of an artifact, as well as directions for its use.

(1) Effective use of time: Is the artifact suitable for the time allotted? Is the learner's time wasted by such things as wordiness or extraneous information unrelated to the learning objectives?

(2) Pace: Is the pace appropriate to the level of the learners, neither too fast nor too slow? Does the pace vary inversely with difficulty of content?

(3) Aids to understanding: Are directions clearly explained? Are unfamiliar terms defined? Are important concepts emphasized?

(4) Visual quality: Do the visuals show all educationally significant details? Is composition uncluttered? Does the composition help the learner to recognize important content? Are essential details identified through appropriate use of highlighting, color, tone, contrasts, position, motion, or other devices? Is the type size of any text legible from the anticipated maximum viewing distance?

(5) Audio quality: Can the audio component be clearly heard?
(6) Physical quality: Is the artifact durable, attractive, and simple? Are size and shape convenient for hands-on use and storage?

In addition to direct supervisory activities to assess and assist probationary teacher skills and development, mechanisms must be put in place to promote professional reflection and collegiality. Figure 10.1 lists several activities that are aimed at this phenomenon. The assignment of an experienced mentor teacher, participation in professional discussion groups and the maintenance of a reflective teaching journal all add to the personal and professional support needed by the probation teacher. These activities should not be voluntary. Instead, all probationary teachers should show evidence of their active participation in the activities described above. Using the wide range of data collected about the probationary teacher, a better decision can be made as to the focus of his or her improvement efforts and, of course, decisions as to continuation of employment.

As a teacher exhibits satisfactory progress in meeting the entry-level school expectations, he or she can then engage in more challenging, self-directed classroom practices. With the recognition of the supervisor (and the teacher) that the probationary teacher has successfully mastered the basic expectations of a professional within the school, the focus of supervision must become less directive. Increasingly, classroom observations should focus less on instructional modeling and more on the teacher's ability to integrate more complex instructional practices into daily lessons. Figure 10.1 identifies two such practices, cooperative learning and technology, that have been consistently shown to enrich student learning. While these serve as just two possible initiatives, the purpose of supervisor practice for the demonstrated competent, advanced teacher should shift to ensuring an awareness and effective implementation of instructional innovations. The model also suggests that classroom observations should be focused on specific, predetermined instructional phenomenon. These could be related to the reinforcement of a particular nuance within the instructional model or toward the introduction of a specific innovation. While the supervisor has summative, evaluatory responsibility, the thrust of the classroom observation must be the ongoing development of new instructional application.

To reinforce and support growth for the competent teacher, peer coaching should be instituted as a vehicle for collegiality. As described in Chapter 9, peer coaching can help provide a non-threatening environment to get feedback about a new or challenging instructional application. It also provides a focus for professional dialogue and reflection. In a practical sense it helps both teachers in the peer coaching relationship gain insight and skill into the integration of classroom improvement strategies. In a conceptual sense, peer coaching provides a vehicle for professionalizing teaching by reducing direct monitoring of the teacher and increasing the trust that, as professionals, teachers can be relied upon for self-assessment and self-improvement.

As the teacher develops into a skilled, experienced professional, supervisory activities should become non-directive. If by state law or district policy a classroom observation is mandated, that observation should be used to reinforce the higher-level abstraction the teacher uses to identify and solve classroom and student problems. To do otherwise would merely reduce the observation to a means of fulfilling a bureaucratic necessity. If state or district rules permit, the direct classroom observation of skilled, experienced teachers should be eliminated.

In its place (or as the major portion of the supervisory system for skilled, experienced teachers), teachers should be actively engaged in independent or collective research to solve classroom or school problems or to better understand a complex learning or instructional construct. Commonly called action research (see Chapter 9 for a detailed description), the teacher becomes his or her own initiator of professional growth and assessment. Figure 10.2 illustrates a simple form that can be used to initiate this practice. Importantly, the nature of action research must be carefully explained to teachers before they decide to engage in this alternative assessment strategy. Additionally, teachers' participation should be voluntary to ensure that the activity is truly participatory, relying on teacher initiative and professionalism.

It is very important that an ongoing assessment of this strategy is conducted. Teachers, not supervisors, should be the ultimate judge as to the appropriateness of their involvement in action research as an alternative to traditional supervisory practices. Figure 10.3 provides a framework for collecting and organizing data about the utility of this activity.

Ultimately, some accountability must be built into the system to ensure compliance of applicable state, district, and contractual directives. Therefore, a simple method of reporting outcomes of this action research project should be developed. Figure 10.4 provides an example of how outcomes can be presented. As you will see, the comments are made by the teacher. The supervisor's role is to facilitate the research or project by providing collegial support and necessary resources. The "assessment" of outcomes is the introspective analysis of the teacher.

INTEGRATED PORTFOLIOS AS TOOLS FOR DIFFERENTIATED TEACHER ASSESSMENT

One emerging method of teacher evaluation that recognizes the complexities of teaching and teacher developmental readiness is portfolio assessment. A portfolio is an accumulation of personal data about an individual teacher. The folder can include a record of achievement; samples of work; observa-

Action Research

<u>Guiding Principles</u>

1. Supervision, to be effective, must be a function that responds to the developmental stages and relative expertise of teachers. Teachers are not alike in their thinking or their motivation for teaching; thus, they should not be treated as a homogeneous group.

2. Supervision, to be effective, must be a function that responds to adult learning characteristics. Adults tend to learn best when they are interested in a concept, are self-directed, and are provided sufficient encouragement and support.

<u>Goal</u>

To design a system of teacher evaluation that ensures a baseline of quality control, adheres to state guidelines and board policies, and provides the opportunity for self-directed professional development.

<u>Process</u>

Skilled, experienced, tenured teachers will have the option of eliminating the second (required) observation in lieu of self-directed, professional development research.

This activity will be agreed upon and will provide mutual benefit to both the teacher and his or her immediate supervisor.

The activity will be voluntary in nature and during the 1994–95 school year will be limited to two (2) teachers at each elementary school, ten (10) teachers (not more than one per supervisor) at the middle school, and ten (10) teachers at the high school.

- -

Please return this form to your immediate supervisor by **December 15, 1994**

Supervisor: _____

I wish to be considered for participation in the Differentiated Supervision Pilot scheduled to be implemented January 4, 1995 to April 13, 1995.

_____

Staff Member Signature

FIGURE 10.2. Differentiated supervision.

In this process of self-directed, professional development research you had an opportunity to:

(1) Hear from colleagues regarding an alternative process to formal observations and evaluations

(2) Understand and participate in the concept of differentiated supervision

(3) Select and develop a topic to enhance your professional growth

In an attempt to assist future participants in the Differentiated Supervision model, please respond to: (If you need more space, attach additional sheets.)

A) How did you select your topic?

B) What did you like about the experience?

C) What problems did you encounter?

D) Would you do it again? If no, why not?

E) Would you be willing to share your experience with other staff?

F) What recommendations would you make for the differentiated supervision process or program?

G) Please circle your overall reaction to your evaluations of the process. On a scale of 1 (poor concept, no benefit to my supervision) to 10 (excellent concept, many positive learning experiences):

   1   2   3   4   5   6   7   8   9   10

_____

Staff Member Signature

FIGURE 10.3. Assessment.

Professional Development Research

Teacher_____

Supervisor_____

  <u>Topic</u>

<u>Activities</u>*

<u>Comments</u> regarding your particular topic:

_____   _____   _____

Teacher Signature   Date   Date

_____   _____   _____

Supervisor Signature   Date   Date

*You may add additional pages, if necessary.

Reprinted with the permission of the Moorestown Township Public Schools.

FIGURE 10.4. Outcome inventory.

tions made by a supervisor, a colleague, or oneself; and parent and student comments or evaluations. Portfolios can help strengthen a faculty member's overall organization, demonstrate progress and innovative work, and provide information that helps improve performance and quality of the overall program (Perkins and Gelfer, 1993).

On a simplistic level, a teacher's portfolio can be defined as a container for storing and displaying evidence of a teacher's knowledge, skills, and accomplishments. Yet on a conceptual level, a portfolio also embodies an attitude that assessment is dynamic and that the portrayals of teacher performance are based on multiple sources of evidence collected over time in authentic settings (Valencia et al., 1990).

CONTENTS OF TEACHER PORTFOLIOS

A teacher portfolio can include a wide variety of materials that are linked to the school's evaluation system and are reflective of both the teacher's efforts and student learning outcomes. In a general way, the contents of the portfolio should provide a balance of (1) information and materials from the teacher, (2) materials and information from others (supervisors, peers, parents, etc.), and (3) products of student learning.

Stowell et al. (1993) provide a framework for topics that should be addressed in the teacher portfolio:

(1) Learning: evidence of growth as a teacher

(2) Teaching: evidence that teaching is guided by sound pedagogy and characterized by reflective practice

(3) Curriculum: evidence of knowledge of curriculum-based content (i.e., what is known about teaching a chosen content area). There are two kinds of knowledge at issue here. One is knowledge of the curriculum. The other kind of knowledge is what is described as "pedagogical content knowledge": knowledge associated with the blending of content with pedagogy into an understanding of how particular topics, problems, or issues are organized, represented, and adapted to the diverse interests and abilities of learners and presented for instruction. It lies in a teacher's ability to transform the content knowledge into forms that are comprehensible and appropriate for students.

(4) Context: evidence of sensitivity to learners (in terms of abilities, gender, home environment, culture, ethnicity, etc.)

(5) Other: provide another lens with which to look at the portfolio or show what else contributes to development as a teacher/learner

(6) Self-evaluation: critique of portfolio outlining its strengths and weaknesses. Includes tags or a table of contents. Explain what is in the portfolio, why each item is important, and what it says about the teacher. Portfolio conferences will be held with the team.

Within this general framework the actual content of the teacher portfolio should be guided by the mission of the school and, of course, the developmental readiness of the teacher. Stowell et al. (1993) provide a series of key questions that help decide decisions related to portfolio contents:

(1) What is the purpose of the portfolio? Is it primary and central to our assessment or peripheral and supplemental?

(2) Who will be the decision makers in the process and how will decisions be made?

(3) What will be the contents of the portfolio?

(4) Who will be the audience(s) of the portfolio?

(5) What form will the final product take?

(6) What will be the criteria for evaluation?

(7) What form will the report back to the teachers take?

As critical decisions are made as to the nature and content of the portfolio, specific entries into the portfolio should demonstrate a teacher's knowledge and skills. Similarly, the portfolio should provide a means of reflection, offering the opportunity for critiquing one's work and evaluating the effectiveness of lessons, relationships with students, professional growth activities, and other meaningful standards as established by the school.

Typical portfolio contents should reflect the established standards and may include:

- teacher background
- class description: time, grade, and content
- written examinations: National Teacher's Exam and state licensure tests
- a personal statement of teaching philosophy and goals
- documentation of effort to improve one's teaching: seminars, programs, etc.
- implemented lesson plans, handouts, and notes
- graded student work such as tests, quizzes, and class projects
- video/audio tape of classroom lessons
- peer observation records
- written reflections on teaching
- photographs of bulletin boards, chalkboards, or projects
- unit plans
- letters from parents
- letters and notes from students
- outcomes of action research projects
- self-evaluations

While not a complete list, the concepts and materials addressed above can be used as a basic guideline in determining the appropriate content of the teacher portfolio.

DIFFERENTIATED TEACHER PORTFOLIOS

Integrated portfolios that apply rigorous and substantive standards can be an effective teacher evaluation tool. Yet as with all elements of the teacher supervision and evaluation process, the portfolio must reflect the developmental readiness of the teacher. To that end, the goals and content of the portfolio should vary along a continuum to provide for different standards for the probationary teacher, the competent, advanced teacher, and the skilled, experienced teacher.

For the probationary teacher the portfolio should include evidence of attainment of base line competencies and standards. Consistent with Figure 10.1, entries into the probationary teacher's portfolio would include selected artifacts, classroom observation reports, indicators of successful induction into the school, selected lesson plans, and evidence of ongoing reflection and professional development consistent with his or her developmental needs. Other entries could and should be included as mutually agreed upon by the teacher and supervisor.

Perkins and Gelfer (1993) describe a series of competencies that are appropriate expectations for the probationary teacher's portfolio:

(1) Content and curriculum coverage
   • Activities promote problem solving, decision making, and creativity.
   • Lessons are related to children's experiences.

(2) Methodology and classroom organization
   • Small groups in the classroom are flexible and related to the needs and interests of different students.
   • Students are given opportunities to explore issues and concepts.

(3) Planning
   • Objectives are stated.
   • Materials and equipment are listed.

(4) Manages classroom instruction and behavior
   • Activities and teacher questions are sufficiently open ended to allow creative and divergent thinking to occur.
   • Teacher has established a set of rules and procedures to prevent disruptive behavior.

(5) Communicates effectively
   • Teacher is sensitive to the needs and concerns of others.
   • Teacher respects the right of others.

(6) Evaluates students' performance
   • Teacher uses a variety of assessment and evaluation procedures.
   • Teacher reports progress to parents.

(7) Uses appropriate resources
   • Media selections match learner variables.

(8) Exhibits professionalism

- Accepts constructive criticism and is willing to admit mistakes.
- Teacher is dedicated and enthusiastic.

The competent, advanced teacher's portfolio may include (based on an assessment of their skill development) items similar to those of the probationary teacher. Yet since base line competencies can be assumed, the portfolio should also include evidence of higher levels of abstraction. While classroom observation reports may still be appropriate as evidence of mastery of the school instructional expectations, entries showing evidence of more innovative classroom techniques and professional development must be used as a standard for teachers in this stage of readiness.

Of particular importance is inclusion of evidence of collegiality and experimentation. Through vehicles such as peer coaching, competent teachers are better able to shape their perspectives on daily work. Little (1981) suggests that teachers derive career rewards and daily satisfaction from conditions of collegiality. Additionally, collegiality provides the soul support needed to reduce the risks from experimentation, as well as establish an ongoing mechanism for professional dialogue and reflection. Additionally, Little (1981), in studying the norms and work conditions that appear to cultivate collegiality and experimentation, describes four conditions that could be included in the competent teacher's portfolio:

(1) Teachers engage in frequent, continuous, and increasingly concrete and precise talk about teaching practice (as distinct from teacher characteristics and failings, the social lives of teachers). By such talk, teachers build up a shared language adequate to the complexity of teaching, capable of distinguishing one's own practice and its virtues from another teacher's practice.

(2) Teachers and administrators frequently observe each other teaching and provide each other with useful (if potentially frightening) evaluations of their teaching. Only such observation and feedback can provide shared referents for the shared language of teaching, and both demand and provide the precision and concreteness that make the talk about teaching useful.

(3) Teachers and administrators plan, design, research, evaluate, and prepare teaching materials together. Even the best observations remain academic ("just theory") without the machinery to act on them. By joint work on materials, teachers and administrators share the considerable burden of development required by long-term improvement—and make rising standards for their work attainable by them and by their students.

(4) Teachers and administrators teach each other the practice of teaching.

Entries into the skilled, experienced teacher's portfolio should include the evidence of self-directed professional growth. Few, if any, external standards of presentation should be imposed. While the teacher and the supervisor should understand the nature of the problem or research the teacher will explore, the supervisor should not have a role in evaluating project outcomes. Instead, evaluation (as indicated in Figure 10.4) should be non-directive, relying more on the teacher's self-evaluation of the utility of the project or research in solving an authentic classroom problem or phenomenon.

Regardless of the teacher's developmental stage, the portfolio should provide evidence of the teacher's thinking as well as the teacher's performance. Additionally, most (if not all) portfolio entries should be linked explicitly to student learning. By this process, portfolios can provide a more sophisticated and substantive dimension to teacher evaluation (Regan, 1993). When implemented appropriately, integrated portfolios offer several advantages over traditional teacher evaluation processes. Regan (1993) describes those advantages:

(1) They generate information about the cognitive aspects of teaching.
(2) They explicitly connect teaching to student outcomes.
(3) They offer differentiated evaluation processes for novice and experienced teachers.
(4) They stimulate rich, intellectual conversations among teachers and between teachers and administrators.
(5) They assume accountability as an accepted professional norm.
(6) They function without inordinate demands on administrator time.
(7) They lead teachers to internalize standards for excellence in teaching that are directly related to student learning.
(8) They shift responsibility for documenting proficiency from the administrator to the teacher.

THE CONTEXT OF SUCCESSFUL TEACHER EVALUATION

McLaughlin (1990) discusses five elements associated with building and sustaining a district culture for successful teacher evaluation:

- Evaluation must be imbedded: In the broader context of school improvement, the mechanisms and standards established for improved teaching, professional dialogue, and personal reflection cannot be ends in themselves.
- Stakeholder involvement: Administrators, teachers, and, if appropriate, students and citizens involved in school improvement committees should understand and agree upon the proposed process and role expectations associated with the evaluation model.

- The superintendent's active commitment: Central administrators must be knowledgeable of concepts and practices associated with the model and actively recognize and support participating staff members.
- Joint training for teachers and administrators: As with any organizational initiative, all stakeholders must be trained to ensure understanding and acceptance of the process.
- Resources to support individual needs: Appropriate financial and personnel resources must be sustained to ensure ongoing commitment to the goals and anticipated outcomes of the process.

Even though a conceptual framework like the one described above is important for framing evaluation practices, the heart of the process must include an appreciation that the structure of teacher knowledge and skills is (and must be) an evolving, developing form. To that end, the teacher's perceived skill level and developmental readiness should ultimately guide supervisory activities.

The illustration presented in Figure 10.5 graphically depicts the ongoing cycle of teacher evaluation and teacher improvement.

This model acknowledges teacher supervision and evaluation as an ongoing phenomenon initiated by the teacher's knowledge and skill base. Moreover, it provides for both individual and collegial reflection and the encouragement of integration of instructional techniques consistent with the teacher's level of abstraction. Finally, it calls for a differentiated system of assessment based on established standards of professional readiness.

The consistent element of the model is its emphasis on showing evidence of meeting differentiated expectations through the use of integrated portfolios. These portfolios illustrate the complexities and breath of teaching–learning. They stimulate professional dialogue, and they effectively enable

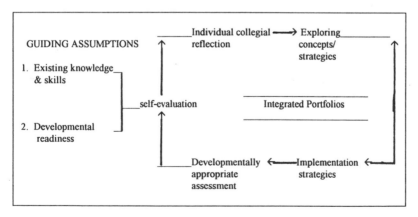

FIGURE 10.5.

supervisors to exert influence on a continuum of directive to non-directive. They incrementally shift responsibility for documenting proficiency from the supervisor to the teacher. Finally, they enable employment decisions (for probationary teachers) to transcend isolated classroom observations to include a wide variety of criteria that describe an effective teacher.

Rather than being a passive recipient of another's inspection and appraisal, teachers begin to observe themselves and their students carefully, to analyze critically the results of particular teaching episodes, and to make determinations about the effectiveness of their teaching as evidenced in the learning of their students. Portfolio assessment, in this context, presents a stimulating professional exercise whereby teachers sharpen skills of thinking about and judging their own performance, become more self-directed, and refine their abilities to modify their own work toward the goal of student success at attaining important and meaningful learning outcomes (Regan, 1993).

SUMMARY

Costa et al. (1988) alerted educators to one of the great myths in our profession—that the traditional teacher evaluation practices improve instruction and student learning. This chapter acknowledges this widely held belief and provides a model for the establishment of new standards and professional improvement. The basic premise that guides the new model for teacher evaluation is the belief that everyone has the potential (and the professional responsibility) to improve. Further, it challenges supervisors to treat teachers differently based on standards of professional knowledge and skills and development readiness. Finally, this chapter describes the relationship between teacher evaluation and professional development as an ongoing, integrative process of reflection and collaboration.

REFERENCES

Blumberg, Arthur. (1980). *Supervisors and Teachers: A Private Cold War,* Second edition. Berkeley, CA: MacCutchan.

Cogan, M. L. (1973). *Clinical Supervision.* Boston, MA: Houghton-Mifflin.

Costar, A. L., Gaviston, R. J. and L. Lambert. (1988). "Evaluation of Teaching: The Cognitive Development View." *Teacher Evaluation: Six Prescriptions for Success.* ed. Sarah J. Stanley and James W. Popham. Alexandria, VA: The Association for Supervision and Curriculum Development.

Denham, C. (1987). "Perspective on the Major Purposes and Basic Procedures for Teacher Evaluation." *Journal of Personnel Evaluation in Education.* (1): 29–32.

Gitlin, Andrew and Karen Price. (1992). "Teacher Empowerment and the Development of Voice." *Supervision in Transition: 1992 Yearbook of the Association for Supervision and Curriculum Development,* ed. Carl Glickman. Alexandria, VA: Association for Supervision and Curriculum Development.

Glanz, J. (1991). *Bureaucracy and Professionalism: The Evolution of Public School Supervision.* London, England: Fairleigh Dickinson University Press.

Glickman, Carl D. (1990). *Supervision of Instruction: A Developmental Approach.* Second edition. Boston, MA: Allyn & Bacon.

Glickman, Carl, ed. *Supervision in Transition: 1992 Yearbook of the Association for Supervision and Curriculum Development.* Alexandria, VA: Association for Supervision and Curriculum Development.

Harris, B. (1986). *Developmental Teacher Evaluation.* Boston, MA: Allyn & Bacon.

Little, Judith W. (1987). "Teachers as Colleagues." *Educators' Handbook: A Research Perspective.* ed. Virginia Richardson-Koehler. White Plains, NY: Longman, pp. 491–518.

Little, Judith W. (1981). "The Power of Organizational Setting: School Norms and Staff Development." Paper presented at the annual meeting of the American Educational Research Association, Los Angeles, CA.

Marczely, Bernadette. (1992). "Teacher Evaluation: Research vs. Practice." *Journal of Personnel Evaluation in Education.* (5): 279–290.

McGreal, Thomas (1983). *Successful Teacher Evaluation.* Alexandria, VA: Association of Supervision and Curriculum Development.

McGreal, Thomas L., Broderick, Eileen and Joyce Jones. (1984). "Artifact Collection." *Educational Leadership.* (41):20–21.

McLaughlin, Milbrey W. (1990). "Embracing Contraries: Implementing and Sustaining Teacher Evaluation." *The Handbook of Teacher Evaluation,* ed. Jason Millman and Linda Darling-Hammond. Newberry Park, CA. pp. 2–8.

Ogden, Evelyn H. and Vito Germinario. (1994). *The Nation's Best Schools: Blueprints for Excellence, Volume I—Elementary and Middle Schools.* Lancaster, PA: Technomic Publishing Co., Inc.

Perkins, Peggy G. and Jeffrey I. Gelfer. (1993). "Portfolio Assessment for Teachers." *The Clearing House.* 66(4): 235–237.

Regan, Helen B. (1993). "Integrated Portfolios as a Tool for Differentiated Teacher Evaluation: A Proposal." *Journal of Personnel Evaluation in Education.* (7): 275–290.

Siens, Catherine Marie and Ebmeier, Howard. (1996). "Developmental Supervision and the Reflective Thinking of Teachers." *Journal of Curriculum and Supervision.* (11)4: 299–319.

Stowell, Laura P., Rios, Francisco A., McDaniel, Janet E. and M. G. Peggy Kelly. (1993). "Casting Wide the Net: Portfolio Assessment in Teacher Education." *Middle School Journal.* (1): 61–67.

Tracy S. and R. MacNaughton. (1989). "Clinical Supervision and the Emerging Conflict Between the Neo-traditionalist and the Neo-progressive." *Journal of Curriculum and Supervision.* (4)3: 246–256.

Valencia, Sheila, McGinley, William and P. David Pearson. (1990). "Assessing Reading and Writing: Building a More Complete Picture." Gerald Duffy, ed., *Reading in the Middle School.* Second edition., International Reading Association, Newark, DE.

CHAPTER 11

Schools for the Twenty-First Century: Planning and Leading for Change

For teachers and administrators to be truly successful in the twenty-first century, change in much of what we now consider standard practice must occur. While much debate exists over the nature of that change, little in the way of systemic reform can be documented.

The nation continues to demand accountability from its schools and value for the increasing financial support they are asked to provide. Yet despite over a decade of rhetoric, most of the nation's high schools have yet to install comprehensive reform plans. In a survey of over 3,000 schools, fewer than half were using techniques such as cooperative learning and standard-based mathematics education, and barely a quarter were experimenting with outcome-based education or school-to-work transition programs (Cawelti, 1994).

Resistance to change, in one form or another, has been a common theme in education. While not unique to organizations, resistance to educational change manifests itself most frequently in relation to policy or curriculum innovations. Typically, the resistance comes from teachers to whom the change has the greatest impact. Interestingly, a corollary of change is the (almost) overwhelming desire of individuals to maintain the status quo. Both formal and informal influences exist to preserve the traditional ways of thinking and acting, as well as the roles and functions of staff members within the school. In a very real way change upsets the balance and order that has been institutionalized over varying lengths of time. The resistance to individual and organizational change can manifest itself in both subtle and not so subtle ways. The behaviors range from illusions of support, to manipulative behaviors, to outright refusal to cooperate. Regardless of the methods of resistance, it is imperative to understand that with the introduction of change will come

183

a certain degree of dissonance. If schools are to change to meet the needs of students in the twenty-first century, major stakeholders in the schools must plan for the dynamics inherent to the change process.

Sashkin and Egermier (1992) have identified the four broad strategies that are most often used in planning for change in schools:

(1) Fix the parts by transferring innovations: Get new information into practice by developing and transferring specific curricular or instructional programs.

(2) Fix the people by training and developing professionals: This includes the comprehensive remodeling of pre-service training of administrators and teachers.

(3) Fix the school by developing the organization's capacities to solve problems: Help people in the school to solve their own problems more successfully. This strategy has grown out of the organization development (OD) movement that has schools collect data to identify and solve problems and to evaluate critical outcomes. Frequently, consultants are brought into the school to guide this strategy.

(4) Fix the system by comprehensive restructuring: Often called systemic change, school districts adopt a multilevel approach involving the school or district's major stakeholders by reaching out to examine and change the fundamental culture of the school community.

Following an examination of the writings and activities of proponents of school improvement, Joyce (1991) has identified five major emphases associated with initiatives for school change:

(1) Collegiality: developing cohesive and professional relations within school faculties and connecting them more closely to their surrounding neighborhoods

(2) Research: helping school faculties study research findings about effective school practices or instructional alternatives

(3) Site-specific information: helping faculties collect and analyze data about their schools and their students' progress

(4) Curriculum initiatives: introducing changes within subject areas or, as in the case of the computer, across curriculum areas

(5) Instructional initiatives: organizing teachers to study teaching skills and strategies

While various strategies have proven successful, there are common themes that cultivate successful change in schools. Primary to this success is the creation of a professional culture, where instructional and curricular decisions are based on informed research, support, inquiry, consultation, and collaboration, that help establish a central focus for the successful achievement of all students (Ogden and Germinario, 1995). These elements are often difficult to achieve unless some key elements are included with the change process. Weischadle and Weischadle (1990) identify these elements as time, trust, team, and training.

(1) Time: In schools, as in other bureaucracies, change comes slowly; school personnel must not act in haste but instead move at a pace consistent with the needs of the group.

(2) Trust: A natural by-product of change is skepticism often voiced by phrases such as, "I've heard that before." All stakeholders in the change process must acknowledge that the innovation will help them and, most importantly, help students.

(3) Team: If collaboration is to work, the decisions of the group must be accepted and implemented.

(4) Training: This element may be the most important component of the four presented; carefully planned training can help use time more effectively and build trust and teamwork.

There is very strong interconnectiveness associated with the major concepts presented in this book. Yet it would be impractical to believe that each of the concepts presented are of equal importance to each school or to each professional within the school. Similarly, it would not be prudent to believe that all major stakeholders in the school will embrace the need for and significance of change. School personnel must realize that without the appropriate planning for change, school improvement is doomed for failure.

As previously discussed, a more prudent way of influencing school improvement efforts may be through a process of "systematic tinkering." Unlike the isolated, nonconnective efforts that many schools have embraced for improvement, systematic tinkering provides a clear vision for where a school wants to go, how it will get there, and, most importantly, how to apply different degrees of emphasis and resources to different elements of the overall improvement model. The basic premise for such an approach lies in the differences in adult and child learning. Adults bring a much more highly developed set of beliefs about what works and doesn't work in a given situation. Educators, like all adult professionals, have been socialized into a set of norms and values specific to ways of doing what is right for them.

While not fashionable in the eyes of some reformers, this more incremental approach embraces the realities of life in today's schools and is built around the following assumptions:

- Use what we already know is supported in the research and operationalized in current practice.

- Keep what is good in our classrooms and schools.
- Recognize organizational constraints, limitations, and the inherent instinct to resist change.
- Accept that teachers are the major participants and contributors in the school improvement process.
- Value the role and participation of parents and community members in the improvement of schools.
- Transform the administrator from manager to collaborative leader.

PLANNING: THE HEART OF THE CHANGE PROCESS

Successful schools have long known the benefits of systematic planning. These schools look upon planning as an organic, ongoing process not initiated by crisis or the need to institutionalize innovations. Instead, successful schools have developed a culture that initiates the planning process by recognizing and accepting what is good about their schools, but they are secure enough to create a level of dissatisfaction that essentially says, "We can always do better" (Ogden and Germinario, 1995).

Taylor and Bullard (1995) explain that planning must be developed in a way that: (a) honors the past but looks forward, (b) solicits involvement of all stakeholders, and (c) scans external and internal environments for relevant data and research findings. By adhering to these three principles, the plan can ensure (among other things) that the school's beliefs, mission, and vision are established or reaffirmed.

Glickman (1992) speaks to a "super vision" for school success. He states that for a school to be educationally successful, it must be a community of professionals working together toward a vision of teaching and learning that transcends individual classrooms, grade levels, and departments. The entire school community must develop a covenant to guide future decisions about goals and operation of the school.

The vision is most often expressed in a mission statement as a broad, general description of purpose. It can be motivational, inspirational, and/or directional (Kaufman and Herman, 1991). In developing a mission statement, no single format works equally well for all schools. Whatever process is used must be agreed upon by and actually involve representatives from all aspects of the school community. Although it can and should be stated in many different ways, it should emphasize that all students in a school are capable of achieving mastery in all areas of the curriculum, and the teachers and administrators accept responsibility for making this a reality (Lezotte and Jacoby, 1992). Rogers (1990) attempts to simplify the definition of a mission statement by describing it as "a statement of an organization's vision of itself that serves to guide program planning, development, and evaluation."

Mission statements are not ends in themselves. Instead, they are clear statements that conceptualize and communicate the vision. The realization of the vision depends upon the successful implementation of workable action plans. Herman (1990) recommends a five-step process to facilitate this activity, which includes the following:

(1) Identify all tasks that must be accomplished.
(2) Rank each task with a sequential number.
(3) Identify the person or persons who are responsible for completing the task.
(4) Identify the resources necessary to accomplish the objective.
(5) State the measurement that will be used to determine whether or not the objective has been achieved.

While planning models help guide the strategic vision of a school, we must recognize that the content of planning must change to meet the needs of students in the twenty-first century. To that end, we must recognize that the mission of the schools must change to meet the challenges of the twenty-first century, that students are different in terms of their academics and emotional needs, and that we know more about teaching and how people learn than at any time in our history. With these tools in hand, we must operate within a model of collaboration. As we create classrooms that value collaboration and the construction of knowledge, so too must we share the same vision of the professionals who establish the framework for school operation and improvement. The most common way to accomplish this end is to decentralize planning through the use of school-based planning teams. Under the general rubric of site-based management, school councils, school improvement committees, etc., major stakeholders within the school community are empowered to strategically plan for school improvement.

According to the American Association of School Administrators (AASA), the National Association of Elementary School Administrators (NAESP), and the National Association of Secondary School Principals (NASSP), school-based planning teams should

- Allow competent individuals in the school to make decisions that affect them with the focus on improving learning.
- Give the entire school community a voice in key decisions.
- Focus accountability for decisions, which leads to a greater creativity in the design of programs and redirection of resources to support the goals developed in the school.

- Generate realistic budgeting as teachers and parents become more aware of the school's financial status, spending limitations, and the cost of its programs.
- Improve morale of teachers and nurture new leadership at all levels of the school organization.

While strategic planning rests with the group, tactical planning or the achievement of classroom objectives clearly resides with the teacher. Although not a new phenomenon, increasingly more responsibility must be placed with the teacher for planning how to assess the needs of students and how to deliver lessons. In a very real sense, teachers must embrace their role as leaders in their respective classrooms. Figure 11.1 describes the salient features that establish what teachers need to know to effectively meet the challenges of this leadership role.

This book is about rethinking what schools have been doing and how practitioners within the schools have been getting things done. Its premise has been that our nineteenth-century model of public education must adapt itself to meet twenty-first-century needs. The scope, nature, and magnitude of the kinds of adaptations that have been suggested will not happen easily or quickly. The existence of a logical, systemic plan for causing this metamorphosis within the school system is the best hope for encouraging those within the organization to undertake the challenge.

An important first step in bringing about such massive change is to create for those closest to the problem—teachers, parents, students, and the commu-

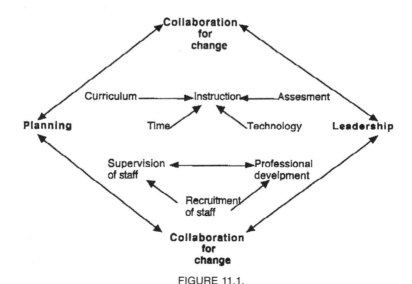

FIGURE 11.1.

nities they serve—a method by which they can become primary participants in the process of redefining the mission and structure of their school.

The increasing diversity of the public school student and the need to prepare them for a competitive and globally interdependent world will require a revision of what students will need to know and be able to do, and it will need to be accomplished through new and innovative ways that will rely on

- what we are learning about how students learn
- how well we can integrate the available technology into the classroom
- how effective we are in coordinating the resources throughout the community to meet student demands—for health services, social services, and job training opportunities

The nature of this kind of collaboration requires a general awareness of the need for change and the acquisition of specific skills to ensure that the cooperative efforts of the primary stakeholders are not awkward and unproductive. Both professionals within the organization and those they will be planning with will need to be trained to engage in this new partnership.

Coming to consensus on what it is they hope to accomplish is a critical first step. A blueprint for the community's aspirations for its children and the role the school is expected to play in achieving those aspirations needs to be created. What a community wants its children to know and to be able to do and what evidence they will accept as proof that those standards have been met are significant guideposts from which all other decisions about change will logically flow.

Recognizing the need for change, preparing participants to plan for the change, and reaching consensus on what the change will eventually lead to set the stage for reconsidering those issues raised throughout the book with regard to curriculum, instruction, assessment, our use of time, the application of technology, collaboration with parents and other community groups, and the need for staff development opportunities to provide the training required to bring these changes to fruition. This restructured learning community will also require alternative ways to assess its effectiveness in terms of staff supervision and may very well require a new breed of professional and a more rigorous program of in-service and professional development to keep pace with the required evolution of the educational process this book suggests. The following steps are suggested:

(1) Recognizing the need for change: Getting people within the school organization and in the community to accept the need for change and to be excited about the prospect of change must begin with a heightening of their awareness of the need to restructure American education if we are to adequately prepare students for the twenty-first century.

(2) Preparing for the change process: Next, both the professionals within the organization and the community members with whom they will be expected to cooperate need to be trained in the collaborative process.

(3) Defining the change: Working collaboratively, an agreement must be reached about
   • what to change
   • how to make those changes
   • how those changes will be measured

All three steps must be taken within the context of what we know and what we anticipate about the future.

Recognizing the need for change must be rooted in what we believe students will be expected to know in the twenty-first century and what we believe to be the inadequacies of the current educational structure. For example, a greater percentage of students will need to meet ever increasing standards at a time when the fastest growing segment of our student population are those students with whom public schools have traditionally been least successful. The future is imposing upon us a mission very different from the one we have had and are prepared for.

Defining the changes to be made and how they should be made must be linked to what we know about teaching and learning and the importance of parent and community investment in the educational process. While these and other issues have been described throughout the book, their relationships and the interrelationship among them suggest an interdependence worth discussing here.

CURRICULUM

The nature and scope of what students will need to know and be able to do in the next century suggests a curriculum that is going to require a deeper understanding from less specific content and the acquisition of skills and behaviors not previously deliberately taught in many schools. We have suggested in Chapter 3 the development of a core concept curriculum that will be authentic and, if practical, interdisciplinary. The curriculum for the twenty-first century should provide a solid background in traditional content and basic skills but complement that background with skills and behaviors we expect will be required by citizens in the next century.

INSTRUCTION

Developing a deeper understanding from a less content-specific curriculum and teaching skills and behaviors in a deliberate and measurable way require alteration of the traditional classroom dynamic of teacher-centered, information-disseminating activities. Building on current cognitive sciences, it was suggested in Chapter 4 that a constructivist approach to instruction be considered. The paradigm of an interactive community of learners seems better suited than other models to delivering the curriculum we believe students will need to know and is most consistent with current understanding of brain functioning, the acquisition of knowledge, and the way students learn.

ASSESSMENT

Measuring student mastery of a curriculum that is concept based, process oriented, interdisciplinary, and delivered through constructivist instructional strategies cannot be adequately accomplished through traditional assessment techniques. In Chapter 5 the issues of alternative and authentic assessments were discussed and should be viewed as logical extensions of the nature of the changes suggested for both the content of the curriculum and the way it is delivered. Student growth in their cognitive ability, their mastery of skills, and their exhibition of behaviors can best be documented as suggested in Chapter 5 through a combination of traditional testing and alternative assessments over an extended period of time.

TIME

A cornerstone in the development of any restructuring of public education is our use of time. The daily structure of the school day may be, as suggested in Chapter 6, the single most important obstacle to redesigning schools for the twenty-first century. Given what is suggested for curriculum, instruction, and assessment adjustments to the school schedule, the length of the school day and school year may be the issue with the greatest potential for bringing about change. Time is not only important as it relates to the instructional process, but it is critical in determining training opportunities for teachers (Chapter 9) and in structuring the opportunities for professionals, parents, and community members to work together (Chapter 8).

TECHNOLOGY

Technology, discussed in Chapter 7, may hold the key to much of what may need to be done to prepare schools for the twenty-first century. In its most obvious application, the computer can facilitate many management aspects of organizing the school, the classroom, and the valuable alternatives for enriching, remediating and individualizing the instructional program. Innovations such as the Internet, interactive long-distance learning, and related technologies have only begun to be appreciated as tools for communications with parents, linkages to community resources, and connections for authentic learning opportunities apart from the school. Technology as a tool may not only revolutionize how and what the student will learn but where that learning will take place.

COLLABORATION

Collaboration is the fuel of reform. In Chapter 8 we discussed the need for collaboration both within the organization and between the school and the communities it serves. Professionals working together to improve instruction, teachers working with parents and students, school personnel working with community members, and students collaborating with each other, teachers, and adults have all been shown to positively influence both student achievement as well as increased public support for education. Students, teachers, and community members must take the time to learn about, acquire the skills for, and participate in this important and powerful tool for qualitative improvement of education.

PROFESSIONAL DEVELOPMENT

Almost everything we have mentioned thus far requires some degree of training or retraining for many if not all of the participants in the educational process. A second fuel in the restructuring process is the availability of a comprehensive and well-designed professional development program. The components of a professional development program were discussed in Chapter 9; the need for both the time and the resources to adequately train teachers and other participants in the change process has been an underlying theme throughout the text.

SUPERVISION

Success for the twenty-first century implies that the nature of the changes suggested in this book will be ongoing. The key to that ongoing and evolutionary process will be those ideas suggested in Chapter 10 regarding the supervisory process. A differentiated supervision model, which encourages ongoing professional development based on the individual differences among teachers, will be needed to institutionalize the change process and ensure that our public schools will remain contemporary well into the future.

LEADERSHIP: THE MUSCLE OF THE CHANGE PROCESS

Planning provides the heart of the change process by establishing a central focus for the life blood of school improvement. Leadership provides the muscle by which plans are initiated and acted upon.

Traditionally, leadership in schools has been vested with the principal, who by the nature of his or her position is charged with managing the daily activities in the building. This perspective has often led to vast differences in the way schools are organized, run, and maintained. These differences reflect the values and beliefs of the principal and the degree to which teachers agree to adhere to the directives of the principal.

Some teachers have engaged in limited leadership activities, but their roles, with the exception of union leadership, have existed as an administrative prerogative within a hierarchical structure of decision making. Most opportunities for teachers have involved minimal levels of collegial or collaborative involvement and little or no training. Thus, to a large degree teachers have not been considered by many principals to be central figures in school leadership. Unfortunately, many twenty-first-century schools will open with twentieth-century principals.

The role of principal in twenty-first-century schools must transcend the traditional notions of management and power. Instead, their most important task is to establish a school culture that values and encourages leadership at all levels of school organization. Whether through formal collaborative teams, consensus building, modeling, or personal influence, the principal must promote a school's vision for success by establishing a culture where staff, students, and community members have school goals that become more important than their own self-interests. In this new role of cultural leader, the principal seeks to define, strengthen, and articulate enduring values and beliefs that give the school its identity and purpose.

This change in the leadership role of the principal has prompted a major shift among those who study leadership and those who practice it. Despite different styles, principals in successful schools have a transformational effect on the people who work in the shadow of their leadership. As Roberts (1985) explains,

> The collective action that transforms leadership generally empowers those who participate in the process. There is hope, there is optimism, there is energy. In essence, transforming leadership is a leadership that facilitates the redefinition of a people's mission and vision, a renewal of their commitment, and the restructuring of their systems for goal accomplishment. (p. 1024)

Leithwood (1992) describes transformational leadership as a form of consensual or facilitative power that is manifested *through* other people instead of *over* other people. The "old" way of leadership is hierarchical and authoritarian; the "new" way seeks to gain overall participation of others.

Walker (1993) defines three dimensions of the research that illustrate transformational leadership, which encompasses the following elements:

(1) A collaborative, shared, decision-making approach: Such leaders believe that organizational goals can be better accomplished by shared commitment and collaboration.

(2) An emphasis on teacher professionalism and teacher empowerment: Such leaders believe all teachers are capable of leadership and encourage them to be self-directed.

(3) An understanding of change, including how to encourage change in others: Such leaders are agents of change and are committed to educating students for the twenty-first century.

John Gardner (1990) concludes that the primary skill for contemporary leaders is to "understand the kind of world it is and have some acquaintance with the systems other than their own with which they must work" (p. 119):

(1) Agreement building: Leaders must have skills in conflict resolution, mediation, compromise, and coalition building. Essential to these activities are the capacity to build trust, judgment, and political skills.

(2) Networking: In a swiftly changing environment, traditional linkages among institutions may no longer serve or may have been disrupted. Leaders must create or recreate the linkages needed to get things done.

(3) Exercising nonjurisdictional power: In an earlier time, corporate or government leaders could exercise almost absolute power over internal decisions. The new leaders must deal on many fronts with groups or constituencies over whom they have no control (for educators, that might be taxpayers with no children in the schools). Their power comes from the ability to build consensus and teamwork and to translate others' ideas into action. They must be sensitive to the media and to public opinion. New leaders use "the power that accrues to those who really understand how the system works and perhaps above all, the power available to anyone skilled in the art of leadership" (Gardner, 1990, p. 119).

Sagar (1992) reports that an increasing trend in schools where teachers and students report a culture conducive to school success is that the principal is a transformational leader. He goes on to suggest that these principals consistently use identifiable strategies:

• a clear and unified focus that empowers professionals to act as both individuals and members of the school

- a common cultural perspective that enables teachers to view other schools through a similar lens
- a constant push for improvement emphasizing the importance of the simultaneous application of pressure and support during educational change

Sergiovanni (1990) discusses the stages of leadership as it relates to the evolution of a transformational perspective. Traditionally, leaders and followers assume that they do not share a common stake in the school and must arrive at some kind of agreement. This bargaining process is viewed metaphorically as *leadership by bartering*. In transformational leadership, by contract, leaders and followers are united in a pursuit of higher-level common goals. Both want to guide school improvement and ultimately improve school life for students. Initially, this transformational leadership takes the form of leadership by building. Here the leader provides the climate and interpersonal support that enhances members' opportunities for fulfillment of needs for achievement, responsibility, competence, and esteem. Eventually, the teacher and leader develop a set of shared values and commitments that bond them together in a common cause. This *leadership by bonding* stimulates awareness and consciousness that elevates school goals to the level of a shared covenant that bonds the leader and follower in a moral commitment. Finally, *leadership by banking* seeks to institutionalize school improvement gains into the every day life of the school.

Schools in the twenty-first century must become more open systems where the principal's (and other traditional school leader's) role is redefined to assume a more facilitative role. In fact, the ability of principals to make this transition from one leadership perspective to another, to perceive power as something that is multiplied rather than reduced when it is shared, seems to be one of the key issues of school improvement (Goldman et al., 1991).

Operationalizing a culture that promotes and sustains collaboration and is focused on a shared mission of school and individual improvement is not easy. Too many principals and teachers in this new role may be viewed as difficult and, at times, threatening. Deal and Peterson (1990) provide a list of guidelines to assist in this process:

- Read the existing culture. Understand the inner workings of the school's history, values, and norms, and reflect on their match with your own hopes and fears for the school.
- Identify the norms, values, and beliefs to reinforce, as well as those to change. Develop a deep sense of new elements that are needed.
- If change needs to be dramatic, make an explicit commitment that is known to others.

- Work with all the school's stakeholders to clarify the mission and purposes of the school.
- Reinforce the core values and norms of the school by consistently modeling, coaching, attending to detail, observing ceremonies, rituals, and traditions, and telling stories that identify "heroes and heroines" that all support the school's mission.
- Confront resistance; don't avoid or withdraw from it. Use conflicts to explain the mission and values of the school.
- Highlight the priority of additional values and beliefs that are not now prominent in the existing culture but that support a vision of the school's mission. Encourage deep structures that support those values, and recognize those whose actions illustrate them.
- Recruit teachers and staff who share the mission of the school and whose values and beliefs are consistent with those trying to be established.
- Encourage the potent school ceremonies and traditions that celebrate the purposes and goals of the school. Recognize and celebrate successes (both small and large) as often as possible, and involve all members of the school and community in doing so.
- Keep track of what's going on. Regularly reevaluate the extent to which students, teachers, parents, and the community share the vision of the school's mission and the degree to which cultural patterns are mutually reinforcing and supportive of the school's mission.

Leadership, while somewhat difficult to describe, has and will be a critical ingredient for school improvement. The new paradigm for school leadership must include the teachers as major stakeholders in creating and implementing the school's vision for its students. The professionalization of teaching must be a center piece of school restructuring efforts to meet the demands of students in the twenty-first century. This professionalization seems warranted for many reasons, among them the failure of traditional forms of administrative influence to contribute to teacher development, the promising effects of teacher leadership initiatives, and the incentive to join the teaching ranks that such a professionalization offers to highly talented prospective teachers (Leithwood, 1994).

TEACHERS AS LEADERS

By the very nature of what they do in their classrooms, teachers are leaders. In their classrooms they develop plans, implement those plans, and manage the diverse needs of as many as 125 students each day. Yet, to a large degree, those leadership abilities have not been utilized outside the classroom.

A common theme within the school restructuring literature is the need to empower teachers to have meaningful ways to influence decisions that directly affect their working environment. Thus, it is highly likely that elevating teachers to leadership roles will result in a variety of positive individual and school outcomes. Pounder and Ogawa (1995), studying leadership as an organizational quality, suggest that the total amount of leadership found in schools will have a positive correlation to their performance. Further, they suggest that all members of the school, including the teachers, can lead and thus affect the performance of their school. Teacher leaders (like other school leaders) affect school performance by shaping the organization of work, developing solidarity among organizational members, managing the school's relation with its external environments, and building members' commitment to their schools. The basic premise for empowering teachers to assume leadership roles is the belief that those persons closest to existing problems have the expertise to solve them. Howey (1988) provides additional support for teacher leadership based on the need for "highly competent leaders who reside where the problems primarily are—in schools—and who can address these in a continuing collective manner" (p. 29).

Teachers in leadership roles will likely lead to a wide range of positive outcomes including self-improvement, a sense of ownership in school decisions, collegiality and the improvement of others, and the initiation of curricular and programmatic change. Similarly, Short and Reinhart (1993) identify six dimensions associated with empowering, which lead to (1) better decision making, (2) professional growth, (3) status, (4) self-efficacy, (5) autonomy, and (6) impact on the organization.

It would seem quite apparent that in preparing teachers for their role as leaders in twenty-first-century schools, appropriate in-service opportunities must be planned. While the specific nature of leadership training remains relatively inexact, training should focus on the need for teachers to develop a collective vision and skills in communication, collaboration, and group dynamics as agents of change. Within this context, specific avenues for teachers to assume leadership must be provided. Henderson and Barron (1995) identify and describe six leadership roles of teachers for effective educational change.

(1) Master teacher: The assumption is that teaching expertise provides a foundation for other leadership roles. The skills inherent to a master teacher are essential to assisting inexperienced and less effective teachers. Similarly, the master teacher's success in designing and implementing effective teaching and learning strategies can initiate professional growth activities leading to other leadership roles.

(2) Curriculum specialist: The knowledge base developed through interest and experience in specific curricular areas make the teacher a valuable resource in designing and evaluating curriculum.

(3) Mentor: The significance of internships and induction processes place additional importance in the teacher's leadership role in the professional development of novice teachers.

(4) Teacher educator: A traditional role of teachers has been providing leadership in the ongoing professional development of other teachers. This role has focused on serving as a model in demonstrating skills and dispositions.

(5) Student advocate: The teacher has the most contact and interaction with students. Information about student achievement, attendance, needs, home life, etc. come from teachers. To that end, teachers have the most significant role in developing leadership skills that address issues related to improving instruction, curriculum, and school climate for the benefit of students.

(6) Researcher: This role provides an important way to link theory and practice, to look anew at everyday activities, and to inform others about the classroom ways in which children learn and teachers teach.

In developing this new paradigm for school leadership, traditional beliefs and hierarchical relations must be challenged. This is by no means an easy task. For decades the structure of schools has done little to allow and encourage teachers to seek new roles in influencing and reshaping educational practices. Interestingly, teachers are held accountable for a system that they have had little to help design. It is no wonder, then, that teachers are reluctant to change, take risks, or challenge the status quo. The inherent distrust that is perpetuated in the isolation of leadership opportunities based on traditional role expectation will only serve to inhibit the type of pervasive change needed to meet the needs of students in the twenty-first century.

The challenge then exists to develop both the culture and the vehicles to thrust teachers into leadership roles. Clearly, concepts related to culture and leadership opportunity are both interactive and cyclical. That is while culture influences risk taking and willingness to change, establishing vehicles for teachers to assume meaningful leadership roles influences school culture. These opportunities for teacher leaders are possible on a broad continuum of informal to formal with an impact on both individual and school-wide practices.

An appropriate starting point for teachers to assume leadership would be in areas associated with their content specialty. Figure 11.2 describes the purpose and formation of a subject advisory committee (SAC), where teachers are empowered within a formal structure to review, analyze, and make decisions about curriculum, textbooks, and subjects they teach.

Formal involvement within an area that a teacher knows provides the sense of security needed to facilitate change. Similarly, valuing teachers as leaders in their subject area provides the opportunity for administrators to help build trust and reshape school culture.

The general purposes of the Subject Advisory Committees are as follows:

A. (1) To review and evaluate existing programs and to determine needs for:

Materials	Equipment
Facilities	Time
Personnel	Content
Coordination among schools and articulation among grades	

   (2) Recommend action to address needs.

B. To assist in formulation of K-12 objectives/proficiencies in the subject area and proficiencies in individual courses.

C. To arrange for the study of promising new materials including author/publisher demonstrations.

D. To recommend adoption of programs/courses and texts:

   – Recommendations for pilot programs
   – Recommendations for district-wide adoptions

E. To assist in the monitoring and evaluation of new materials and programs.

F. To plan for and recommend in-service training and curriculum development.

The responsibilities of members of Subject Advisory Committees are as follows:

A. Attend SAC meetings.

B. Be thoroughly familiar with the program in the school.

C. Contribute input that furthers the purposes of the SAC.

D. Discuss the program with other staff and share the ideas of staff with the SAC.

E. Take a leadership role in the school in orienting staff to recommendations, plans, and programs in the subject area.

F. Report to staff on the activities of the SAC.

Reprinted with the permission of the Moorestown Township Public Schools, Moorestown, New Jersey.

FIGURE 11.2. Subject advisory committees.

Throughout this book examples of professional development activities, alternative supervision and educational practices, technology applications, curriculum writing, selection of instructional strategies, assessment techniques, and working with the major stakeholders within the school community all lead to the realization that teachers will and must be the focal point for change and leadership in the school of tomorrow. It is only when we embrace and operationally promote this concept that educators will truly be prepared for the twenty-first century.

SUMMARY

This chapter examined the dynamics of planning and leadership in twenty-first-century schools. Specifically, the need for an appreciation and understanding of the change process was emphasized. Finally, the unique role of teachers as leaders both in and now outside of the classroom was highlighted as the central focus for both individual professional development and school-wide improvement.

REFERENCES

Cawelti, Gordon. (1994). *High School Restructuring: A National Study.* ERS Report. Arlington, VA: Educational Research Service.

Deal, Terrence E. and Kent D. Peterson (1990). *The Principal's Role in Shaping School Culture.* Washington, D.C.: United States Department of Education, Office of Research and Improvement.

Gardner, John (1990). *On Leadership.* New York, NY: The Free Press.

Glickman, Carl D. (1992). "The Essence of School Renewal: The Prose Has Begun." *Educational Leadership,* 50(1): 24–27.

Goldman, Paul, Diane Dunlap and David Darley (1991). "Administrative Facilitation and Site-Based School Reform Project." Paper presented at the *Annual Conference of the American Educational Research Association,* Chicago, April 4, 1991.

Henderson, Martha V. and Bennie Barron (1995). "Leadership Challenges for the Classroom Teachers." *Education,* 116(1): 62–65.

Herman, Jerry J. (1990). "Action Plans to Make Your Vision a Reality." *NASSP Bulletin.* 74(523): 14–17.

Howey, K. (1988). "Why Teach Leadership?" *Journal of Teacher Education.* 39(1): 28–30.

Joyce, Bruce R. (1991). "The Doors to School Improvement." *Educational Leadership,* 48(8): 59–62.

Kaufman, Roger and Jerry Herman. (1991). *Strategic Planning in Education: Rethinking Restructuring, Revitalizing.* Lancaster, PA: Technomic Publishing Co., Inc.

Leithwood, Kenneth (1992). "The Move Toward Transformational Leadership." *Educational Leadership.* 49(5): 34–35.

Leithwood, Kenneth (1994). "Leadership for School Restructuring." *Educational Leadership Quarterly.* 30(4): 498–518.

Lezotte, Lawrence, W. and Barbara C. Jacoby. (1992). *The District Content for School Improvement.* Okemos, MI: Effective Schools Products, Ltd.

Ogden, Evelyn H. and Vito Germinario. (1995). *The Nation's Best Schools: Blueprints for Excellence. Volume 2—Middle and Secondary Schools.* Lancaster, PA: Technomic Publishing Co., Inc.

Pounder, Diana G. and Rodney T. Ogawa (1995). "Leadership as an Organization-wide Phenomena: Its Impact on School Performance." *Educational Administrative Quarterly.* 31(4): 564–588.

Roberts, N. (1985). "Transforming Leaders: A Process of Collective Action." *Human Relations.* 38(11): 1023–1046.

Rogers, Joseph F. (1990). "Developing a Vision Statement—Some Considerations for Principals." *NASSP Bulletin.* 74(523): 14–17.

Sagar, Richard D. (1992). "Three Principals Who Make a Difference." *Educational Leadership.* 49(5): 13–18.

Sashkin, M. and J. Egermier. (1992). *School Change Models and Processes: A Review and Synthesis of Research and Practice.* Washington, D.C.: United States Department of Education, Office of Educational Research and Improvement, Programs for the Improvement of Practice.

Sergiovanni, Thomas J. (1990). *Value-Added Leadership: How to Get Extraordinary Performance in Schools.* New York: Harcourt Brace Jovanovich.

Short, Paula M. and James S. Reinhart (1993). "Teacher Empowerment and School Climate." *Education.* 113(4): 592–597.

Taylor, Barbara O. and Pamela Bullard. (1995). *The Revolution Revisited: Effective Schools and Systematic Reform.* Bloomington, IN: Phi Delta Kappa Educational Foundation.

Walker, Bradford L. (1993). "What It Takes to Be An Empowering Principal." *Principal.* (March): 41–42.

Weischadle, David E. and Mary Ann P. Weischadle. (1990). "School-Based Management: School Restructuring and Shared Leadership." *New Jersey ASCD Focus on Education Journal,* 1990 Edition.

Ackland, Robert (1991). "A Review of the Peer Coaching Literature." *Journal of Staff Development.* 12(1): 22–27.

Adler, M. (1984). *The Paideia Program.* New York: Macmillan.

Allum, K. F. (1991). "Partners in Innovation: School–College Collaborations." *EDUCOM Review,* 26(3–4): 29–33.

Anderson, E. M. and A. L. Shannon (1988). "Toward a Conceptualization of Mentoring." *Journal of Teaches Education.* 39(1): 38–42.

Asayesh, Gelareh (1993). "Staff Development for Improving Student Outcomes." *Journal of Staff Development.* 14(3): 24–27.

Aschblacher, Pamela R. (June 1994). "Helping Educators to Develop and Use Alternative Assessments: Barriers and Facilitators." *Educational Policy,* 8 (2): 202–223.

Baker, Eva L. (December 1993). "Questioning the Technical Quality of Performance Assessment." *The School Administrator,* Arlington, VA: American Association of School Administrators, 12–16.

Beane, James A. (1995). *Toward a Coherent Curriculum. The 1995 ASCD Yearbook.* Alexandria, VA: Association for Supervision and Curriculum Development.

Blumberg, Arthur. (1980). *Supervisors and Teachers: A Private Cold War,* Second edition. Berkeley, CA: McCutchan.

Bowman, Gerald and Kirkpatrick, Barbara (May 1995). "The Hybrid Schedule: Scheduling to the Curriculum." *NASSP Bulletin.* Alexandria, VA: National Association of Secondary School Principals: 42–52.

Boyer, Earnest. (1995). "The Educated Person." *Toward a Coherent Curriculum.* Alexandria,VA: The Association for Supervision and Curriculum Development: 16.

Bracey, Gerald (December 1993). "Testing the Tests." *The School Administrator.* Arlington, VA: American Association of School Administrators, 8–11.

Bracey, Gerald (1994). *Transforming America's Schools: An Rx for Getting Past Blame.* Arlington, VA: American Association of School Administrators.

Brooks, J. G. and Brooks, M. G. (1993). *In Search of Understanding: The Case for Constructivist Classrooms.* Alexandria, VA: Association for Supervision and Curriculum Development.

Buday, Mary Catherine and James A. Kelly. (1996). "National Board Certification and the Teaching Profession's Commitment to Quality Assurance." *Kappan.* 78(3): 215–219.

Canady, Robert L. and Michael D. Rettig (1995). *Block Scheduling: A Catalyst for Change in High Schools*

Canady, Robert L. and Rettig, Michael D. (1996). *Teaching in the Block Strategies for Engaging Active Learners.* Princeton, NJ: Eye on Education.

Canady, Robert Lynn and Rettig Michael D. (September 1996). "All Around the Block: The Benefits and Challenges of a Non-Traditional School Schedule." *The School Administrator,* Arlington, VA: American Association of School Administrators, 53(8): 8–12.

Caro-Bruce, Cathy and Jennifer McCreadie (1996). "Educational Author Research." *Practically Critical: An Invitation to Action Research in Education.* ed. Sue Noffke. New York: Teachers College Press.

Carroll, Joseph M. (1994). *The Copernican Plan Evaluated: The Evolution of a Revolution.* Topsfield, MA: Copernican Associates.

Cawelti, Gordon and Art Roberts. (1993). *Redesigning General Education in American High Schools.* Alexandria, VA: Association for Supervision and Curriculum Development.

Cawelti, Gordon. (1994). *High School Restructuring: A National Study.* ERS Report. Arlington, VA: Educational Research Service.

Cheek, Dennis W. (November 1993). "Plain Talk About Alternative Assessment," *Middle School Journal.*

Cogan, M. L. (1973). *Clinical Supervision.* Boston, MA: Houghton-Mifflin.

Corey, Stephen M. (1953). *Action Research to Improve School Practices.* New York: Teachers College Press.

Costar, A. L., Gaviston, R. J. and L. Lambert. (1988). "Evaluation of Teaching: The Cognitive Development View." *Teacher Evaluation: Six Prescriptions for Success.* eds. Sarah J. Stanley and James W. Popham. Alexandria, VA: The Association for Supervision and Curriculum Development.

Cuban, Larry (1995). "Reality Bytes." *Electronic Learning,* 14(8): 18–19.

Cummings, Carol (1990). *Managing a Cooperative Classroom: A Practical Guide for Teachers.* Edmonds, WA: Teaching Incorporated.

Cunningham, R. Daniel and Nogle, Sue Anne. (March/April 1996). "Implementing A Semesterized Block Schedule: Six Key Elements." *The High School Magazine for Principals, Assistant Principals and All High School Leaders.* Alexandria, VA: National Association of Secondary School Principals, 3(3): 28–33.

Cushman, Kathleen. (March,1993). *Horace.* Providence, RI: The Coalition of Essential Schools, 9 (4): _____.

Cushman, Kathleen. (March, 1996). *Horace.* Providence, RI: The Coalition of Essential Schools, 12(4): 2.

Danielson, Charlotte (1996). *Enhancing Professional Practice: A Framework for Teaching.* Alexandria, VA: Association for Supervision and Curriculum Development.

Darling-Hammond, Linda. (1996). "What Matters Most: A Competent Teacher for Every Child." *Kappan.* 78(3): 193–200.

David, J. L. (1990). "Restructuring and Technology: Partners in Change." In K. Shangold and M. S. Ticker (Eds.) *Restructuring for Learning with Technology* (pp. 75–89). New York: Center for Technology in Education, Bank Street College, and the National Center on Education and the Economy.

Deal, Terrence E. and Kent D. Peterson (1990). *The Principal's Role in Shaping School Culture.* Washington, D.C.: United States Department of Education, Office of Research and Improvement.

DeBolt, Gary P. (1992). *Teacher Induction and Monitoring.* Albany, NY: State University of New York Press.

Denham, C. (1987). "Perspective on the Major Purposes and Basic Procedures for Teacher Evaluation." *Journal of Personnel Evaluation in Education.* (1): 29–32.

Dilworth, Mary E. and David G. Imig. (1995). "Professional Teacher Development." *The EIRC Review,* 3(3): 5–11.

Dryfoos, Joy G. (April 1996). "Full Service Schools." *Educational Leadership.* Alexandria, VA: Association for Supervision and Curriculum Development. 53(7): 18–23.

DuFour, Richard and Eaker, Robert (1992). *Creating the New American School: A Principal's Guide to School Improvement.* Bloomington, IN: National Education Service.

Duke, Daniel L. (1990). "Setting Goals for Professional Development." *Educational Leadership,* 71–75.

Educational Research Service (1983). *Effective Schools: A Summary of Research.* Arlington, VA.

Edwards, June (January 1991). "To Teach Responsibility Bring Back the Dalton Plan." *Phi Delta Kappan.* Bloomington, IN: Phi Delta Kappa, 398–401.

Ellis, Nancy H. (1988). "Job Redesign: Can It Influence Teacher Motivation?" Paper presented at the *Annual Meeting of New England Educational Research Organization.* Rockport, ME. April 1988.

Epstein, Joyce (1988). "How Do We Improve Programs for Parent Involvement?" *Educational Horizons* (66): 58–59.

Evans, Robert (1993). "The Human Face of Reform." *Educational Leadership,* 51(1): 19–23.

Everston C. and A. Harrison (1992). "What We Know About Managing Classrooms." *Educational Leadership,* 49(7): 74–78.

Fielder, Donald J. (1993). "Wanted: Minority Teachers—Strategies for Increasing Staff Diversity." *The Executive Educator.* 15(5): 33–34.

Finn, Chester. (1991). *We Must Take Charge Our Schools and Our Future.* New York: Free Press.

Fowler, R. Clarke and Corley, Kathy Klebs (April 1996). *Educational Leadership.* Alexandria, VA: Association for Supervision and Curriculum Development. 53(7): 24–26.

Fullan, M. and M. Miles (1992). "Getting Reform Right: What Works and What Doesn't." *Phi Delta Kappan.* 745–752.

Galvey-Hjornevik, C. (1985). *Teacher Mentors: A Review of the Literature.* Austin, TX: The University of Texas at Austin, The Research and Development Center for Teacher Education, ERIC No. ED 263105.

Gardner, John (1990). *On Leadership.* New York, NY: The Free Press.

Gitlin, Andrew and Karen Price. (1992). "Teacher Empowerment and the Development of Voice." *Supervision in Transition: 1992 Yearbook of the Association for Supervision and Curriculum Development,* ed. Carl Glickman. Alexandria, VA: Association for Supervision and Curriculum Development.

Glanz, J. (1991). *Bureaucracy and Professionalism: The Evolution of Public School Supervision.* London, England: Fairleigh Dickinson University Press.

Glatthorn, Allen. (1994). *Developing a Quality Curriculum.* Alexandria, VA: The Association for Supervision and Curriculum Development.

Glickman, Carl D. (1990). *Supervision of Instruction: A Developmental Approach.* Second edition. Boston, MA: Allyn & Bacon.

Glickman, Carl D. (1992). "The Essence of School Renewal: The Prose Has Begun." *Educational Leadership,* 50(1): 24–27.

Glickman, Carl, ed. (1992). *Supervision in Transition: 1992 Yearbook of the Association for Supervision and Curriculum Development.* Alexandria, VA: Association for Supervision and Curriculum Development.

Glickman, Carl D. (1993). *Reviewing America's Schools: A Guide for School-based Action.* San Francisco, CA: Jossey-Boss.

Goldman, Paul, Diane Dunlap and David Darley (1991). "Administrative Facilitation and Site-Based School Reform Project." Paper presented at the *Annual Conference of the American Educational Research Association,* Chicago, April 4, 1991.

Goodlad, John L. (1984). *A Place Called School.* New York: McGraw-Hill.

Gordon, Stephen P. (1991). *How to Help Beginning Teachers Succeed.* Alexandria, VA: Association for Supervision and Curriculum Development.

Goswani, Dixie and Peter Stillman (1987). *Reclaiming the Classroom: Teacher Research as an Agency for Change.* Upper Montclair, NJ: Boynton Cook.

Haberman, Martin. (1995). "Selecting Star Teachers for Children and Youth in Urban Poverty." *Kappan.* 777–781.

Hall, G. and S. Loucks. (1978). "Teacher Concern as a Basis for Facilitating and Personalizing Staff Developing." *Teacher College Record.* 80(1): 36–53.

Harm, Merrill (1994). *Inspiring Active Learning: A Handbook for Teachers.* Alexandria, VA: Association for Supervision and Curriculum Development.

Harris, B. (1986). *Developmental Teacher Evaluation.* Boston, MA: Allyn & Bacon.

Hartzell, Gary and Marc Wenger. (1989). "Manage to Keep Teachers Happy." *The School Administrator.* 46(10): 22–24.

Haney, Walt (1991). "We Must Take Care: Fitting Assessments to Functions." *Expanding Student Assessment,* Vito Perrone, ed. Alexandria, VA: Association for Supervision and Curriculum Development, pp. 142–163.

Haselkorn, David. (1996). *Breaking the Class Ceiling: Paraeducator Pathways in Teaching.* Belmont, MA. Recruiting New Teachers, Inc.

Henderson, Martha V. and Bennie Barron (1995). "Leadership Challenges for the Classroom Teachers." *Education,* 116(1): 62–65.

Herman, Jerry J. (1990). "Action Plans to Make Your Vision a Reality." *NASSP Bulletin.* 74(523): 14–17.

Herman, John, Aschbacher, Pamela and Winters, Lynn (1992). *A Practical Guide to Alternative Assessment.* Alexandria, VA: Association for Supervision and Curriculum Development.

Howey, K. (1988). "Why Teach Leadership?" *Journal of Teacher Education.* 39(1): 28–30.

Huling-Asten, L., S. J. Odell, P. Ishler, L. S. Kay, and R. A. Edelfet. (1989). *Assisting the Beginning Teacher.* Reston, VA: Association of Teacher Educators.

Jervis, Kathe (1991). *Expanding Student Assessment,* Vito Perrone, ed. Alexandria, VA: Association for Supervision and Curriculum Development.

Johnson, R. W. (1993). "Where Can Teacher Research Lead? One Teacher's Daydream." *Educational Leadership.* 50(9): 66–68.

Johnson, Susan Moore (1990). *Teachers at Work.* New York: Basic Books.

Jones, Linda T. (1991). *Strategies for Involving Parents in Their Children's Education,* Fastback, No. 315, Bloomington, IN. Phi Delta Kappan Educational Foundation.

Jorgensen, Margaret (December 1993) "The Promise of Alternative Assessment." *The School Administrator.* Arlington, VA: American Association of School Administrators, 17–23.

Joyce, Bruce R. (1991). "The Doors to School Improvement." *Educational Leadership,* 48(8): 59–62.

Joyce, Bruce and Beverly Showers (1981). "Transfer of Training: The Contribution of Coaching." *Boston University Journal of Education.* 1(2): 163–172.

Joyce, Bruce and Beverly Showers (1995). *Student Achievement Through Staff Development.* 2nd ed. White Plains, NY: Longman.

Kasonovic, Gerald (1994). *Retooling the Instructional Day: A Collection of Scheduling Models.* Reston, VA: National Association of Secondary School Principals.

Kaufman, Roger and Jerry Herman. (1991). *Strategic Planning in Education: Rethinking, Restructuring, Revitalizing.* Lancaster, PA: Technomic Publishing Co., Inc.

Kean, Michael (December 1996). "Multiple Measures." *The School Administrator.* Arlington, VA: American Association of School Administrators, 53(11): 14–15.

Kemmis, S. and R. McTaggart (1982). *The Action Research Planner.* Victoria, Australia: Deakin University Press.

Killon, Joellen P. (1990). "The Benefits of Induction Programs for Experienced Teachers." *Journal of Staff Development.* 11(4): 32–36.

Kobus, Marc and Toenders, Liny (1993). *School 2010.* Arnhem, The Netherlands: Interstudie, Center for Education Management.

Kruse_____- and Kruse,_____ (May 1995). "Reforming the Use of Time." *NASSP Bulletin,* Alexandria, VA: National Association of Secondary School Principals: 1–8.

Lee, Valerie E. and Smith, Julia B. (Fall 1994). "High School Restructuring and Student Achievement." *Issues in Restructuring Schools.* Madison, WI: University of Wisconsin. 7: 4.

Leithwood, Kenneth (1992). "The Move Toward Transformational Leadership." *Educational Leadership.* 49(5): 34–35.

Leithwood, Kenneth (1994). "Leadership for School Restructuring." *Educational Leadership Quarterly.* 30(4): 498–518.

Lezotte, Lawrence, W. and Barbara C. Jacoby. (1992). *The District Content for School Improvement,* Okemos, MI: Effective Schools Products, Ltd.

Liberman, A. (1986). "Collaborative Research: Working With, Not Working On. . . ." *Educational Leadership.* 41: 4–9.

Little, Judith W. (1981). "The Power of Organizational Setting: School Norms and Staff Development." Paper presented at the *Annual Meeting of the American Educational Research Association,* Los Angeles, CA.

Little, Judith W. (1987). "Teachers as Colleagues." *Educators' Handbook: A Research Perspective.* ed. Virginia Richardson-Koehler. New York: Longman, pp. 491–518.

Longstreet, _____and Shane, _____(1995). *Curriculum for a New Millennium.* Boston, MA: Allyn & Bacon: 185–201.

Lortre, D. C. (1975). *Schoolteacher: A Sociological Study.* Chicago, IL: University of Chicago Press.

Marczely, Bernadette. (1992). "Teacher Evaluation: Research vs. Practice." *Journal of Personnel Evaluation in Education.* (5): 279–290.

Marzano, Robert, Pickering, Debra and McTighe, Jay (1993). *Assessing Student Outcomes.* Alexandria, VA: Association for Supervision and Curriculum Development, 11–13.

McGreal, Thomas. (1983). *Successful Teacher Evaluation.* Alexandria, VA: Association of Supervision and Curriculum Development.

McGreal, Thomas L., Broderick, Eileen and Joyce Jones. (1984). "Artifact Collection." *Educational Leadership.* 20–21.

McKay, Jack A. (1992). "Professional Development Through Action Research." *Journal of Staff Development.* 13(1): 18–21.

McKenzie, J. "Taming the Minotaur." *Now On,* April 1992.

McLaughlin, Milbrey W. (1990). "Embracing Contraries: Implementing and Sustaining Teacher Evaluation." *The Handbook of Teacher Evaluation,* ed. Jason Millman and Linda Darling-Hammond. Newberry Park, CA. pp. 2–8.

Miere, Deborah (Summer 1992). "Reinventing Teaching." *Teachers College Record,* New York: Teachers College Press.

Miller, Edward. (April 1992) "Breaking the Tyranny of the Schedule." *The Harvard Education Letter,* Cambridge, MA: Harvard Graduate School of Education.

A Nation Prepared: Teachers for the 21st Century (1986). Washington, D.C.: Carnegie Task Force on Teaching.

National Association of Secondary School Principals (1991). "Individual Staff Development for School Renewal." *The Practitioner.* 17(4): 1–6.

National Association of Secondary School Principals (1996). *Breaking Ranks: Changing an American Institution.* Alexandria, VA.

National Board for Professional Teaching Standards. (1994). *What Teachers Should Know and Be Able to Do.* Southfield, MI: Author.

The National Commission on Teaching and America's Future (1956). *What Matters Most: Teaching for America's Future.* Woodbridge, VA: Author.

Office of Technology Assessment (1995). *Teachers and Technology: Making the Connection.* Washington D.C.: United States Government Printing Office.

Ogden, Evelyn H. and Vito Germinario. (1994). *The Nation's Best Schools: Blueprints for Excellence, Volume I—Elementary and Middle Schools.* Lancaster, PA: Technomic Publishing Co., Inc.

Ogden, Evelyn H. and Vito Germinario. (1995). *The Nation's Best Schools: Blueprints for Excellence, Volume II—Middle and Secondary Schools.* Lancaster, PA: Technomic Publishing Co., Inc.

O'Neil, John (November 1995). "Finding Time to Learn." *Educational Leadership* Alexandria, VA: Association for Supervision and Curriculum Development, 53(3): 11–15.

Pawlas, George E. (1995). "The Structured Interview: Three Dozen Questions to Ask Prospective Teachers." *NASSP Bulletin.* 62–65.

Perkins, Peggy G. and Jeffrey I. Gelfer. (1993). "Portfolio Assessment for Teachers." *The Clearing House.* 66(4): 235–237.

Peters, Thomas (1987). *Thriving on Chaos.* New York: Alfred A. Knopf.

Pilon, G.H. (1991). *Workshop Way.* New Orleans, LA: Workshop Way Incorporated.

Place, A. William and Thelbert L. Drake. (1994). "The Priorities of Elementary and Secondary Principals for the Criteria Used in the Teacher Selection Process." *Journal of School Improvement.* (4)1: 87–93.

Pounder, Diana G. and Rodney T. Ogawa (1995). "Leadership as an Organization-wide Phenomena: Its Impact on School Performance." *Educational Administrative Quarterly.* 31(4): 564–588.

Piaget, J. (1973). *To Understand Is to Invent.* New York: Grossman.

Regan, Helen B. (1993). "Integrated Portfolios as a Tool for Differentiated Teacher Evaluation: A Proposal." *Journal of Personnel Evaluation in Education.* (7): 275–290.

Resnick, L. and Klopfer, L. (1989). *Toward a Thinking Curriculum: Current Cognitive Research.* Alexandria, VA: Association for Supervision and Curriculum Development.

Richardson, Michael D., Lane, Kenneth E., and Flanagan, Jackson L. (1995). *School Empowerment.* Lancaster, PA: Technomic Publishing Co., Inc.

Roberts, N. (1985). "Transforming Leaders: A Process of Collective Action." *Human Relations.* 38(11): 1023–1046.

Rogers, Joseph F. (1990). "Developing a Vision Statement—Some Considerations for Principals." *NASSP Bulletin.* 74(523): 14–17.

Rubin, L. J. (1971). *Inservice Education of Teachers: Trends, Processes, and Prescriptions.* Boston, MA: Allyn & Bacon.

Rudiger, Charles W. and Ira W. Krinsky (1992). "Getting to 2001." *International Journal of Educational Reform,* 1(3): 285–290.

Sagor, Richard (1992). *How to Conduct Collaborative Action Research.* Alexandria, VA: Association for Supervision and Curriculum Development.

Sagar, Richard D. (1992). "Three Principals Who Make a Difference." *Educational Leadership.* 49(5): 13–18.

Sardo-Brown, Deborah (1994). "Description of Six Classroom Teachers' Action Research." *People and Education.* 2(4): 458–467.

Sashkin, M. and J. Egermier. (1992). *School Change Models and Processes: A Review and Synthesis of Research and Practice,* Washington, D.C.: United States Department of Education, Office of Educational Research and Improvement, Programs for the Improvement of Practice.

Sergiovanni, Thomas J. (1990). *Value-Added Leadership: How to Get Extraordinary Performance in Schools.* New York: Harcourt Brace Jovanovich.

Shaten, Lewis N. (1983). "Merit Does Not Have to be a Four Letter Word." *NASSP Bulletin.* 56–63.

Short, Paula M. and James S. Reinhart (1993). "Teacher Empowerment and School Climate." *Education.* 113(4): 592–597.

Shubert, William H. (1993). "Curriculum Reform." *Challenges and Achievements of American Education.* Alexandria, VA: The Association for Supervision and Curriculum Development: 80-84.

Siegel, Jessica (1995). "The State of Teacher Training." *Electronic Learning.* 14(8): 43–53.

Siens, Catherine Marie and Ebmeier, Howard. (1996). "Developmental Supervision and the Reflective Thinking of Teachers." *Journal of Curriculum and Supervision.* (11)4: 299–319.

Smith, M. and J. O'Day. (1990). Position Paper on Education Reform Decade. Stanford University Center for Policy Resources in Education.

Smith, Stuart C. and Scott, Janis J. (1990). *A Work Environment for Effective Instruction.* Alexandria, VA: National Association of Secondary School Principals.

Smylie, Mark A. and John G. Conyers (1991). "Changing Conceptions of Teaching Influence the Future of Staff Development." *Journal of Staff Development,* 12(1): 12–16.

Snider, Robert C. (1992). "The Machine in the Classroom." *Phi Delta Kappa,* 74(4): 316–323.

Sparks, Dennis and Susan Loucks-Horsley (1989). "Five Models of Staff Development for Teachers." *Journal of Staff Development,* 10(4): 40–57.

Speck, Marsha (1996). "Best Practices in Professional Development for Sustained Educational Change." *ERS Spectrum.* 14(2): 33–41.

Stanley, Sarah J. and Popham, James W., eds. (1988). *Teacher Evaulation: Six Prescriptions for Success.* Alexandria, VA: ASCD.

Steffy, Betty E. (1995). *Authentic Assessment and Curriculum Alignment: Meeting the Challenge of National Standards.* Rockport, MA: Pro-Active Publications.

Steffy, Betty and English, Fenwick W. (1997). *Curriculum and Assessment for World-Class Schools.* Lancaster, PA: Technomic Publsihing Co., Inc.

Steuteville-Brodinsky, Burbank, Russ, and Charles Harrison. (1989). *Selecting, Recruiting and Keeping Excellent Teachers.* AASA Critical Issues Report: Arlington, VA.

Stowell, Laura P., Rios, Francisco A., McDaniel, Janet E. and M. G. Peggy Kelly. (1993). "Casting Wide the Net: Portfolio Assessment in Teacher Education." *Middle School Journal.* (1): 61–67.

Strommen, Erik F. and Bruce Lincoln (1992). "Constructivism, Technology, and the Future of Classroom Learning." *Education in Urban Society,* 24(4): 466–476.

Sykes, Gary (1996). "Reform Of and As Professional Development." *Phi Delta Kappan,* March: 465–467.

Sylwester, Rober (1995). *A Celebration of Neurons: An Educators Guide to the Human Brain.* Alexandria, VA: Association for Supervision and Curriculum Development.

Taylor, Barbara O. and Pamela Bullard. (1995). *The Revolution Revisited: Effective Schools and Systematic Reform.* Bloomington, IN: Phi Delta Kappa Educational Foundation.

The Teacher Institute (1994). Fairfax Station, VA. *Working with Parents*

Thies-Sprinthall, Lois M. and Edwin Gerler, Jr. (1990). "Support Groups for Novice Teachers." *Journal of Staff Development.* 11(4): 18–22.

Tonnesen, Sandra and Susan Paterson. (1992). "Fighting First-Year Jitters." *The Executive Educator.* 14(1): 29–30.

Tonnesen, Sandra and Susan Patterson (1992). "Fighting First-Year Jitters." *The Executive Educator,* 14(1): 29–30.

Tracy S. and R. MacNaughton. (1989). "Clinical Supervision and the Emerging Conflict Between the Neo-traditionalist and the Neo-progressive." *Journal of Curriculum and Supervision.* (4)3: 246–256.

Uchida, Donna L., Cetron, Marvin, and McKenzie, Floretta. (1996). *Preparing Students for the 21st Century.* Alexandria, VA: American Association of School Administrators.

United States Department of Education, *Advanced Telecommunications in U.S. Public Schools, K–12*. (Washington, D.C.: United States Department of Education, OERI, February 1995).

U.S. Department of Labor (June 1991). *What Work Required of Schools: A Scans Report for America 2000,* Secretary's Commission on Achieving Necessary Skills. Washington, D.C..

Valencia, S. W. and J. P. Killion (1988). "Overcoming Obstacles to Teacher Change: Direction From School-Based Efforts." *Journal of Staff Development.* 9(2): 168–174.

Valencia, Sheila, McGinley, William and P. David Pearson. (1990). "Assessing Reading and Writing: Building a More Complete Picture." Gerald Duffy, ed., *Reading in the Middle School.* Second edition., International Reading Association, Newark, DE.

Walker, Bradford L. (1993). "What It Takes to Be An Empowering Principal." *Principal.* (March): 41–42.

Weischadle, David E. and Mary Ann P. Weischadle. (1990). "School-Based Management: School Restructuring and Shared Leadership," *New Jersey ASCD Focus on Education Journal,* 1990 Edition.

Wells, Scott. (November 1992). *Interdisciplinary Learning—Movement to Link Disciplines Gains Momentum.* Alexandria, VA: ASCD Curriculum Update.

Wiggins, Grant (July 1994). "None of the Above." *Executive Educator,* Arlington, VA: American Association of School Administrators, 15.

Wise, Arthur E., Darling-Hammond, Linda, and Barry Barnett. (1987). *Effective Teacher Selection: From Recruitment to Retention—Case Studies.* Rand Corporation's Center for the Study of the Teaching Profession.

Wiske, M. S. (1989). A Cultural Perspective on School–University Collaborative Research. Report No. ETC-TP-89-3. Topical paper. Cambridge, MA: Educational Technology Center.

Wood F. and P. Kleine (1987). "Staff Development Research and Rural Schools: A Critical Appraisal." Unpublished paper, University of Oklahoma, Norman, OK.

Wood, F. H. and S. R. Thompson (1993). "Assumptions About Staff Development Based on Research and Practices." *Journal of Staff Development,* 14(4): 52–56.

Wraja, William G. (September 1994). *Performance Assessment: A Golden Opportunity to Improve the Future.* Alexandria, VA: National Association of Secondary School Principals.

Young, I. P. and D. Ryerson. (1986). "Teacher Selection: Legal, Practical and Theoretical Analysis." *UCEA Monograph Series.* Tempe, AZ.

Zeichner, Kenneth M. (Spring 1991). "Contradictions and Tensions in the Professionalization of Teaching and the Democratization of Schools." *Teachers College Record.* New York: Teachers College Columbia University.

214 *Index*